NATIVE PLANTS
of the
NORTHEAST

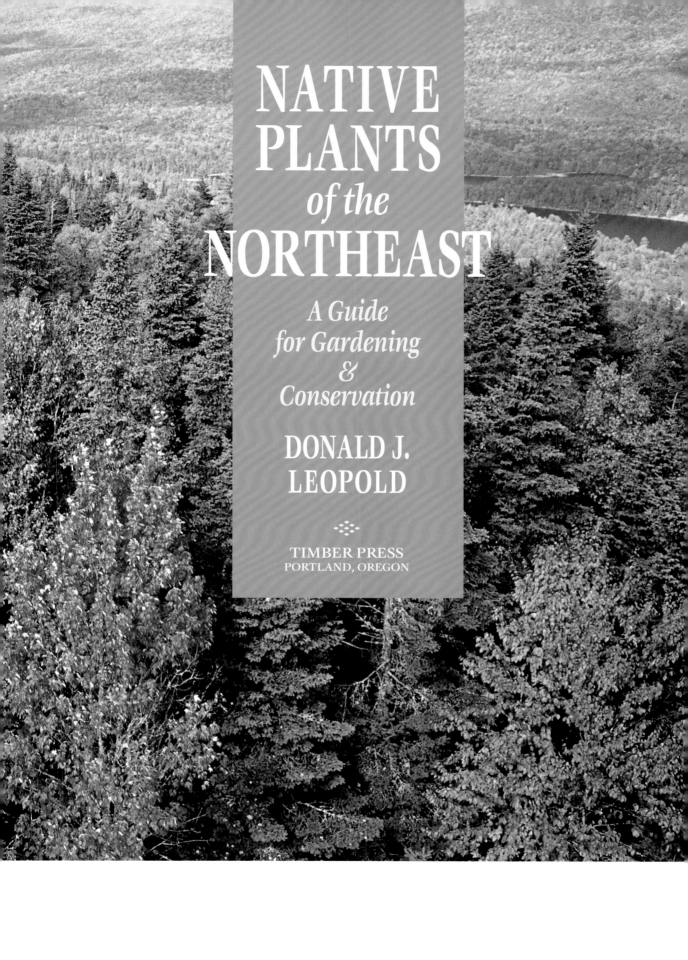

NATIVE PLANTS of the NORTHEAST

A Guide for Gardening & Conservation

DONALD J. LEOPOLD

❖

TIMBER PRESS
PORTLAND, OREGON

Published in 2005 by Timber Press, Inc.

The Haseltine Building
133 S.W. Second Avenue, Suite 450
Portland, Oregon 97204-3527
timberpress.com

Ninth printing 2019

Printed in China
Designed by Susan Applegate

Library of Congress Cataloging-in-Publication Data

Leopold, Donald Joseph, 1956–
    Native plants of the northeast: a guide for gardening and conserva-
        tion / Donald J. Leopold.
            p. cm.
    Includes bibliographical references (p.   ) and index.
    ISBN-13: 978-0-88192-673-6 (hardcover)
    1. Native plants for cultivation—Northeastern States. 2. Native plant
        gardening—Northeastern States. I. Title.
    SB439.24.N67L46 2005
    635.9′5174—dc22   2004015732

A catalog record for this book is also available from the British Library.

CONTENTS

PREFACE

Why another native plant book? Such books generally focus on herbaceous species with showy flowers, i.e., "wildflowers." Occasionally ferns are included. Rarely are woody plant species—typically included in many horticultural guides (where nativeness is usually not emphasized)—mentioned. And in one popular guide to wildflowers, published by one of North America's most well-known conservation groups, the most exotic and invasive species (tatarian honeysuckle, *Lonicera tatarica*, for example) are included with no mention of these crucial facts: they are not native to North America, they need to be eradicated, and they should never be planted, *regardless* of circumstances; furthermore, users of said guide who do not carefully read its text will see multiflora rose (*Rosa multiflora*), purple loosestrife (*Lythrum salicaria*), and many other noxious species and may not appreciate the serious threat these species are to our native plant heritage. Such popular guides quickly undo decades of conservation education.

The region this book is centered on is the entire northeastern portion of North America: all of eastern Canada and the eastern U.S., with relevance west to and including the Plain states and south into northern Florida. The intent of this book is to compile, in one place, basic horticultural information on the many trees, shrubs, and herbaceous species (including wildflowers, grasses, and ferns) native to this region that are particularly well suited for the garden or for restoration projects. This book is a result of my own personal experiences with—and the sustained interest by the public in—these native species. When I am asked about plant selection for the most difficult sites (very dry, very wet, very shaded), I invariably think of the variety of native plants that are ideally suited to these conditions,

7

because they become established, grow, and reproduce under these same conditions in nature.

As a very young boy I recall planting a sour cherry tree in my parents' backyard in northern Kentucky because I loved cherry pies. I loved cherry pies so much that on an occasional late night in mid summer, long after my parents went to bed, I would "borrow" enough cherries from a neighborhood tree to make a pie. But my own planted tree died.

After years of failure to establish a sour cherry tree in my yard, I stumbled across a very small river birch at a local garden center. I think I was just beginning high school at the time; I did not know much about trees, other than which ones were good to climb and had tasty fruit (sour cherry trees were both). This river birch was in an old tin can and cost only a few dollars, so I bought it and planted it in my parents' backyard. Like Jack's magic beans, the river birch grew at a tremendous rate on the same site that killed every sour cherry tree I had carefully planted. At the time, I thought the difference in survival was simply chance; I did not realize that the poorly drained soil conditions killed the cherry but provided excellent growing conditions for the river birch.

A few years later, after summers of landscape and garden maintenance jobs, I needed some plants for the rock garden below this rapidly expanding river birch. I transplanted some of the showy wildflowers common along the bluffs of northern Kentucky, overlooking the Ohio River, which occur in the deep shade of many large, tall deciduous trees. Of course, I now know I should not have done this: such digging threatens populations of many wildflower species. But the wildflowers thrived in the rock garden, where the various annuals planted in previous years did not.

Later, as an undergraduate in a horticulture program at a midwestern university, I recall learning about the ornamental traits and landscape use of hundreds of plants but hardly ever heard about where these plant species naturally occurred, although many were native to the region. Still later, as a graduate student in forest ecology, I began to see many of these species in the woods, prairies, marshes, and swamps where they were native. These experiences were the foundation of my interests and professional training: I learned the value and beauty native plant species give to our gardens, regardless of site characteristics or scale.

So, there are numerous reasons for wanting to write this book. Another strong motivation is that I have seen too many large planting projects along major eastern U.S. travel corridors that include little if any native plants, despite signage (like "Do Not Mow—Wildflowers") suggesting otherwise. For example, a multimillion-dollar federal project along an interstate in Pennsylvania relied on nonnative exotic trees and shrubs in an area otherwise dominated by many beautiful, functional native plants, among them gray birch, pitch pine, scrub oak, mountain-laurel, and rosebay rhododendron. Millions of dollars could have been redirected to truly needed projects if such local, native species had been used; signage could have educated the public, explaining why these native species had been selected—instead of the forsythia, burning bush, spiraea, and purple-leaf plum there now.

Even more recently, along a stretch of interstate south of Syracuse, New York, literally miles of Scotch and Austrian pine, Norway spruce, and other nonnative trees were planted, when facilitating natural regeneration of sugar maple, white ash, eastern white pine, nannyberry, staghorn sumac, gray dogwood, and many other locally abundant native tree and shrub species would have cost a fraction of the amount for this project. Scotch pine and Norway spruce are already escaping cultivation in the Northeast and are beginning to occupy sites that otherwise would have supported native species. There are already too many examples of nonnative species displacing native plants. Whether the planting scenario is a modest one around one's house or involves substantial acreage and public funds, native plants should be given first consideration.

I have written this book in a style that is most useful to me: I like to browse, and when I see something I like, I want to know immediately how to grow it without wading through pages of extraneous material. And I do believe that a good photograph can say so much more—and better—than many lines of text. While the color images should be strong enough justification for selecting these species, the text should inform the reader of other key species traits and to which site conditions they are well suited. For readers who want to go beyond the basic material here, I recommend many books and other readings in the bibliography.

I thank Maija Benjamins, Matt Buff, Jodi Forrester, Alison Halpern, and Sara Scanga for reviewing an earlier draft of the introduction, and Sandra Polimino for assisting me with many tasks here at SUNY-ESF, giving me the time needed to do this project. I thank Timber Press for the opportunity to pursue this project as I wanted to, and especially Dale Johnson and Franni Farrell for their editorial guidance (and wit!). And I really appreciate the willingness of my family (Nancy, Kay, and Mark) to go on so many detours for so many years to see plants, during trips in which they were clearly anxious to do something else.

DONALD J. LEOPOLD
Syracuse, New York

INTRODUCTION

Many readers of this book undoubtedly already know about the incredible beauty, diversity, and versatility of our native plants. I hope that these readers still can learn something about these plants in the following pages. I have visited the darkest, brightest, driest, wettest, coldest, and hottest natural areas throughout eastern North America. Regardless of how good or poor the site conditions are, I have seen an array of native plant species, many of which at the right time of year are quite attractive. Some put on a show two or three times each year, with flowers, fruit, fall color, or perhaps an interesting form. Unfortunately, many people know little about our native plants and how they can function in garden or restoration projects. I especially hope that these readers quickly discover our natural plant heritage and how one can use these native plants in the landscape.

It is interesting to read about many of these species, especially in books written by outstanding horticulturists from Great Britain and other temperate areas. These authors often will save their best strings of superlatives for the species that are the subject of this book, and mention how they have seen these species in gardens around the world. How unfortunate that these species are so often ignored in the region in which they naturally occur.

Rationale for selecting species

Nearly all flowering plants (except artificially created hybrids) are "wildflowers" or "native" species somewhere in the world; but a plant species that naturally occurs somewhere is not necessarily native to that region. For example, when dame's rocket (*Hesperis matronalis*) blooms in moist, open areas throughout the Northeast each year, many people assume it is native, a species of phlox. However, dame's rocket is in the mustard family (four petals, versus five for phlox flowers) and is native to southern Europe and western Asia. Ox-eye daisy (*Leucanthemum vulgare*) is another example of a widely naturalized species (again from Europe) that many observers assume is native to this region. In fact, many European species that are naturalized in the eastern U.S. are substantial components of "wildflower" seed mixes. The term "wildflower" should be restricted to those species that are truly native to a specific region. "Native" means that as best as botanists can determine, a species naturally occurred in an area prior to European settlement. While species included in this book are indeed native to some portion of the Northeast, they are not necessarily native to every county, state, or province in this region.

If one wants to learn more about which plant species are native to a particular region in the U.S., and about their identification characteristics and ecological requirements, an excellent source of information is the USDA PLANTS Database Web site (http://plants. usda.gov). For many of the species listed here, county distribution maps are included, along with much additional information on the plants. State heritage programs (accessed through http://www.natureserve.org/index.htm) also have important information about native plant species, especially those of most concern.

As I reviewed many of the books listed in the bibliography to supplement my personal observations, I often found myself grumbling about species that other authors included or excluded. I suspect the most informed readers will do the same here. I include plants that are native to a good portion of this region, have one or more ornamental attributes, can be found at one or more nurseries (often specialty native plant nurseries), and typically do not require routine incantations to grow. I have not emphasized those that are relatively naturally rare, just too difficult to grow, or too expensive to purchase. And I have excluded hundreds of other species that—while native and likely to fill important natural niches— simply do not compare with the species included here for gardening and restoration purposes. To give some idea of the number of native vascular plant species in this region, relative to the number included here: there are 2078 native, and another 1117 nonnative vascular plant species in New York state alone (Mitchell and Tucker 1997). Although few plant species remain to be discovered in the wild in this region, many wait for gardeners to find and appreciate them.

I have done little justice to the many graminoids—true grasses and grasslike plants, such as sedges and rushes—found in this region. One could easily fill another volume with the many native graminoid species that have roles in gardens, and especially restoration projects, and I highly recommend the reference by Darke (1999) for anyone interested in this ecologically, economically, and horticulturally significant group of plants.

Ecology of natural communities

A group of species (plants and animals) constrained to an array of physical, chemical, and biological factors is a natural community. Natural communities can be forested or open canopy (no trees above). Forested communities generally comprise distinct groups of tree, shrub, and herbaceous species, and are typically referred to by the dominant tree species of that community (e.g., oak-hickory forest). Some open canopy communities are cattail (*Typha* spp.) marshes and old fields dominated by asters (*Aster* spp.) and goldenrods (*Solidago* spp.).

Natural communities are not necessarily diverse; for example, cattail marshes and aspen (*Populus tremuloides* and *P. grandidentata*) stands have few other plant species. But some natural communities, like the cove hardwood forests of the southern Appalachians, rival the composition, structure, and aesthetics of any garden. And natural communities generally are highly dynamic—within any year, as species grow, flower, produce seeds, and become dormant, and from one year to the next, as plants mature and die over time, and their space is colonized by new plants.

Growing native plants simply as a collection of individual plant species can be quite satisfactory. Throughout my garden I have many native fern and wildflower species that likely have never occurred naturally together. In some places, these species are mixed with ferns and wildflowers that are native, but to places like Japan; for example, growing next to my devil's bit (*Chamaelirium luteum*) is the Japanese beech fern (*Thelypteris decursive-pinnata*). Only a few of my most accomplished colleagues would notice this incongruity. Why not plant a native fern, like marsh fern (*T. palustris*) alongside this rather rare native wildflower, especially because both native species would thrive under similar growing conditions? Actually this and many other native ferns are dispersed throughout my garden in other patches of native and nonnative plant species. Having limited space for the large number of plant species that I would like to grow, I add plants that I like (and eliminate others) no matter where they originate. As a conservation-oriented botanist, ecologist, and teacher, the mix of native and nonnative plants serves many professional and personal purposes. But what if one wants to create a natural community, and has the space or opportunity to at least plant the woody and herbaceous species that define the plant portion of a natural community? Proceeding to this next level of complexity, one must appreciate the regional and local factors that underlie natural communities.

At every specific point in the landscape the combination of these factors result in the growing conditions for a plant. Some of these factors have such a profound effect on plant species distributions that they act as a coarse filter for species over very large geographical areas. Some of these large-scale factors, like climate, are relatively stable between years but within a year make the pronounced change of seasons. Climate is the most important factor that determines if a species can survive, grow, mature, and reproduce on a site, once it has successfully reached that location. The boundaries of many natural communities are first constrained by climate variables, especially those related to temperature. Other climatic factors can be equally important; for example, the raised bogs of coastal Maine and farther north develop because precipitation amounts in this region are greater than hydrologic losses due to evapotranspiration, which is greatly affected, but not solely, by temperature. The geographical distribution of many species, and hence the natural communities they constitute, are controlled first by climate factors.

While one has the least control on climatic factors, some plant species can be sited so they are less affected by cold, heat, etc. Extending a plant species into the next higher horticultural zone is often possible by placing that species near the foundation of a house, especially on the south side. But a broadleaf evergreen species that is otherwise cold hardy might be damaged growing at the same location.

The manifestations of climate at any point in time and space, or weather, can vary minimally to substantially, one day to the next. We make decisions about what to plant largely based on our understanding about the climate in an area. But weather, especially extremes in heat, drought, and cold, is the most humbling physical factor to which every gardener must eventually surrender.

Many large-scale factors change little over decades, centuries, and millennia. For example, although soils develop over thousands of years, the underlying surficial and bedrock geology will not change until some catastrophic event (like plate tectonics, glaciation, or other paleoevents) occurs. The bedrock geology can directly influence soil (and water) pH, which is demonstrated so strongly in central New York by the large outcrops of limestone bedrock that provide ideal growing conditions for so many fern species, at least those that thrive under circumneutral conditions. Some of the forested natural areas near Syracuse have over two dozen fern species—some glued to the tops of the limestone blocks, others in deeply shaded nooks filled with rich, organic materials. Not far away from these uplands are calcareous wetlands (fens) that receive groundwater that has moved through this bedrock and glacial deposits enriched by high levels of calcium. These fens, which hold so many unusual plants and animals, and some plants very well known among gardeners, like the shrubby cinquefoil (*Potentilla fruticosa*), are a result primarily of the climate, bedrock geology, and surficial geology, which provide a unique hydrogeological setting in the landscape. It is important to understand these major factors locally before embarking on ambitious plans to create certain natural communities.

Bedrock and surficial bedrock geology maps for eastern North America are available from a variety of sources. These should be examined, especially for regions that exhibit much variation in these features. For instance, the surficial geology in central New York can vary greatly due to many glacial features that promote very different natural communities—drumlins dominated by oak (*Quercus*) and hickory (*Carya*) species if facing south or west, and sugar maple (*Acer saccharum*) and American beech (*Fagus grandifolia*) if facing north or east. In contrast, fens often develop in low areas of the landscape fed by groundwater that arises from kame deposits. Surficial geology has such a significant influence on the occurrence of some natural communities, like fens in central New York, that one can use this information to find these wetlands.

Natural communities are greatly influenced by regional physiography, or physical geography. The physiography of eastern North America varies from north to south and east to west, but also creates substantial variation in climatic conditions in mountainous physiographic regions. Within a mountain range, increasing elevations result in climatic conditions found farther north. The southern Appalachians, primarily in the Blue Ridge physiographic region, are well known for their great diversity of plant species, which coincide with the many distinct natural communities, including the major forest types of oak-pine, oak-hickory, and northeast hardwood (see map on page 18). One of my favorite native trees, Fraser fir (*Abies fraseri*), occurs in extensive, nearly pure stands at 6000+ feet in the southern Appalachians. But it does not grow very well at low elevations unless much farther north. The climate imposed by the physiography of the southern Appalachians is the primary reason Fraser fir and the associated American mountain-ash (*Sorbus americana*) thrive where they do. A gardener in the Midwest will waste much time and money not appreciating this relationship and trying to amend soils and so forth in an effort to grow this beautiful tree species.

Physiography, climate, bedrock and surficial geology, and time since last glaciation—all influence the type of soils that develop in a region. At relatively small spatial scales, soil characteristics have substantial control of which natural communities can develop. Paying attention to these characteristics is especially worthwhile because soils can be readily amended (covered later in this introduction) to provide ideal growing conditions. Much important local soil information can be found in county soil surveys, which give information about depth to bedrock, pH, drainage, and many other basic features. Having soil tested, especially for pH, by local county cooperative extension services is important if there are potential pH problems.

Soils can be of two general types, mineral or organic. Mineral soils are composed of one or more of three groups of particles: sand, silt, clay. Particle size is largest for sand, smallest for clay. Because even the space between sand particles is relatively large, water more readily moves through sand. Consequently, sandy soils are well-drained and prone to drought. Many, over long time periods, also become infertile and acidic because of extensive leaching. Clay particles, by contrast, are so small that porosity is minimal, and water moves very slowly through. The percentage of each group of mineral soil particles has a great influence on the soil's water-holding capacity and nutrient availability. Additionally, mineral soils in natural systems have a layer of organic matter (decaying leaves and twigs, often processed by earthworms) near their surface, which improves soil structure, fertility, and moisture-holding capacity.

Acer saccharum, fall color

Organic soils develop under poorly drained, anaerobic conditions, and result from the accumulation of partially decomposed plants. Substantial deposits of these soils, also known as peat, occur especially in the more northern portions of our region because colder temperatures here further slow the rate of decomposition. Barely decomposed peat is well known among gardeners as sphagnum peat, because *Sphagnum* moss species constitute a large portion of the volume. Very decomposed peat, which is black in color and nearly homogenous, is termed "muck." Extensive areas of muck soil occur throughout the Great Lakes Basin in poorly drained areas. Organic soils have a high availability of nitrogen when aerobic (drained). Organic soils, and mineral soils high in clay, generally hold water well—sometimes too well, relative to a plant root system's need for oxygen.

Another highly significant soil property is its pH, or degree of acidity or alkalinity, because soil pH greatly controls the availability of many nutrients and minerals, and plant symbiotic relationships with fungi (mycorrhizae). Many plant species require acidic conditions (a pH range of 4.5 to 6.0). Some other species tolerate alkaline soils or soils naturally high in calcium, with a pH greater than 6.5. Most plants listed in this guide grow best in circumneutral soils, those with a pH around 6.5. Unfortunately, for so many of us with circumneutral or basic soils, many of the most choice native plant species, like mountain-laurel (*Kalmia latifolia*) and many other members of the heath family (Ericaceae), are also some of the most difficult to grow due to their requirements for acidic, moist, well-drained soil high in organic matter.

Sandy, mineral soils and rocky soils tend to subject plants to occasional extreme drought. Excessively drained, coarse sandy soils also tend to be highly infertile and acidic. While it might seem that native species that thrive on these soils—like gray birch (*Betula populifolia*), pitch pine (*Pinus rigida*), scrub oak (*Quercus ilicifolia*), and bearberry (*Arctostaphylos uva-ursi*)—are less likely to thrive under "opposite" conditions (poorly drained, fertile, alkaline), many species grow well on soils providing either of the "opposite" extreme conditions, except for one factor: many of these species will indeed grow well under dramatically different soil drainage and fertility conditions, but most species do not well tolerate extremes in pH. Gray birch on circumneutral and higher pH soils readily becomes chlorotic because it is not able to acquire sufficient amounts of certain nutrients on these soils.

Ecosystem divisions or ecoregions integrate climate, geology, physiography, and general soil types into a single, coarse scale measure of what natural communities can be supported in a region. The four primary ecoregion divisions in our region are prairie, hot continental, warm continental, and subarctic (Bailey 1996, 1998). Forest-steppes, prairies, and savannas are the broad vegetation types in the prairie ecoregion. The hot continental zone is dominated by broad-leaved (i.e., typically deciduous) forests. Mixed deciduous-coniferous forests characterize the warm continental. Forest-tundra, open woodland, and taiga occupy the subarctic.

To understand why a natural community has developed at a point in the landscape one has to appreciate how the factors that operate at so many temporal and spatial scales affect species within the natural community. The relationships among these coarse scale factors and species are fairly well understood. Successful gardening depends on knowing a plant species' cold hardiness zone. As individual species are constrained to combinations of coarse scale factors, so are natural communities that comprise these species; for example, mature boreal upland forests, dominated by white spruce (*Picea glauca*) and balsam fir (*Abies balsamea*), thrive under the cold climate of Canada and higher elevations of the Northeast. Although one might maintain these species much farther to the south, they will not become a self-replacing community outside of boreal climatic conditions.

These large-scale factors—climate, geology, physiography, and soils—produce regional plant communities (see map, next page), which, because of the coarse scale upon which they are based, are also very general for each region. Species composition within each type can vary greatly within and especially across a region due to local site factors (especially soil moisture) and successional stage. Well-recognized community types within these broadly defined types are discussed in much greater detail elsewhere (e.g., Braun 1950, Leopold et al. 1998, Barbour and Billings 2000). Here I will summarize the defining vegetation components and some common associated species of these regional vegetation types.

Southeast pine forests have one or more of these as canopy dominants: loblolly pine (*Pinus taeda*), slash pine (*P. elliottii*), and longleaf pine (*P. palustris*). Longleaf pine is favored on the driest, deepest sands and by natural fire events on soils that are relatively wet in the spring. Loblolly and slash pines were once naturally restricted to wetter soils, where they were protected from the regular fires that swept through this region, but both species have aggressively colonized abandoned agricultural and other bare lands. Inkberry (*Ilex glabra*), wax-myrtle (*Myrica cerifera*), and saw palmetto (*Serenoa repens*) may be common understory species. The herbaceous layer of the longleaf pine-wiregrass (*Aristida stricta*) savannas is among the richest herb layers in North America, including many insectivorous and orchid species. Southeast pine forests barely reach into our region.

Riverbottom cypress-tupelo-sweetgum forests are deeply and permanently flooded swamps that are dominated by baldcypress (*Taxodium distichum*) and water tupelo (*Nyssa aquatica*). Pondcypress (*T. ascendens*) becomes more common

Betula populifolia bark and *Pinus rigida* foliage

Regional plant communities of eastern North America

than baldcypress further south. Sweetgum (*Liquidambar styraciflua*) is prominent on sites that are not flooded as long during the growing season, along with red maple (*Acer rubrum*), laurel oak (*Quercus laurifolia*), overcup oak (*Q. lyrata*), water hickory (*Carya aquatica*), honeylocust (*Gleditsia triacanthos*), American elm (*Ulmus americana*), and many other deciduous tree species. Common shrubs include Virginia sweet spire (*Itea virginica*), southern swamp dogwood (*Cornus stricta*), and winterberry (*Ilex verticillata*). Many of these forests are lacking baldcypress today because this species was harvested heavily due to its timber value. The cypress-tupelo-sweetgum community, like the previous one, is really a southern U.S. forest type, and barely reaches our region in the middle Mississippi River Valley.

Oak-pine forest is dominated by shortleaf (*Pinus echinata*) and loblolly (*P. taeda*) pines, and white (*Quercus alba*), northern red (*Q. rubra*), black (*Q. velutina*), post (*Q. stellata*), southern red (*Q. falcata*), and scarlet (*Q. coccinea*) oaks. Mockernut (*Carya tomentosa*) and shagbark (*C. ovata*) hickories are also important. Toward the northern portion of this community's range, pitch pine (*Pinus rigida*) and blackjack (*Quercus marilandica*) and scrub oaks (*Q. ilicifolia*) often dominate. Characteristic shrubs in oak-pine forests include mountain-laurel (*Kalmia latifolia*) and huckleberry (*Gaylussacia* spp.).

The most widespread species in **oak-hickory forests** include white, northern red, and black oaks, and shagbark and bitternut (*Carya cordiformis*) hickories. Sugar maple (*Acer saccharum*) and American beech (*Fagus grandifolia*) often dominate more mesic sites. The more mountainous, eastern portion of this forest type was once dominated by American chestnut (*Castanea dentata*), but since the introduction of the causal agent of chestnut blight in the early 1900s, many other tree species have replaced this species. Flowering dogwood (*Cornus florida*), eastern redbud (*Cercis canadensis*), pawpaw (*Asimina triloba*), serviceberry (*Amelanchier arborea*), and eastern hophornbeam (*Ostrya virginiana*) are often in the subcanopy. On mesic sites, spicebush (*Lindera benzoin*) can be common.

Also known as the northern hardwood or beech-maple forest, **northeast hardwood forests** have two main dominant trees, American beech and sugar maple. Yellow birch (*Betula alleghniensis*) is also quite important, and occasionally American basswood (*Tilia americana*) is common. White ash (*Fraxinus americana*) and black cherry (*Prunus serotina*) occur abundantly in stands that are more heavily disturbed by natural windthrow events and timber harvest. Striped maple (*Acer pensylvanicum*) is a common subcanopy tree, and hobblebush (*Viburnum alnifolium*) is a common shrub. Mountain-laurel, witch-hazel (*Hamamelis virginiana*), mapleleaf viburnum (*Viburnum acerifolium*), American fly-honeysuckle (*Lonicera canadensis*), and alternate-leaf dogwood (*Cornus alternifolia*) are common woody understory species in the northeasternmost portions of this forest type.

Transition pine-aspen forests are dominated by jack (*Pinus banksiana*), red (*P. resinosa*) and eastern white (*P. strobus*) pines, and quaking (*Populus tremuloides*) and bigtooth (*P. grandidentata*) aspens. Pin cherry (*Prunus pensylvanica*) and paper birch (*Betula papyrifera*) may also be important components. Sweetfern (*Comptonia peregrina*), blueberries (*Vaccinium* spp.), bush-honeysuckle (*Diervilla lonicera*), and beaked hazelnut (*Corylus cornuta*) are often common shrubs.

Mixed forests are composed primarily of eastern hemlock (*Tsuga canadensis*), eastern white pine and a variety of northeast hardwood forest species (American beech, yellow birch, sugar maple, black cherry, white ash, and occasionally northern red and white oaks). Hobblebush and Canada yew (*Taxus canadensis*) may be common shrubs.

Acadian forests are dominated by spruce and northeast hardwood species. The most common spruce is red spruce (*Picea rubens*), but black spruce (*P. mariana*), white spruce (*P. glauca*), and balsam fir (*Abies balsamea*) may be abundant. American beech, yellow birch, sugar maple, and paper birch are the most abundant hardwood species. Hobblebush is the most common shrub. Other woody understory species include mountain maple (*Acer spicatum*), American mountain-ash (*Sorbus americana*), Canada yew, and bunchberry (*Cornus canadensis*).

Boreal forests comprise mostly white and black spruce, eastern tamarack (*Larix laricina*), balsam fir, jack and lodgepole (*Pinus contorta*) pines, quaking aspen, balsam poplar (*Populus balsamifera*) and paper birch. Following fire, jack pine, quaking aspen, and paper birch are especially abundant. Black spruce and tamarack form extensive forests on saturated, acidic, organic soils. Balsam poplar is common along streams. Common shrubs include American green alder (*Alnus viridis* subsp. *crispa*), mooseberry (*Viburnum edule*), and bunchberry.

Subarctic forests are primarily dominated by white and black spruce. Labrador tea (*Ledum groenlandicum*), sheep-laurel (*Kalmia angustifolia*), low sweet blueberry (*Vaccinium angustifolium*), and American mountain-ash are common woody understory species.

Tall grassland, also known as the tall-grass prairie (versus the short-grass prairie to the drier west), is dominated by big bluestem (*Andropogon gerardii*), switch grass (*Panicum virgatum*), little bluestem (*Schizachyrium scoparium*), and Indian grass (*Sorghastrum nutans*). Toward the eastern extent of this type of natural community, bur oak (*Quercus macrocarpa*) is the main tree component.

Natural heritage programs across the region (see the following Web site for links to each program: http://www.natureserve.org/index.htm) have documented one hundred to two hundred or more natural communities in each state, and have described the key plant (and animal) species that define each natural community. These many, additional natural communities occur in response to local microsites (due to differences in slope aspect, position, and percent, for instance), microclimate, unusual soil characteristics, and type of and time since last disturbance. These detailed descriptions are built on earlier state (e.g., Bray 1915, Curtis 1959) and regional (e.g., Braun 1950) accounts that describe the plant species of more broadly recognized communities. An excellent state-by-state summary of the broad natural community types that should exist given the regional physical characteristics of that area is by Harper-Lore and Wilson (2000; based on Küchler 1985).

A simple example of this regional mosaic of natural communities is displayed in the western Adirondacks, not far from where I teach each summer at our college's biological station. Within a 50-mile radius of the station, one can readily find the following (and more) natural communities: floodplain forest, emergent marsh, boreal acid bog, black spruce–tamarack swamp, northern white-cedar swamp, rich shrub fen, rich graminoid fen, poor fen, shrub swamp, beech-maple mesic forest, hemlock northeast hardwood forest, pine northeast hardwood forest, and successional northeast hardwood forest.

To discuss the floristic elements of these many finer scale natural communities throughout eastern North America is beyond the scope of this book, but one can readily find descriptions of the plants and animals that make up these communities, and information about their affinities to site characteristics, at each state's program Web pages (http://www. natureserve.org/ index.htm). Some states have published these important summaries (e.g., Fike 1999, Thompson and Sorenson 2000).

Within eastern North America, about five to ten percent of each state (and a higher percentage of the Canadian provinces) are wetlands and generally do not show up on coarse scale regional vegetation maps. Yet, these natural communities hold a disproportionate number of species of concern and many of the showiest native plants. The three main types of wetlands in this region—forested, scrub-shrub, and emergent marsh wetlands—are nontidal and freshwater, and occur primarily on mineral soils, although extensive peatlands exist in the northern portion of the region. The species composition of wetlands is most influenced by various hydrological factors, but especially depth and duration of flooding.

Forested wetlands along streams in this region may be dominated by boxelder (*Acer*

Young northeast hardwood forest

negundo), silver maple (*A. saccharinum*), river birch (*Betula nigra*), green ash (*Fraxinus penn-sylvanica*), American sycamore (*Platanus occidentalis*), eastern cottonwood (*Populus deltoides*), swamp white oak (*Quercus bicolor*), bur oak, and to a lesser extent today due to disease, American elm. In swamps, where water from spring snow melt is held in topographic depressions, balsam fir, red maple, shellbark hickory (*Carya laciniosa*), black ash (*Fraxinus nigra*), pin oak (*Quercus palustris*), and northern white-cedar (*Thuja occidentalis*) may dominate in some combination, depending on how far north the location is and whether the substrate is primarily mineral or peat. In acidic swamps, or bogs, tamarack and black spruce are the primary tree species, together with many species from the heath family (Ericaceae) like blueberries and cranberries (*Vaccinium* spp.), insectivorous species like the northern pitcher plant (*Sarracenia purpurea*), and a solid carpet of various *Sphagnum* (moss) species.

Scrub-shrub wetlands include acidic peatlands that lack the tree canopy of black spruce and tamarack but are instead dominated by numerous shrubs, mostly in the heath family; the alder (*Alnus incana* subsp. *rugosa*) and willow (*Salix* spp.) wetlands that line so many streams; and other wetlands dominated by buttonbush (*Cephalanthus occidentalis*), dogwoods (*Cornus sericea* and *C. amomum*), winterberry (*Ilex verticillata*), mountain-holly (*Nemopanthus mucronatus*), and meadowsweet (*Spiraea alba*).

Emergent marsh wetlands may be quite diverse, including many graminoid species,

Goldenrods and Joe-pye weed in old field

such as sedges (*Carex* spp.), rushes (*Juncus* spp.), and bulrush (*Scirpus cyperinus*), and other herbaceous plant species like marsh fern (*Thelypteris palustris*), swamp milkweed (*Asclepias incarnata*), flat-topped aster (*Aster umbellatus*), turtlehead (*Chelone glabra*), spotted Joe-pye weed (*Eupatorium maculatum*), boneset (*E. perfoliatum*), sneezeweed (*Helenium autumnale*), northern blue flag (*Iris versicolor*), and great blue lobelia (*Lobelia siphilitica*). Or they may be dominated by cattail (*Typha* spp.). Unfortunately, many wetlands in this region are monocultures of the exotic purple loosestrife (*Lythrum salicaria*) and common reed (*Phragmites communis*), the former often an escape from local gardens.

Community composition versus structure relative to function

Composition is the array and abundance of plant species at a location, whereas structure is the size, age, and spatial orientation of these species. There is ongoing debate among ecologists and conservationists about whether each plant (and animal) species has a unique, critical role to the functioning and resiliency of natural communities. Certainly, some species, like the group of *Sphagnum* moss species that carpet acidic peatlands, have such a profound effect on so many ecological patterns and processes, they are referred to as "ecosystem engineers." But the ecological role of most species is much more subtle and is poorly understood.

Cinnamon fern and sedges in red maple swamp

Ecological processes are strongly affected by the structure of a community. For example, evapotranspiration is controlled largely by the total amount of living leaves, which in turn controls soil moisture patterns, which affect microbial activity, which affects nutrient availability, which affects primary production of the community. These, and so many more, complex interactions among the biotic and abiotic elements are not fully understood for even the most simple natural communities. But the functional importance of some structural elements are widely appreciated; for example, if one wants to grow some of the many beautiful native spring wildflowers of the eastern deciduous forest, the site must have shade, ideally provided by a deciduous tree canopy.

I was reminded of this basic requirement a few years ago when a group of graduate students, faculty, and I spent many months planning to create a northeast hardwood forest in a small nook between two buildings on our campus. After intensive planning and ameliorating the soils, we transplanted (from another college property) dozens of native plants, including white trillium (*Trillium grandiflorum*), bloodroot (*Sanguinaria canadensis*), foamflower (*Tiarella cordifolia*), and Canada violet (*Viola canadensis*), to this site, which had about everything we thought it needed except a fully closed canopy of deciduous trees above—a feature that cannot just be plopped onto a site. I also added thousands of seeds from these and other native species common to this community. Although there was one large sugar maple near the center of the site, and scattered pole-size natives elsewhere, the site was simply too open to maintain the microclimate in which these spring wildflowers thrive. Wild ginger (*Asarum canadense*), large Solomon's seal (*Polygonatum commutatum*),

Bloodroot in early spring

and some of the other understory species have grown quite well here, but the site has apparently been too dry for the small yellow ladyslipper (*Cypripedium parviflorum* var. *parviflorum*), trilliums, bloodroot, twinleaf (*Jeffersonia diphylla*), and other spring wildflowers of this forest type.

These deciduous forest spring wildflowers grow best under a deciduous tree canopy, but they do not need to be planted under the tree species with which they would naturally be found. Such relationships between the various layers of natural communities need to be understood if one or more of these layers are to be created.

Dynamics of natural communities

Natural communities are highly dynamic over space and time. Some, like freshwater marshes, are invisible until they emerge anew each spring. Others, like forests dominated by evergreen conifers, appear to change little during the year. Most deciduous forests in this region have a pronounced emergence of spring wildflowers, followed by canopy and subcanopy leaf out, disappearance of these spring vernals, emergence of summer- and fall-blooming herbaceous species, development of fall leaf color, then leaf fall. It is important to understand the ecological role of species when deciding what to plant. For example, although many showy spring wildflowers like trilliums, bloodroot, and twinleaf will tolerate a dense tree canopy above them, that canopy must be deciduous to maintain these species. An evergreen canopy provides constant shade, to which few understory species are well adapted, and results in drier conditions beneath because evergreen canopies generally intercept more precipitation during the year than deciduous trees.

Dramatic changes happen within natural communities from one year to the next as species become established, grow, mature, and eventually die. As years pass, one natural community can be transformed into another due to natural succession or disturbance. A simple example of such a transformation are the extensive stands of paper birch and quaking aspen throughout the Adirondacks and Northeast. In the Adirondacks, these stands originated in the early 1900s after intense fires (a result of heavy loads of timber slash ignited by locomotives) burned much of the Adirondacks down to the bare mineral soil. Prior to these fires and timber harvest decades earlier, paper birch and quaking aspen were quite uncommon in this region. But the raw mineral soils in full sunlight provided the perfect seed bed for these trees, and they quickly colonized the burned-over land. Today, these stands, now approaching a hundred years old, are as beautiful as any natural community in the Northeast. But they will not remain for long, as these species do not have the longevity of the sugar maples and other species that currently make up the subcanopy layer and await their opportunity to emerge into the canopy. Without new, catastrophic fires in this region (unlikely because environmental and societal conditions do not favor this event), these striking communities of paper birch and aspen will be more common as postcards sold throughout this region than as real places to visit.

Our life spans are short relative to the time natural communities require to develop. Many wetlands throughout the glaciated portions of this region have been developing since the massive ice sheets retreated over ten thousand years ago. Even upland forests in this region need millennia to include the woody and herbaceous species that ultimately will migrate into them. To expect any created natural community to immediately resemble those that have taken millennia to develop is unreasonable. But, just as Japanese bonsai suggest a more complex natural setting, any created natural community can be much more than a group of native species and do much more by promoting natural processes, even if immature.

Creating natural communities

Increasingly there are significant opportunities to create and restore natural communities as local, state, and federal agencies attempt to reclaim badly degraded landscapes. "Creation" is done where the target community did not previously exist, whereas "restoration" is done where the community once occupied the site. A specific suite of site conditions must be met for the target community to be successful. Some communities are not particularly demanding in their site requirements, while others are—for example, prairies, various kinds of wetlands, and groups of species that require acidic or alkaline soils. One should first assess the site conditions and decide what species are best suited for the specific conditions, or determine the extent to which the site must be modified to support other species of interest. While some critical site characteristics (acidity/alkalinity, drainage, light) are not too difficult to modify, it is impossible to create a wetland community without an area of impeded drainage. At a small scale, shallow pools suffice, but for larger areas the soil must be naturally saturated for prolonged periods or there must be a way to flood the site. Creating and restoring natural communities, regardless of scale, is the ultimate form of native plant gardening, typically replete with much trial, error, learning, and eventual success.

The easiest natural communities to create are those that occur locally on sites that already have soil conditions that naturally support these communities. The elements to constitute a community can come from natural seed sources, both from nearby sites and from seeds that have laid dormant in the soil on the site. If it were not for the natural regenerative capacity of natural communities, much of the Northeast today would not be as heavily forested. For example, in the early 1920s New York was about twenty percent forested, whereas now that figure is around sixty-two percent, mostly due to natural regeneration. The northeast hardwood, oak-hickory, and elm-ash-maple (now minus the elm) forests throughout the state arose on their own on agricultural lands that had become badly eroded and were abandoned. In fact, many of the dominant species that define these forest types are regenerating in the thousands of acres of plantations—typically of exotic species like Norway spruce (*Picea abies*) and European larch (*Larix decidua*) or native species like red pine (*Pinus resinosa*) but on atypical site conditions—established during this same period.

But although these forests appear to have recovered, many important plant species are still missing; many *Trillium* species and other spring wildflowers, for example, have not colonized these former agricultural sites as readily as many woody species have. Seeds of tree, shrub, and vine species are dispersed by two primary agents, wind and birds, whereas dispersal of many wildflowers depends on small mammals and ants. So if one wants to create a natural community on a site that appears to have no biological legacy to the desired community, many tree and shrub species will arrive to a site much more quickly (assuming the desired natural community is not far away) than will the herbaceous species.

Species that are desired but not likely to arrive on their own can be planted by seed or as transplants, either bought or grown from seed or cuttings. Propagule source is a concern to many native plant enthusiasts because of the natural variation in so many traits within a species over large geographical ranges. A simple example of this variation and its importance is the failure of marginally cold hardy species to survive at their limits of cold hardiness when that individual has come from southernmost sources. Ideally, one should be able to purchase native plants propagated from local sources, but such idealism is rarely reality.

Another potential problem (besides time and how many native species arrive on their own) with relying on natural regeneration to compose a natural community is that non-native, aggressive—that is to say, invasive—species can defeat any attempts to promote native species. Some of the most serious invasive plant species produce very large pools of widely dispersed, long-lived seeds that tolerate a great range of site conditions. Few native plants can compete with the Asian honeysuckles (*Lonicera maackii*, *L. tatarica*, and others) and European buckthorn (*Rhamnus cathartica*) among many very serious invasive plant species in this region. Throughout this region some of the most unusual natural communities, including those of great conservation concern, are being seriously threatened by exotic species. Tremendous effort has been expended by government agencies and non-governmental organizations to keep these natural communities from becoming biological wastelands.

Depending on spatial scale and objectives, soils are relatively easy to alter. My very small bog thrives because it is growing in acidic peat moss that barely drains. It was easy to create because of its small scale. What specific soil amendments are needed depends primarily on how far existing soil conditions are from those that a native species or natural community will tolerate, or better yet, thrive on. Nearly all gardening guides discuss how important the addition of organic materials is to soil because organic matter improves soil structure, including porosity, water-holding capacity, and nutrient availability. Indeed, most plant species grow faster and larger on soils enriched with organic matter. But native plant species naturally restricted to infertile, acidic, barrens perform well on a substrate that is basically a mix of fine gravel and sands, and may grow too large and spread too rapidly on rich, moist soils.

One should not be intimidated about the many ways to amend soils. Gardening is much more forgiving than baking. When amendments are added, the addition should be half to equal the volume of soil being amended, for best results. However, the actual volume of amendment depends on how different the soil is from the soil on which the species would naturally occur. Amendments should be worked to a minimum depth of 6 to 9 inches for herbaceous species, 18 to 30 inches minimum for woody species.

If a species or community needs rich, moist soils, then the generous addition of a variety of organic materials is likely necessary. Soil amendments to improve fertility and moisture-holding capacity can include peat moss, highly decomposed peat (muck), compost, bark mulch (relatively fine-textured), aged wood chips, manure, and a variety of locally available organic materials.

For species that require a saturated soil, if the site is not poorly drained, one should sink some type of pool or liner into the ground. Depth to the artificial water table can be easily controlled by piercing small holes in the pool liner at the desired height of the water table.

To improve drainage, add inorganic materials like coarse perlite and vermiculite to heavy clay soils. The addition of sand and gypsum will also improve soil aeration. However, if the water table is near the soil surface and the soil is saturated for extended periods during the growing season, amendments are ineffective, and site engineering (e.g., ditching or installation of tile drains) is necessary. Instead, why not plant the species that naturally occur under these conditions? Perhaps by altering the light to the site, or changing the pH, a group of desired native wetland plants can be grown.

Species that require acidic, well-drained soils high in organic matter, like the many beautiful native species in the heath family (Ericaceae), should be planted on sites that have been highly amended with peat moss and composted vegetation, and acidified if soil pH is higher than 5.5. To maintain acidic conditions long-term, sulfur chips are very effective. For sandy loam soils it takes about 0.5 to 0.8 pounds of sulfur per 100 square feet to lower the pH by 1 unit, 2.5 pounds of sulfur in heavy clay soils. Fertilizers like ammonium sulfate can be used to quickly lower soil pH, and provide nitrogen simultaneously. Iron and aluminum sulfate also are good soil acidifiers, but do not provide any other major plant nutrient. Five pounds of peat moss per 100 square feet will also gradually lower the pH by 1 unit.

If the goal is to ameliorate the acidity of the soil, pulverized (agricultural) lime is highly effective. It takes about 5 pounds of lime per 100 square feet to raise the pH in sandy loams by 1 unit, 8 pounds in heavy clay soils. After application the change will take weeks to months. County agricultural extension offices will give more specific recommendations based on the soil tested.

Amendments may not be sufficient, especially for more large-scale projects. For example, if one living in a new housing development wanted to grow some of the many showy spring woodland wildflowers, like large white trillium, and the native soils were stripped away or were not conducive to growing these species anyway, then a truckload or more of rich, loamy top soil (free of weed seeds) may be satisfactory.

One does not need an elaborate restoration project or extensive amount of land to grow the main plant elements of many natural communities. For example, in a 4-foot-wide kiddie pool sunken in the ground in my backyard, I have created a snapshot of one type of acidic, organic soil community in the Northeast, a "bog," in which Virginia chain fern (*Woodwardia virginica*), marsh fern (*Thelypteris palustris*), the insectivorous northern pitcher plant (*Sarracenia purpurea*), and many other interesting species are growing quite well.

Just a few feet away I made an elliptical mound of mostly sand and gravel, with a little soil, on which I planted bearberry (*Arctostaphylos uva-ursi*), blue lupine (*Lupinus perennis*), wild bergamot (*Monarda fistulosa*), butterfly weed (*Asclepias tuberosa*), eastern prickly pear (*Opuntia humifusa*), wild columbine (*Aquilegia canadensis*), wild stonecrop (*Sedum ternatum*), and barren strawberry (*Waldsteinia fragarioides*). Although only some of these species would typically occur beside each other naturally, all thrive on the rather barren nature of this mound, which is similar to the raw sands and gravels on which these species are often naturally found. These conditions are ideally suited to the seed germination and establishment of especially the blue lupine and butterfly weed, and the bearberry stems root freely along the surface. Even this modest planting, the size of a typical bathtub, is highly dynamic and always interesting.

Some garden groupings of native species do not necessarily ever occur together naturally but grow quite well together under certain conditions. For example, in a wet, sunny ditch in my backyard I planted ostrich fern (*Matteuccia struthiopteris*), swamp milkweed (*Asclepias incarnata*), cardinal flower (*Lobelia cardinalis*), great blue lobelia (*L. siphilitica*), Oswego tea (*Monarda didyma*), northern blue flag (*Iris versicolor*), spotted Joe-pye weed (*Eupatorium maculatum*), buttonbush (*Cephalanthus occidentalis*), and other wetland species—all are thriving. From a native plant species perspective, this planting is one hundred percent successful, but from a natural communities standpoint—I cannot recall ever seeing this exact grouping of plant species together in any of the hundreds of wetlands I have visited. But this planting is quite successful aesthetically, and ecologically, in terms of attracting butterflies and hummingbirds, and for occupying a site that many people would not have attempted planting, because it is flooded to some extent much of the spring and throughout the summer. An additional ecological function is the large amount of evapotranspiration carried out by this planting, thus greatly lowering the water level, minimizing mosquito problems, and allowing less tolerant flood species to coexist.

Similarly, a shade garden can be composed entirely of native species, but a blending of natives and nonnatives may be suitable for some sites and gardeners' objectives—for example, strong foliage contrasts can be attained by planting the large, glaucous, crinkled leaves of *Hosta sieboldiana* 'Elegans' (species native to Japan) next to the small, dark green leaves

Blue lupine in spring

of the native wild ginger (*Asarum canadense*). Both species have been thriving now for over twelve years in a deeply shaded portion of my garden, partially beneath a northern white-cedar (*Thuja occidentalis*) and near the north-facing side of my house, a setting that is so dark that it is nearly impossible to photograph.

There has been much debate among native plant enthusiasts regarding the use of non-natives. The objectives of a project should guide one's plant selections, with attention toward which nonnative plant species are likely to become serious invasive species in the future. Exotic, invasive species have traits that make them highly competitive, widely dispersed, and able to dominate a great range of site conditions. For example, many invasive species produce large numbers of long-lived seeds that are bird- or wind-dispersed; form dense clumps locally by vegetative spread (e.g., stolons, rhizomes, and root suckers); can tolerate deep shade, full sun, and dry and wet soils; are favored by land disturbances; and, have few if any serious pest problems away from their natural range. If in doubt about which nonnative species may become a nuisance, check the USDA PLANTS Database (http://plants.usda.gov). Another good Web site on invasive species biology, problems, and management can be found at http://www.invasivespecies.gov/. Location of the planting in the context of a larger landscape also can facilitate the dispersal of exotic, invasive species. For example, an invasive aquatic plant a group of us has been studying initially spread decades ago via a canal from an otherwise contained site in Canada. This potentially serious plant is now abundant throughout the eastern Great Lakes basin and continues to spread. Other travel corridors for invasive species include ditches, roads, and fencerows.

Explanation of categories

ZONES Cold hardiness given for each species refers to zones shown in the USDA Plant Hardiness Zone Map (see back matter), which is undergoing revision (for the most recent version, visit http://www.usna.usda.gov/Hardzone/). One of the many challenges and rewards of gardening is to find special places in one's garden that support plants that otherwise would not survive at a particular latitude or elevation.

SOIL Wet soil is saturated: it has water near or even above the surface. When "wet" is used here, plant species for these sites will generally thrive with even a few inches of water above the surface during the growing season. "Dry" soils are those that subject plants to prolonged periods of drought because they are excessively drained (coarse sands, for instance) or have little soil on top of bedrock.

LIGHT While so many ecological and horticultural studies confirm the great significance of light as a major plant growth factor, a specific light level under which a plant grows best is especially difficult to characterize. Deep-shade plants will grow where sunlight never reaches them, for example, beneath canopy cover or on north-facing sites near buildings; some plants thrive in places that are brightly lit, even sunny, in early spring, but receive little if any direct sunlight during the majority of the growing season—"shade" is used to describe the ideal light conditions for these species. "Sun" is direct sunlight nearly all day; "partial sun" is more direct sunlight than "partial shade." Light and soil moisture have interacting effects on many plant species; for instance, many wetland plant species thrive in full sun if on saturated soils, but need increasing shade with decreasing wetness.

ATTRIBUTES Attributes listed are the most relevant horticultural ones, that is, I did not include detailed botanical descriptions of each species, which are readily available elsewhere (e.g., Gleason and Cronquist 1991). If a feature—the flowers, fruit, fall leaf color, or bark—is not noteworthy, then no information is listed for it. A plant's overall form will be highly influenced by whether it is crowded by neighbors, uncrowded but beneath shade, or is in the open and allowed to spread. Tree crown shapes are especially affected by neighboring trees. Crown shapes given here are usually for a plant in uncrowded spaces. A plant's ultimate height and spread are affected by soil characteristics, light, and, of course, age. Tree heights given here are what one would generally expect for a mature specimen in a landscape setting, but many of these trees will increase fifty to one hundred percent in height in their natural stands. Fall color is another attribute that can vary greatly within a species, especially due to light and seasonal climatic conditions. Some species have fairly consistent fall color from year to year and among individuals of the species. Other species are quite variable, which is why many cultivars of our native woody plant species have been selected. In general, fall colors develop best in full sun.

PROPAGATION While every species here can be grown from seed, some seeds have rather difficult pregermination requirements. Many species require some kind of stratification—storage in moist (not wet) peat moss for one to three months, for example. For seeds of species that require a pregermination treatment, cold stratification (generally 33 to 41°F) for one to three months is often sufficient. Seeds in moist peat moss can be put into a refrigerator (not freezer) to meet this requirement or sown outdoors in the autumn, ideally in a cold frame or other location that is protected from extreme freezing and thawing, and herbivores. Species with double dormancy may not germinate unless first given warm stratification (generally 68 to 86°F) for one to three months followed by cold stratification (generally 33 to 41°F).

The seed coats of some species are extremely resistant to water absorption and need to be scarified before germination can occur. Scarification can be done mechanically, by nicking the seed coat (e.g., with a file or sandpaper), or by soaking the seeds in concentrated sulfuric acid.

Many woody species are easily propagated by softwood or hardwood stem cuttings. Softwood cuttings are taken in early to mid summer before wood hardens. Hardwood cuttings are taken after leaf fall. Softwood cuttings often require commercially available rooting hormone, and mist (or some other method to maintain one hundred percent humidity) to establish roots. Propagation by cuttings is necessary if one wishes to maintain a particular cultivar. Many perennials are most readily propagated by clump division, which to a novice gardener probably seems a bit brutal, but is a very easy way to quickly have new plants.

Other references on propagation should be consulted for details lacking here. For example, although many fern species can be simply propagated by dividing existing clumps, all can be grown from spores to various degrees of success. Explaining different techniques for fern spore culture is beyond the scope of this book, but there are complete details in Mickel (1994) and Hoshizaki and Moran (2001). Cullina (2000) is a fine source for propagation information about herbaceous wildflowers. For propagating woody species, Dirr and Heuser (1987) and Dirr (1998) should be consulted.

NOTES I have included this miscellaneous category for occasional ramblings, comments about related species, and information about cultivated varieties, or cultivars. Many cultivars are naturally occurring variants of native species, while others have come about through hybridization in natural or garden settings. Additional cultivars have been produced by horticulturists who have artifically crossed various species, sometimes one native, the other not. And in some cases, the parentage of some cultivars is unknown; for example, some bee balm cultivars are likely the result of crosses between two natives, *Monarda didyma* and *M. fistulosa*.

I have listed cultivars for many of the native plants in this guide. I include only cultivars that are selections from straight native species: they are not hybrids of species, native or not. I have seen enough natural variation in many of these species throughout the region to believe that many more horticultural selections await to be discovered, propagated, and made available to the native plant gardener. Should cultivars be planted? It depends on a person's objectives. If conserving native gene pools is the single most important reason for planting these species, then one should collect seeds from specimens throughout a species' range of interest (county, state, region) and grow a genetically diverse mix of each species. If one primarily wants to derive the many benefits of native plants (preserving natural heritage, having plants succeed on a difficult site, attracting a diversity of insects), then a cultivar selected from the natural variation within a plant species seems appropriate.

NATURAL RANGE offers the natural geographical range for each species (taken directly from Gleason and Cronquist 1991), but many species occur far outside these boundaries, in extended ranges which often suggest their relative cold tolerances (or lack thereof). In a few cases—for example, *Hamamelis vernalis* (vernal witch-hazel) and *Hydrangea quercifolia* (oakleaf hydrangea)—I have ignored the geographical limits of this book to include otherwise excellent plant species that occur just a bit to the south but will grow well throughout most of the Northeast. I hope the reader will accept this lack of discipline on my part, and consider using these species if one objective is to select species native to the eastern U.S, rather than particular areas within the Northeast.

Sources of native plant species

In the preface I mentioned transplanting showy native wildflowers from natural woodlands along the bluffs of the Ohio River to my parents' house in northern Kentucky when I was still in high school and certainly ignorant about plant conservation issues. Perhaps I have long wanted to write this book as part of a catharsis for these actions. After decades of reading and research in the fields of forest ecology and conservation biology, I have realized that transplanting wildflowers from natural areas can have serious consequences for many species. During the past twenty years or so, most states have enacted laws to protect native plants that are vulnerable to exploitation or are rare (e.g., see Raynal and Leopold 1999). These laws generally protect plants on public and private property, but a landowner can dig up any plant species or give permission to others for such digging. Even if allowed to dig native plants, one should become informed about which native species are protected or may even locally be in danger of being extirpated.

There are significant opportunities to "rescue" native plants, especially when a parcel of land is going to be cleared for farming or development. Years ago I learned of a large tract of land that was in the process of being cleared for agriculture north of Syracuse, New York. This site had thousands of individuals of many state-protected species, among them white and purple trilliums (*Trillium grandiflorum*, *T. erectum*), over a dozen fern species, and over one hundred small yellow ladyslippers (*Cypripedium parviflorum* var. *parviflorum*). With permission of the landowner I transplanted about two dozen of these ladyslippers to my garden, where they have thrived since, in soil generously enriched with muck (well-decomposed peat) and *Sphagnum* peat moss. Most native orchids are not well suited to gardens because the site conditions usually must be exact for the mycorrhizal fungi that each

White trillium in rich, mesic hardwood forest

orchid species requires. But I have included yellow ladyslipper in this guide because it is regarded as the easiest native orchid to grow and it is becoming more readily available from select nurseries, being propagated primarily by tissue culture. One should not buy protected and rare plant species collected from the wild, unless under the circumstances described above.

Native plants are relatively easy to obtain today. Many nurseries sell some of the most showy species, often unaware that these species are native. And increasingly there are more nurseries devoted exclusively to propagating, growing, and selling native plants. Local farmers' markets often sell native plants too, but buyers should avoid wild-dug plants that sometimes are available.

Some of the best places to see large collections of native plants—Bowman's Hill Wildflower Preserve (New Hope, Pa.) and Garden in the Woods (Framingham, Mass.), for instance—also propagate and sell native plants. Many nature centers hold annual native plant sales for fundraising purposes. Many communities have native plant societies that visit native plant collections and facilitate trading among their members. An outstanding sourcebook for native plants is the Native Plants Material Directory, from the publisher of *Native Plants Journal*. This directory includes over a thousand suppliers of native plants in North America. Information about these and other important native plant resources can be found at this Web site: www.nativeplantnetwork.org. Two other resources that will likely be of interest are *Wildflower* magazine (www.wildflowermag.com) and the North American Native Plant Society (www.nanps.org).

Some of my favorite native plant species

When asked about my favorite native woody and herbaceous species, I avoid giving a specific answer because so many of these species have numerous unique attributes and natural niches. However, I do enjoy reading what others most recommend and why. With the caveat that I would be much more comfortable listing my fifty favorite in each category, here are my top ten or so favorite native species in each category. These choices are based primarily on aesthetic factors; some (e.g., American hart's-tongue fern and painted trillium) are great challenges to grow, and others (e.g., lady fern and red maple) are nearly foolproof. More detailed justifications for these choices should be evident from each species' entry in the species descriptions that make up the heart of this book.

Ferns and fernlike plants: maidenhair fern (*Adiantum pedatum*), American hart's-tongue fern (*Asplenium scolopendrium* var. *americanum*), maidenhair spleenwort (*Asplenium trichomanes*), lady fern (*Athyrium filix-femina*), oak fern (*Gymnocarpium dryopteris*), royal fern (*Osmunda regalis*), rock polypody (*Polypodium virginianum*), Christmas fern (*Polystichum acrostichoides*), New York fern (*Thelypteris noveboracensis*), and Virginia chain fern (*Woodwardia virginica*).

Grasses and grasslike plants: big bluestem (*Andropogon gerardii*), northern sea oats (*Chasmanthium latifolium*), plantain sedge (*Carex plantaginea*), broad-leaf sedge (*C. platyphylla*), tussock sedge (*C. stricta*), tufted hairgrass (*Deschampsia cespitosa*), little bluestem (*Schizachyrium scoparium*), Indian grass (*Sorghastrum nutans*), and prairie dropseed (*Sporobolus heterolepis*).

Wildflowers: wild columbine (*Aquilegia canadensis*), wild ginger (*Asarum canadense*), yellow ladyslipper (*Cypripedium parviflorum*), shooting star (*Dodecatheon meadia*), crested iris (*Iris cristata*), Turk's cap (*Lilium superbum*), cardinal flower (*Lobelia cardinalis*), blue lupine (*Lupinus perennis*), foamflower (*Tiarella cordifolia*), and painted trillium (*Trillium undulatum*).

Vines: Dutchman's pipe (*Aristolochia macrophylla*), cross-vine (*Bignonia capreolata*), American bittersweet (*Celastrus scandens*), twinflower (*Linnaea borealis*), partridgeberry (*Mitchella repens*), trumpet honeysuckle (*Lonicera sempervirens*), and Kentucky wisteria (*Wisteria macrostachya*).

Shrubs: red chokeberry (*Aronia arbutifolia*), New Jersey tea (*Ceanothus americanus*), fringetree (*Chionanthus virginicus*), summersweet clethra (*Clethra alnifolia*), bunchberry (*Cornus canadensis*), dwarf fothergilla (*Fothergilla gardenii*), Virginia sweet spire (*Itea virginica*), mountain-laurel (*Kalmia latifolia*), flame azalea (*Rhododendron calendulaceum*), and highbush blueberry (*Vaccinium corymbosum*).

Trees: serviceberry (*Amelanchier arborea*), pawpaw (*Asimina triloba*), river birch (*Betula*

Cypripedium parviflorum and emerging *Thelypteris palustris*

nigra), yellowwood (*Cladrastis kentukea*), blackgum (*Nyssa sylvatica*), sourwood (*Oxyden-drum arboreum*), swamp white oak (*Quercus bicolor*), sassafras (*Sassafras albidum*), mountain stewartia (*Stewartia ovata*), and eastern hemlock (*Tsuga canadensis*).

Tough native plant species

Some of my other favorites are also very easy to cultivate under a wide range of conditions. Once established under their ideal conditions, these are especially able to persist without further attention. The appendix offers lists of the best species for specific, difficult growing conditions.

Ferns and fernlike plants: hay-scented fern (*Dennstaedtia punctilobula*), scouring rush (*Equisetum hyemale*), ostrich fern (*Matteuccia struthiopteris*), sensitive fern (*Onoclea sensibilis*), and bracken fern (*Pteridium aquilinum*).

Grasses and grasslike plants: broomsedge (*Andropogon virginicus*), blue gramma (*Bouteloua gracilis*), buffalo grass (*Buchloe dactyloides*), softrush (*Juncus effusus*), switch grass (*Panicum virgatum*), prairie cord-grass (*Spartina pectinata*), purpletop (*Tridens flavus*), and cattails (*Typha* spp.).

Wildflowers: purple coneflower (*Echinacea purpurea*), hardy ageratum (*Eupatorium coeles-*

Mature eastern hemlock with various northeast forest species in the understory

tinum), Jerusalem artichoke (*Helianthus tuberosus*), oxeye (*Heliopsis helianthoides*), Oswego tea (*Monarda didyma*), sundrops (*Oenothera fruticosa*), false dragonhead (*Physostegia virginiana*), mayapple (*Podophyllum peltatum*), large Solomon's seal (*Polygonatum commutatum*), and Canada goldenrod (*Solidago canadensis*).

Vines: trumpetcreeper (*Campsis radicans*), Virginia creeper (*Parthenocissus quinquefolia*), and grapes (*Vitis* spp.).

Shrubs: gray dogwood (*Cornus racemosa*), horizontal juniper (*Juniperus horizontalis*), northern bayberry (*Myrica pensylvanica*), eastern ninebark (*Physocarpus opulifolius*), shrubby cinquefoil (*Potentilla fruticosa*), scrub oak (*Quercus ilicifolia*), staghorn sumac (*Rhus typhina*), buffalo berry (*Shepherdia canadensis*), meadowsweet (*Spiraea alba*), and prickly-ash (*Zanthoxylum americanum*).

Trees: red maple (*Acer rubrum*), gray birch (*Betula populifolia*), hackberry (*Celtis occidentalis*), hawthorns (*Crataegus* spp.), green ash (*Fraxinus pennsylvanica*), honeylocust (*Gleditsia triacanthos*), eastern redcedar (*Juniperus virginiana*), eastern hophornbeam (*Ostrya virginiana*), pitch pine (*Pinus rigida*), American sycamore (*Platanus occidentalis*), eastern cottonwood (*Populus deltoides*), pin cherry (*Prunus pensylvanica*), black locust (*Robinia pseudoacacia*), black willow (*Salix nigra*), and northern white-cedar (*Thuja occidentalis*).

Canada goldenrod with New England aster and other native old-field species

SPECIES DESCRIPTIONS

FERNS

Treating both ferns and fernlike plants, such as scouring rushes

Adiantum pedatum

MAIDENHAIR FERN
PTERIDACEAE

ZONES 2 to 8

SOIL moist, rich, well drained

LIGHT partial shade to shade

ATTRIBUTES 12 to 20 inches tall; unfurling fronds on wiry, black and pink stems; fronds consist of twice-branched, flattened sprays of numerous bright to dark bluish green leaflets; deciduous, clump-forming

PROPAGATION spores; easy to divide

NOTES Maidenhair fern is best suited for rich, moist soils in substantial shade. Clumps expand by rhizomes. Cultivars include 'Miss Sharples' (yellow-green new growth) and 'Imbricatum' (crowded, stiffly erect fronds). The southern maidenhair fern, *A. capillus-veneris,* is native to the southernmost portions of this region, and further south into the tropics.

NATURAL RANGE Newfoundland to Alaska and adjacent Asia, south to Georgia, Louisiana, Oklahoma, and California

Asplenium platyneuron

EBONY SPLEENWORT
ASPLENIACEAE

ZONES 4 to 8

SOIL moist, well drained

LIGHT shade

ATTRIBUTES 5 to 12 inches tall; small dark green, leaflets along erect, single, unbranched, dark stem; frond sword-shaped and evergreen

PROPAGATION spores; division

NOTES Many of the ten or so *Asplenium* species native to this region are fine additions to the shaded rock garden, including *A. bradleyi* (Bradley's spleenwort), *A. montanum* (mountain spleenwort), *A. rhizophyllum* (= *Camptosorus rhizophyllus,* walking fern), *A. ruta-muraria* (wall-rue), and *A. viride* (green spleenwort). Because the walking fern and wall-rue grow best on sloping, deeply shaded, calcareous rock faces, they are the most difficult of this group to establish. The natural cross between the ebony spleenwort and walking fern, known as the dragontail fern (*A.* ×*ebenoides*), is an excellent fern for the very shaded rock garden.

NATURAL RANGE Quebec and Ontario to southeastern Minnesota, Kansas, and Colorado, south to Florida, Texas, and Arizona

Asplenium scolopendrium var. *americanum*

AMERICAN HART'S-TONGUE FERN
ASPLENIACEAE

ZONES 5 to 9

SOIL moist, well drained, circumneutral

LIGHT shade

ATTRIBUTES 8 to 18 inches tall; bright to dark green, straplike, leathery fronds

PROPAGATION spores

NOTES One of the most challenging but rewarding native ferns to grow, the American hart's-tongue fern is also one of the rarest ferns in the U.S. (federally listed as threatened). About ninety percent of the U.S. population occurs in two counties in upstate New York, where this variety of the species was originally discovered in North America in 1807. In upstate New York, it is generally found on north-facing slopes at mid slope position, under deciduous tree canopy; it is also found on sites that are glacial plunge basins or narrow meltwater channels, or other enclosed glacial features that maintain very high humidity. Under these conditions, this variety grows in the calcium-enriched humus that settles into rock crevices. *Asplenium scolopendrium* var. *scolopendrium* is quite common in Great Britain, often emerging from sidewalk and building crevices; the European variety of hart's-tongue fern (also listed as *Phyllitis scolopendrium*) has about two hundred cultivars.

Adiantum pedatum

Asplenium platyneuron

Asplenium scolopendrium var. *americanum*

NATURAL RANGE New Brunswick, Bruce Peninsula of Ontario, Upper Peninsula of Michigan, central New York, and eastern Tennessee and northern Alabama

Asplenium trichomanes
MAIDENHAIR SPLEENWORT
ASPLENIACEAE

ZONES 2 to 9

SOIL moist, well drained, high in organic matter

LIGHT shade

ATTRIBUTES 4 to 6 inches tall; once compound, evergreen frond of very small, nearly rounded leaflets on blackish stem

PROPAGATION spores

NOTES Maidenhair spleenwort naturally thrives in deeply shaded, narrow crevices of limestone bedrock so is especially well suited for shaded portions of the rock garden. No matter how often I see it deep in permanently shaded rock crevices in central New York, I always marvel at the fine-textured beauty of this evergreen species. A few cultivars that have more deeply cut or crested fronds are available.

NATURAL RANGE interruptedly circumboreal, and nearly throughout our range, south to Georgia and Texas

Athyrium filix-femina
LADY FERN
DRYOPTERIDACEAE

ZONES 2 to 8

SOIL moist, rich

LIGHT sun to shade

ATTRIBUTES 16 to 36 inches tall; bright green frond with very lacy texture

PROPAGATION spores; easy by division

NOTES Lady fern occurs naturally throughout Europe and Asia, as well as North America. Over three hundred cultivars are recognized. It is one of the easiest and more attractive ferns to grow, especially in moist soil and partial shade.

NATURAL RANGE Newfoundland and Quebec to Ontario and South Dakota, south to Florida and eastern Texas

Botrychium virginianum
RATTLESNAKE FERN
OPHIOGLOSSACEAE

ZONES 4 to 9

SOIL rich, moist, well drained

LIGHT partial sun to shade

ATTRIBUTES fronds about 12 inches tall, erect, bright green, broadly triangular, broken into three major divisions; fertile stalk much higher than frond, arising from same stem, spore cluster resembles open cluster of grapes (but much smaller)

PROPAGATION spores

NOTES Of the eleven or so *Botrychium* species in our region, this is the largest and most common. Another rather common species is *B. dissectum* (dissected grape fern), which has leathery, evergreen leaves that turn purplish in winter.

NATURAL RANGE Newfoundland and Labrador to Alaska, south to Florida and California

Cheilanthes lanosa
HAIRY LIP FERN
PTERIDACEAE

ZONES 5 to 8

SOIL dry

LIGHT partial sun to sun

ATTRIBUTES fronds upright, 6 to 16 inches tall

PROPAGATION spores

NOTES Especially suited to the dry, sunny rock garden; well-drained soils are necessary to maintain this species. Of the four other lip fern species in this region, *C. tomentosa* (woolly lip fern) occurs on both acidic and calcareous, rocky sites.

NATURAL RANGE Connecticut and New York to Wisconsin and Minnesota, south to Georgia and Texas

Cryptogramma stelleri
SLENDER ROCK BRAKE
ADIANTACEAE

ZONES 3 to 5

SOIL cool, moist, calcareous rock

LIGHT shade

ATTRIBUTES fronds 3 to 6 inches tall, arching, bright green, variable in shape depending on whether frond bears spores

PROPAGATION spores

NOTES This species, also known as slender cliff brake, is best suited to very shaded conditions of the rock garden, as long as the rocks, like limestone, are high in calcium.

NATURAL RANGE circumboreal, in America from Newfoundland to Alaska, south to northern New Jersey, northern Pennsylvania, West Virginia, Illinois, Iowa, Utah, and Washington

Cystopteris bulbifera
BULBLET BLADDER FERN
DRYOPTERIDACEAE
ZONES 3 to 7

SOIL moist, rich, circumneutral
LIGHT shade to partial sun
ATTRIBUTES 18 to 30 inches tall; narrow, tapering, yellow-green, arching fronds that are twice pinnate
PROPAGATION reproduces readily from bulblets that fall from the fronds; easy to divide
NOTES Naturally found among wet limestone rocks, bulblet bladder fern will grow under more average garden conditions.
NATURAL RANGE New Brunswick west to Minnesota, south to central Arkansas, northern Alabama,

Asplenium trichomanes

Athyrium filix-femina

Cryptogramma stelleri

Cystopteris fragilis leaflets showing spore clusters

Cystopteris bulbifera

Deparia acrostichoides

Dennstaedtia punctilobula

and Georgia; disjunct in western Texas, eastern New Mexico, and northern Arizona, Utah

Cystopteris fragilis

FRAGILE FERN
DRYOPTERIDACEAE

ZONES 2 to 7

SOIL moist

LIGHT shade to partial sun

ATTRIBUTES fronds bright green, 5 to 12 inches tall, deciduous

PROPAGATION spores; division

NOTES Fragile fern naturally occurs in moist, rocky crevices that are quite shaded. It grows best when soils are enriched with lime. *Cystopteris protrusa*, lowland bladder fern, is common in mesic woods in much of this region, but it is more commonly found growing in soil rather than on rock.

NATURAL RANGE Nova Scotia and New Brunswick and southern Quebec to Minnesota and Nebraska, south to Virginia, southern Illinois, and Missouri, and in the mountains to northern Georgia

Dennstaedtia punctilobula

HAY-SCENTED FERN
DENNSTAEDTIACEAE

ZONES 3 to 8

SOIL moist to dry, acidic

LIGHT sun to partial shade

ATTRIBUTES fronds 15 to 30 inches tall; pale green, twice or thrice pinnate fronds with very lacy texture, deciduous

PROPAGATION spores; easy to divide

NOTES One of easiest ferns to grow, especially on sunny sites, where it may become invasive. This fern rapidly invades brightly lit, disturbed areas where trees have been cut in northeastern forests. Few other herbaceous species can compete with dense stands of hay-scented fern.

NATURAL RANGE Newfoundland and Nova Scotia to Ontario and Minnesota, south to Georgia, Alabama, and Arkansas

Deparia acrostichoides

SILVERY SPLEENWORT
DRYOPTERIDACEAE

ZONES 4 to 9

SOIL moist, rich

LIGHT shade

ATTRIBUTES fronds 18 to 36 inches tall, bright green on upper side, silvery on lower side due to clusters of spores, deciduous

PROPAGATION spores; division

NOTES Also listed as *Diplazium acrostichoides* and *Athyrium thelypteroides*, silvery spleenwort grows best on rich, moist soils under a fair amount of shade.

NATURAL RANGE Nova Scotia and New Brunswick to Ontario and Minnesota, south to Georgia, Louisiana, and Oklahoma

Diplazium pycnocarpon

NARROW-LEAVED SPLEENWORT
DRYOPTERIDACEAE

ZONES 4 to 9

SOIL rich, moist to wet, circumneutral

LIGHT shade

ATTRIBUTES fronds 18 to 36 inches tall, with twenty to forty pairs of lance-shaped leaflets along stalk, deciduous

PROPAGATION spores; easy to divide

NOTES Also listed as *Athyrium pycnocarpon*. Fronds of narrow-leaved spleenwort, also known as the glade fern, are somewhat similar in appearance to the Christmas fern (*Polystichum acrostichoides*) except they are more upright, not leathery, and are deciduous. The narrow-leaved spleenwort should be planted in rich, moist soils that are well shaded.

NATURAL RANGE southern Quebec to Ontario and Minnesota, south to Florida and Louisiana

Diplazium pycnocarpon

Dryopteris campyloptera
MOUNTAIN WOOD FERN
DRYOPTERIDACEAE

ZONES 4 to 7

SOIL moist

LIGHT shade to partial sun

ATTRIBUTES fronds 24 to 36 inches tall, deciduous

PROPAGATION spores; division

NOTES The mountain wood fern is a fertile hybrid of the northern or arching wood fern (*D. expansa*) and the evergreen wood fern (*D. intermedia*). It is a robust, beautiful fern that is fairly easy to cultivate on partially shaded to shaded sites. The northern wood fern has a broader, finer-textured, and more upright frond than the mountain wood fern. The fragrant wood fern (*D. fragrans*) is a relatively rare fern of dry to moist shaded cliffs and slopes in the more northern states of our region.

NATURAL RANGE Labrador and Newfoundland to southern Quebec, western Massachusetts, New York, and Pennsylvania, and south in the mountains to North Carolina and Tennessee

Dryopteris carthusiana
SPINULOSE WOOD FERN
DRYOPTERIDACEAE

ZONES 2 to 7

SOIL moist to wet, acidic

LIGHT shade to partial sun

ATTRIBUTES fronds 12 to 36 inches tall, twice and thrice pinnate

PROPAGATION spores; division

NOTES Also listed as *D. spinulosa*. Similar to the evergreen wood fern (*D. intermedia*), except the spinulose wood fern has deciduous fronds and a hairless blade, among other distinguishing features. The spinulose wood fern thrives in moist to even wet, rich soils in full to partial shade.

NATURAL RANGE interruptedly circumboreal, in America south to South Carolina, Arkansas, and Washington

Dryopteris celsa
LOG FERN
DRYOPTERIDACEAE

ZONES 5 to 9

SOIL rich, moist to wet, acidic

LIGHT partial sun to partial shade

ATTRIBUTES fronds 24 to 36 inches tall, shiny, dark green, deciduous

PROPAGATION spores; division

NOTES Log fern is one of the rarest native ferns in this region; it is a fertile hybrid between Goldie's fern (*D. goldiana*) and southern wood fern (*D. ludoviciana*). *Dryopteris clintoniana*, Clinton's wood fern, is much more common in this region than log fern and looks similar except its leaves are rarely over 8 inches wide, whereas log fern leaves are generally 8 to 12 inches wide. Both ferns grow best in moist to wet soil.

NATURAL RANGE New Jersey and southeastern Pennsylvania to Virginia, South Carolina, and northern Georgia, west to southern Illinois, eastern Missouri, and Texas; disjunct in western New York and southwestern Michigan

Dryopteris cristata
CRESTED WOOD FERN
DRYOPTERIDACEAE

ZONES 3 to 7

SOIL rich, wet to moist

LIGHT shade to partial shade

ATTRIBUTES fronds 12 to 36 inches long, twice pinnate, leaflets spear-shaped, dark green

PROPAGATION spores; division

NOTES Native to forested wetlands in this region and will therefore tolerate substantial soil wetness.

NATURAL RANGE Newfoundland to Saskatchewan and British Columbia, south to North Carolina, Tennessee, Iowa, Nebraska, and Idaho; also Europe

Dryopteris filix-mas
MALE FERN
DRYOPTERIDACEAE

ZONES 4 to 8

SOIL moist, calcareous

LIGHT shade to partial sun

ATTRIBUTES 24 to 48 inches tall

PROPAGATION spores; division

NOTES Male fern will tolerate dry, poor soils but looks best if soils are moist. While this species is naturally uncommon in the eastern U.S., male fern and bracken fern are the most common ferns of Great Britain. Dozens of cultivars are available.

Dryopteris celsa

Dryopteris clintoniana

Dryopteris cristata

Dryopteris filix-mas

Dryopteris filix-mas leaflets showing spore clusters

NATURAL RANGE circumboreal, extending south to Vermont, northern Michigan, northeastern Illinois, South Dakota, and Mexico

Dryopteris goldiana
GOLDIE'S FERN
DRYOPTERIDACEAE
ZONES 3 to 8
SOIL moist
LIGHT shade to partial sun

ATTRIBUTES fronds 36 to 48 inches tall, arching, deciduous
PROPAGATION spores; division
NOTES The largest native *Dryopteris* species and one of the tallest native ferns for shaded, moist conditions. Will grow fine in moist, sunny conditions, but fronds will be yellowish rather than the rich green they are when grown in shade.
NATURAL RANGE New Brunswick to southern Ontario and Minnesota, south to South Carolina, northern Georgia, Tennessee, and Iowa

Dryopteris intermedia
EVERGREEN WOOD FERN
DRYOPTERIDACEAE
ZONES 3 to 8
SOIL moist to dry
LIGHT shade
ATTRIBUTES fronds evergreen, 18 to 36 inches tall; very lacy texture
PROPAGATION spores
NOTES Also known as the common wood fern. A beautiful fern for very shaded conditions.

Dryopteris goldiana

NATURAL RANGE Newfoundland to Georgia, west to Minnesota and Arkansas

Dryopteris marginalis
MARGINAL SHIELD FERN
DRYOPTERIDACEAE

ZONES 2 to 8
SOIL moist to dry

Dryopteris intermedia

Dryopteris marginalis

LIGHT shade to partial shade
ATTRIBUTES 18 to 30 inches tall; fronds twice pinnate, leathery, bluish green, evergreen; single-crowned specimen having vase-shaped appearance
PROPAGATION spores
NOTES A robust fern that is relatively easy to grow; once established, it is very drought-tolerant.
NATURAL RANGE Newfoundland to South Carolina and Georgia, west to southern Ontario, Minnesota, Kansas, and Oklahoma

Equisetum fluviatile
WATER HORSETAIL
EQUISETACEAE

ZONES 1 to 6

Equisetum fluviatile

SOIL wet, including shallow, standing water

LIGHT sun to partial shade

ATTRIBUTES 24 to 36 inches tall; sparsely branched, slender stems

PROPAGATION easy to divide

NOTES Few plant species offer the striking vertical architecture that horsetail species do. They are often grown in the garden in sunken pots to limit their spread. Water horsetail is especially effective in shallow, standing water.

NATURAL RANGE circumboreal, in America south to Pennsylvania, Illinois, Iowa, Nebraska, and Washington

Equisetum hyemale

SCOURING RUSH

EQUISETACEAE

ZONES 2 to 10

SOIL moist or wet

LIGHT sun

ATTRIBUTES 24 to 48 inches tall; evergreen, stiff, erect, jointed, light green stem

Equisetum hyemale

PROPAGATION easy to divide

NOTES Can become too successful in the garden and be invasive. Besides *E. fluviatile* and *E. hyemale,* eight other species of scouring rush or horsetails are native to this region including field horsetail (*E. arvense*), dwarf scouring rush (*E. scirpoides*), woodland horsetail (*E. sylvaticum*), and variegated scouring rush (*E. variegatum*). The field horsetail, which resembles a cut pine tree sprouting from its base, is the most aggressive of this latter group.

NATURAL RANGE circumboreal, in America south to Florida, California, and Central America

Gymnocarpium dryopteris

OAK FERN

DRYOPTERIDACEAE

ZONES 2 to 5

SOIL rich, moist to wet, acidic

LIGHT shade

ATTRIBUTES 6 to 12 inches tall; three-parted fronds that are very delicate-looking

PROPAGATION spores; division

NOTES The oak fern is better suited to the northern half of this region as it does not tolerate heat. It is one of the most distinctive ferns because of its diminutive size and three-parted fronds (similar to bracken fern, *Pteridium aquilinum,* but significantly shorter and more finely textured). A similar native species, *G. robertianum* (limestone oak fern), grows on shaded, limestone rocks.

NATURAL RANGE circumboreal, south to Virginia, North Carolina, Ohio, Illinois, Iowa, and Arizona

Gymnocarpium dryopteris

Lycopodium lucidulum

SHINING CLUBMOSS
LYCOPODIACEAE

ZONES 2 to 7

SOIL rich, moist, well drained, acidic, and high in organic matter (although often on very rocky sites)

LIGHT partial shade to shade

ATTRIBUTES 6 to 10 inches tall; dark green, evergreen, foliage arranged along stem, resembling a bottlebrush

PROPAGATION division of clumps

NOTES Seventeen species of clubmoss are native to this region. They are fernlike plants, typically resembling very small evergreen trees with either very narrow or spreading crowns. All are very difficult to grow, generally requiring moist, well-drained, and acidic soils. Recent taxonomic treatments place some species, like *L. lucidulum,* in the genus *Huperzia.* Clubmoss species are legally protected in many states because they are popular to harvest, especially for Christmas garland and wreaths. Some of the more common species in this region include *L. alopecuroides* (foxtail clubmoss), *L. annotinum* (stiff or

Lycopodium complanatum

Lycopodium tristachyum

bristly clubmoss), *L. clavatum* (running pine), *L. complanatum* (northern ground-cedar), *L. digitatum* (southern ground-cedar), *L. obscurum* (ground-pine), and *L. tristachyum* (ground-pine, ground-cedar).

NATURAL RANGE Newfoundland to Ontario and Minnesota, south to South Carolina, northern Georgia, northern Alabama, and northwest Arkansas

Matteuccia struthiopteris

OSTRICH FERN
DRYOPTERIDACEAE

ZONES 2 to 6

SOIL moist to wet, occasional standing water is fine

LIGHT shade to partial sun

ATTRIBUTES 24 to 72 inches tall; erect, dark green fronds that are once compound and emerge from central crown; structures that holds spores (i.e., the fertile fronds) are much shorter, woody, and persist through the winter

Matteuccia struthiopteris

PROPAGATION spores, or transplant new shoots in spring as they emerge throughout the garden

NOTES Ostrich fern occurs in forested wetlands or along creeks and rivers and can reach extraordinary heights, spreading well (sometimes too well) by rhizomes on wet, rich soils. I probably remove about half of all the new shoots that emerge each spring in my garden, otherwise it would take over a very large area completely. This is also the most delicious species from which to harvest fiddleheads, where such harvest is permissible or if it becomes a problem in one's garden. I have also grown it in large clay pots; the pot should stand in a saucer of water during the growing season, and be protected from strong winds.

NATURAL RANGE circumboreal, in America south to Virginia, Missouri, South Dakota, and British Columbia

Onoclea sensibilis

SENSITIVE FERN
DRYOPTERIDACEAE

ZONES 2 to 10

SOIL moist to wet

Matteuccia struthiopteris fronds emerging in early spring

LIGHT sun (if soil constantly moist) to shade
ATTRIBUTES 12 to 36 inches tall; pale green, triangular frond that is coarsely segmented; fertile fronds resemble a cluster of woody, very small grapes
PROPAGATION spores; easy to divide
NOTES An attractive, easy fern to grow on wet sites

Onoclea sensibilis

(where it naturally occurs), and less aggressive on drier sites. Fronds are adversely affected by drought and frost.
NATURAL RANGE Newfoundland and Labrador to Florida, west to Minnesota, Arkansas, Texas, and irregularly to Colorado; eastern Asia

Osmunda cinnamomea
CINNAMON FERN
OSMUNDACEAE

ZONES 2 to 10
SOIL moist to wet
LIGHT shade to sun (if wet)
ATTRIBUTES 30 to 60 inches tall; fiddleheads large, densely hairy, and very prominent in spring; once pinnate fronds; spores along separate and shorter structure that turns a bright cinnamon color when mature
PROPAGATION spores
NOTES Cinnamon fern is common in many swamps of this region, where it grows on hummocks between pools of water and is often at least head-high. Like many ferns, its foliage tends to be much shorter,

Osmunda cinnamomea

more leathery, and yellow-green when grown in full sun (where it needs moist to wet soils) versus shade. The naturally occurring variety in our area is var. *cinnamomea.*

NATURAL RANGE Labrador to Minnesota, south to Florida, Texas, New Mexico, and tropical America; eastern Asia

Osmunda claytoniana

INTERRUPTED FERN
OSMUNDACEAE

ZONES 2 to 8

SOIL moist

LIGHT shade to partial shade

ATTRIBUTES 24 to 48 inches tall; spores in dark sacs about midway along leaf frond

PROPAGATION spores

NOTES Of the three native *Osmunda* species in this region, interrupted fern occurs on the best-drained soils, including upland sites. The naturally occurring variety in our region is var. *claytoniana.*

NATURAL RANGE Newfoundland to Ontario and Minnesota, south to Georgia, Tennessee, and Arkansas; eastern Asia

Osmunda claytoniana fronds emerging in spring

Osmunda regalis

ROYAL FERN
OSMUNDACEAE

ZONES 2 to 10

SOIL wet to moist

LIGHT shade to partial shade

ATTRIBUTES 24 to 60 inches tall; bluish green, twice pinnate fronds

PROPAGATION spores

NOTES Royal fern occurs naturally in forested wetlands of this region and thrives in saturated soils, including sites wetter than those in which cinnamon fern occurs. Its common name is most appropriate as there are few, if any, more majestic ferns. A few cultivars are available. The naturally occuring variety in our range is var. *spectabilis.*

NATURAL RANGE circumboreal, in America from Newfoundland to Saskatchewan, south to Florida, Texas, and tropical America

Pellaea atropurpurea

PURPLE CLIFF BRAKE
PTERIDACEAE

ZONES 4 to 9

SOIL dry, circumneutral

LIGHT shade

ATTRIBUTES 8 to 20 inches tall; hairy stem that holds bluish green leaves is dark purple to black

PROPAGATION spores

NOTES An excellent species for the rock garden, especially in limestone rocks. A similar species in this region, the smooth cliff brake (*P. glabella*) has nearly hairless stems and will grow under the same conditions as *P. atropurpurea* (i.e., well-drained, basic substrate).

NATURAL RANGE southern Quebec, Vermont, and Rhode Island to Minnesota and Wyoming, south to Florida, Arizona, and Mexico; disjunct in Saskatchewan, Alberta, and British Columbia

Phegopteris connectilis

NARROW BEECH FERN
THELYPTERIDACEAE

ZONES 2 to 5

SOIL moist, acidic

LIGHT shade to partial sun

ATTRIBUTES 8 to 18 inches tall; triangular frond

PROPAGATION spores; division

Osmunda regalis

Osmunda regalis sterile and fertile fronds

Phegopteris connectilis

NOTES Also listed as *Dryopteris phegopteris, Thelypteris phegopteris.* The narrow beech fern, also known as the northern beech fern, makes a good ground cover or edging plant for the northern half of this region, spreading by rhizomes.

NATURAL RANGE circumboreal, south in America to North Carolina, Tennessee, Iowa, and Oregon

Phegopteris hexagonoptera
BROAD BEECH FERN
THELYPTERIDACEAE

ZONES 5 to 9

SOIL moist

LIGHT partial shade

ATTRIBUTES 15 to 24 inches tall; triangular frond

PROPAGATION spores; division

NOTES Also listed as *Dryopteris hexagonoptera, Thelypteris hexagonoptera.* Although the stem (rachis) of the leaf blade is generally winged on both beech ferns, the stem of the broad beech fern is also winged along the lowest set of leaves (pinnae). The broad beech fern is better suited to planting in the southern portions of this region than is the narrow beech fern.

Phegopteris hexagonoptera

NATURAL RANGE Quebec and Maine to Ontario and Minnesota, south to northern Florida and Texas

Polypodium virginianum
ROCK POLYPODY
POLYPODIACEAE

ZONES 5 to 9

SOIL moist, well drained

LIGHT shade

ATTRIBUTES 3 to 10 inches tall; evergreen

PROPAGATION spores; division

NOTES Often "glued" to rock surfaces, on which it can form impressively large mats. I must admit, it is very frustrating for me to see such mats thriving on top of large rocks in the Adirondacks and Catskills, as I have found this species difficult to grow (with and without rock) in the garden. Some taxonomists consider this species a variety of *P. vulgare. Polypodium polypodioides* (resurrection fern) is also native to this region (and further south), occurring commonly on rocks and trees.

NATURAL RANGE Newfoundland to the Yukon, south to Georgia, Alabama, Arkansas, and South Dakota

Polystichum acrostichoides
CHRISTMAS FERN
DRYOPTERIDACEAE

ZONES 3 to 9

SOIL rich, moist to dry

LIGHT shade to partial sun (if moist)

ATTRIBUTES 12 to 24 inches tall; evergreen, once pinnate, dark green, leathery fronds

PROPAGATION spores; division

NOTES Christmas fern is a beautiful, very dark green, evergreen fern that thrives on moist, rich soils in partial shade. Cultivars include 'Crispum' (ruffled edges) and 'Incisum' (deeply cut leaflets).

NATURAL RANGE Nova Scotia to Wisconsin, south to Florida, Texas, and Mexico

Polystichum braunii
BRAUN'S HOLLY FERN
DRYOPTERIDACEAE

ZONES 3 to 8

SOIL rich, moist, well drained

LIGHT shade to partial sun (if moist)

Polypodium virginianum

Polystichum acrostichoides fronds in early spring

Polystichum braunii

Polystichum acrostichoides

ATTRIBUTES 10 to 28 inches tall; shiny, dark green, twice pinnate fronds with lacy texture; the stem that holds the leaves is covered with a dense layer of golden brown scales that contributes to this species' ornamental appearance

PROPAGATION spores; division

NOTES *P. lonchitis*, northern holly fern, also naturally occurs in this region and differs from *P. braunii* by having a narrower frond. Both have dark green, leathery, fine-textured fronds and are well suited to circumneutral soils in at least moderate shade.

NATURAL RANGE circumpolar, south to Massachusetts, New York, Pennsylvania, Michigan, Wisconsin, and northern Minnesota

Pteridium aquilinum

Pteridium aquilinum

BRACKEN FERN
DENNSTAEDTIACEAE

ZONES 3 to 10

SOIL dry, sandy

LIGHT sun to partial shade

ATTRIBUTES 18 to 60+ inches tall; coarse, three-branched, triangular fronds on sturdy stems

PROPAGATION spores; easy to divide

NOTES An exceptional fern species for large, open areas of dry, sandy, infertile soils—even under these conditions, it will readily out-compete any shorter plant species; spreads extensively by deep rhizomes. A number of varieties are recognized, including three in our region, differing by hairiness of fronds and other frond traits. Variety *latiusculum* is the common form of this species in our region.

NATURAL RANGE widespread in the northern hemisphere

Selaginella apoda

MEADOW SPIKEMOSS
SELAGINELLACEAE

ZONES 5 to 10

SOIL moist to wet

LIGHT sun

ATTRIBUTES creeping, mosslike, bright green foliage

PROPAGATION divide clumps or root branchlets in moist sand

NOTES The meadow spikemoss is a very small plant but would be effective between stones, especially in moist to wet soil, or in pots. Three other species of these fernlike plants are native to this region, includ-

Selaginella apoda

ing the rock spikemoss (*S. rupestris*), which forms dense mats on exposed rocks.

NATURAL RANGE southern Quebec to Wisconsin, south to Florida and Texas

Thelypteris noveboracensis
NEW YORK FERN
THELYPTERIDACEAE

ZONES 4 to 8

SOIL moist

LIGHT sun to partial shade

ATTRIBUTES 12 to 24 inches tall; yellow-green frond that tapers at both ends

PROPAGATION spores; easy to divide

NOTES Spreading widely by rhizomes, New York fern is an aggressive plant, especially in light shade.

NATURAL RANGE Newfoundland to Virginia and West Virginia; disjunct in the driftless areas of Wisconsin

Thelypteris palustris
MARSH FERN
THELYPTERIDACEAE

ZONES 2 to 10

Thelypteris noveboracensis

Thelypteris palustris

SOIL moist to wet, including standing water

LIGHT sun (if wet) to shade

ATTRIBUTES 12 to 30 inches tall; bluish green fronds

PROPAGATION spores; easy to divide

NOTES Although I have often seen marsh fern growing in shallow water in shade to full sun, it grows well (sometimes too well) in moist but well-drained garden soils in sun or shade. Marsh fern is one of the best fern species for wet soils, although not as robust as cinnamon, royal, and ostrich ferns. As with many ferns, its fronds are typically wider and longer when grown under shaded conditions. Massachusetts fern (*T. simulata*) is much less common in this region, occurring on very acidic, wet soils in swamps.

NATURAL RANGE widespread in the northern hemisphere

Woodsia obtusa

BLUNT-LOBED WOODSIA
DRYOPTERIDACEAE

ZONES 4 to 9

SOIL moist to dry (with light shade)

LIGHT partial shade to partial sun

ATTRIBUTES 5 to 16 inches tall; grayish green, erect, semievergreen fronds

PROPAGATION spores; division

NOTES An excellent fern for the rock garden. Another woodsia native to this region and well suited to rock gardens is the rusty woodsia (*W. ilvensis*). Two less common native species are the alpine cliff-fern or woodsia (*W. alpina*) and the smooth cliff-fern or woodsia (*W. glabella*). The latter species should be grown in crevices of calcareous rocks.

NATURAL RANGE Maine to Minnesota and eastern Nebraska, south to Florida and Texas

Woodwardia areolata

NETTED CHAIN FERN
BLECHNACEAE

ZONES 3 to 9

SOIL moist to wet

LIGHT shade to sun (if wet)

ATTRIBUTES 12 to 24 inches tall; fronds triangular and dark, glossy green

PROPAGATION spores; division

NOTES Also listed as *Lorinseria areolata*. A vigorous fern for the garden, and ideally suited for wet, acidic conditions.

NATURAL RANGE Nova Scotia to northern Florida, west to Michigan, Missouri, and eastern Texas

Woodwardia virginica

VIRGINIA CHAIN FERN
BLECHNACEAE

ZONES 3 to 10

SOIL moist to wet, including standing water

LIGHT shade to sun (if wet)

ATTRIBUTES 18 to 24 inches tall; fronds initially bronze-colored, becoming glossy and very bright green in full sun; deciduous

Woodsia obtusa leaflets showing spore clusters

Woodwardia areolata

PROPAGATION spores; division

NOTES Also listed as *Anchistea virginica*. Virginia chain fern will thrive under the wettest acidic conditions. Despite its common name, which suggests a rather restricted, southern geographical distribution, this species is also very cold-tolerant and occurs naturally throughout southeastern Canada. If the soil is not permanently saturated, the netted chain fern is a better choice.

NATURAL RANGE Nova Scotia to Florida, west to Ontario, Michigan, Illinois, and Texas; Bermuda

Woodwardia virginica

GRASSES

Treating graminoids—true grasses and grasslike plants, such as sedges and rushes

Acorus calamus

SWEETFLAG
ARACEAE

ZONES 5 to 9

SOIL moist to wet, including permanent, shallow, standing water

LIGHT sun to partial shade

ATTRIBUTES sword-shaped, bright green, spreading leaves 24 to 36 inches high; "flower" a slender packed cluster about 3 inches long of very small flowers—interesting, but not showy

PROPAGATION divide clumps in spring

NOTES The leaves and rootstock smell sweetly of cinnamon when crushed. The cultivar 'Variegatus' has prominently white and green variegated leaves.

NATURAL RANGE irregularly circumboreal, in America from Nova Scotia and Quebec to Minnesota, Alberta, and eastern Washington, south to Florida, Texas, and Colorado

Andropogon gerardii

BIG BLUESTEM
POACEAE

ZONES 3 to 9

SOIL moist to dry

LIGHT sun

ATTRIBUTES a robust, clumped grass 5 to 8 feet high; leaves up to 2 feet long and 1/2 inch wide; stems round, stout, frequently bluish or purplish

PROPAGATION seed, cold stratify for a short period to improve germination; divide in early spring

NOTES Big bluestem is a major component of our prairies and is very well suited to the driest soils. It is most attractive in autumn, when its leaves turn bronze-red. Broomsedge (*A. virginicus*), also native to this region, is shorter (to 4 feet high), very drought-resistant, and has bright orange foliage in autumn. Elliott's broomsedge (*A. gyrans*) also tolerates dry, poor soils and is often found with broom-sedge. Another attractive drought-tolerant native species in this genus is the split-beard broomsedge (*A. ternarius*). The bushy beardgrass (*A. virginicus* var. *abbreviatus* = *A. glomeratus*) naturally occurs on wet soils and sunny sites in this region, so is better suited to poorly drained conditions.

NATURAL RANGE Quebec to Saskatchewan, south to Florida and Arizona

Aristida purpurea

PURPLE THREE AWN
POACEAE

ZONES 6 to 9

SOIL well drained to dry

Acorus calamus

62

LIGHT sun

ATTRIBUTES fine-textured mound of sage-green leaves that are $1/16$ inch or less wide and 6 to 12 inches long; greenish purple flowers in nodding clusters on erect spikes to 30 inches long

PROPAGATION seed or division

NOTES Found naturally across the plains of North America, purple three awn is very heat- and drought-tolerant.

NATURAL RANGE Minnesota and Iowa to Washington, California, and northern Mexico

Andropogon gerardii and other native species in restored prairie

Bouteloua gracilis

BLUE GRAMMA
POACEAE

ZONES 3 to 10

SOIL dry, poor

LIGHT sun

ATTRIBUTES about 12 inches tall; foliage fine-textured, light green-gray, turning purple after first frost

PROPAGATION seed or division

NOTES Blue gramma will withstand regular mowing and is also grown for unmown lawns. It does well in containers and rock gardens, too. It is one of key components of North American short-grass prairies and will withstand considerable drought. Side oats gramma (*B. curtipendula*) is also very drought-tolerant but reaches about twice the height of blue gramma.

NATURAL RANGE Illinois to Alberta, south to Texas and southern California

Buchloe dactyloides

BUFFALO GRASS
POACEAE

ZONES 3 to 9

SOIL dry

LIGHT sun

ATTRIBUTES foliage gray-green, fine-textured, to about 6 inches tall

PROPAGATION seed or division

NOTES Buffalo grass is another key component of North American short-grass prairies. It can be mowed and maintained as lawn, or left to grow without any maintenance. It is very tolerant of drought, cold, and infertile soils.

NATURAL RANGE western Minnesota and western Iowa, north to Alberta, west to the mountains, south to Arizona and New Mexico

Carex muskingumensis

PALM SEDGE
CYPERACEAE

ZONES 5 to 8

SOIL moist to wet

LIGHT sun to partial shade

ATTRIBUTES numerous upright stems with medium-textured foliage; leaves narrow, bright green, up to

Carex muskingumensis

20 inches long, some radiating from top of rigid stems

PROPAGATION seed, cold stratify for three months; divide in spring or fall

NOTES A few cultivars of palm sedge may be available, including 'Oehme', which has leaves with a narrow, yellow margin, and 'Silberstreif', which has green and white variegated leaves and is slightly shorter in stature than the species. Of the literally hundreds of *Carex* (sedge) species that naturally occur in this region, the majority are found in wetlands, some even in aquatic habitats. Of these many, a few others that are sometimes available are *C. aurea* (golden-fruited sedge, grows to only 6 inches high), *C. crinita* (fringed sedge, to 4 feet tall), *C. grayi* (especially the selection 'Morning Star', to 3 feet tall), *C. lupulina* (hop sedge, to 30 inches tall), and *C. stricta* (tussock sedge, 3 to 4 feet tall).

NATURAL RANGE Ohio and Kentucky to Michigan, Minnesota, Manitoba, Kansas, and Oklahoma

Carex stricta

Carex nigra
BLACK SEDGE
CYPERACEAE

ZONES 4 to 8

SOIL moist to wet, including saline (salty)

LIGHT sun to shade

ATTRIBUTES loosely packed, narrow leaves forming clumps to about 2 feet tall; leaves often waxy bluish

PROPAGATION seed, cold stratify for three months; divide in spring

NOTES Black sedge naturally occurs in salt marshes, among other wet habitats, and is therefore well adapted to high concentrations of salt in the soil.

NATURAL RANGE Labrador to Connecticut and Vermont; disjunct in northern Michigan; widespread in Europe

Carex pensylvanica
SEDGE
CYPERACEAE

ZONES 4 to ?

SOIL moist, well drained to dry

LIGHT sun to shade

ATTRIBUTES delicate clumps of very slender leaves, to about 9 inches high

PROPAGATION seed, or divide clumps in spring

NOTES Dozens of additional *Carex* species naturally occur in upland, forested habitats of this region, and tolerate deep shade and rather dry conditions. Some additional species that are well suited to the dry, shaded garden and are becoming more available are *C. eburnea* (fine foliage to 12 inches tall), *C. flaccosperma* (medium texture, basically evergreen leaves), and *C. laxiculmis* (narrow, long, bluish green leaves).

NATURAL RANGE New York and southern Maine to Virginia (and in the mountains to North Carolina and Tennessee), west to Saskatchewan, British Columbia, Washington, California, Oregon, and New Mexico

Carex plantaginea
PLANTAIN SEDGE
CYPERACEAE

ZONES 5 to 9

SOIL moist

LIGHT partial shade to shade

ATTRIBUTES clump of bright green, somewhat crinkled leaves to 12 inches long and about 1 inch wide; terminal cluster of small, yellow flowers on slender purplish stalks in very early spring

PROPAGATION seed, or divide clumps in spring

NOTES I have been growing this and *C. platyphylla* in

Carex pensylvanica

Carex flaccosperma

Carex laxiculmis

Carex plantaginea

a very shaded portion of my garden for many years and have really enjoyed their color, texture, and ease of cultivation. Recently, I have seen these species offered for sale. They are nice additions to a shade garden, providing an interesting contrast to hostas and ferns.

NATURAL RANGE New Brunswick and southern

Quebec to Minnesota, southern Indiana, Kentucky, New Jersey, Maryland, and in the mountains to northern Georgia

Carex platyphylla
BROAD-LEAF SEDGE
CYPERACEAE

ZONES ?, but certainly grows well throughout its native range

SOIL moist, well drained to dry

LIGHT partial shade to shade

ATTRIBUTES clump of light, somewhat waxy, bluish green leaves about 1 inch wide and about 8 inches long

PROPAGATION seed or division

NOTES This species has been expanding beyond where I planted it in my garden, not too far from the seed source, wherever there is deep shade. I have seen this species many times throughout the shaded, calcareous, often dry woods of upstate New York and have always wondered why it was not more readily available. Some nurseries have finally started to appreciate the color, texture, and shade-tolerance of this species.

NATURAL RANGE Maine and southern Quebec to

Carex platyphylla

Chasmanthium latifolium

Virginia and in the mountains to North Carolina, west to Wisconsin and Missouri

Chasmanthium latifolium

NORTHERN SEA OATS
POACEAE

ZONES 4 to 8

SOIL moist

LIGHT sun to partial shade

ATTRIBUTES dense clump of dark green leaves (lighter green when grown in full sun) along 30- to 36-inch-long stems that end in a large (5- to 10-inch-wide), open cluster of flowers in late summer, followed by flat, persistent fruit that becomes showy when it turns bronze in autumn. Foliage also turns bronze in autumn

PROPAGATION seed is very easy; divide clumps in spring or autumn

NOTES Northern sea oats is a robust, true grass that is well adapted to moderate shade. I have had to remove dozens of new plants from my garden, as this species self-sows readily.

NATURAL RANGE New Jersey to Georgia and northwestern Florida, west to southern Ohio, Indiana, Illinois, Kansas, and Texas

Deschampsia cespitosa

TUFTED HAIRGRASS
POACEAE

ZONES 4 to 9

SOIL best on organic soils, moist to wet

LIGHT sun to partial shade

ATTRIBUTES densely tufted clump 2 to 3 feet high; leaf blades dark green, $1/5$ inch wide, up to 2 feet long; flowers in open clusters to 8 inches wide and 20 inches long, and in a range of colors (silvery, light green, or purple)

PROPAGATION seed, or divide clumps in spring or fall

NOTES An excellent, relatively fine-textured grass for poorly drained soils in the more northern portions of this region. Several cultivars have been selected for various foliage looks, including a straw-yellow color and variegated, as well as unique inflorescence colors. The crinkled hairgrass (*D. flexuosa*) occurs on much drier, sunny and shaded sites in this region.

NATURAL RANGE circumboreal, south to the higher mountains of New Hampshire and New York, and to Colorado

Elymus glaucus

BLUE WILD RYE
POACEAE

ZONES 4 to 8

SOIL moist to dry

LIGHT sun

ATTRIBUTES clump of arching, light waxy blue, arching leaves to 36 inches high

PROPAGATION divide in spring or autumn

NOTES Whereas most species of wild rye spread aggressively by stolons, this native species does not.

Deschampsia cespitosa

Elymus glaucus

Two other native, ornamental species of *Elymus* in this region are the Canada wild rye (*E. canadensis*) and bottlebrush-grass (*E. hystrix* = *Hystrix patula*). Canada wild rye is well adapted to a wide range of soil conditions in full sun. Bottlebrush-grass naturally is found on dry soils under shaded conditions.

NATURAL RANGE widespread in western mountains, east less commonly to Arkansas, Iowa, northern Michigan, Ontario, and western New York

Eragrostis spectabilis
PURPLE LOVEGRASS
POACEAE

ZONES 5 to 9

SOIL dry to moist, well drained

LIGHT partial sun to sun

ATTRIBUTES compact, mound-forming plant to about 2 feet high and wide; leaves light green, 1/4 to 1/2 inch wide and to 12 inches long; reddish purple flowers in open, fine-textured cluster 12 to 18 inches above foliage

PROPAGATION seed or division

NOTES Purple lovegrass grows especially well on

sandy soils. Another attractive native species in this genus is sand lovegrass (*E. trichodes*), which thrives on dry, sandy soils in full sun; sand lovegrass will reach 4 feet in height.

NATURAL RANGE Maine to North Dakota, south to Florida and Texas

Hordeum jubatum

FOXTAIL BARLEY
POACEAE

ZONES 5 to 9

SOIL moist to wet

LIGHT sun

ATTRIBUTES open clumps 1 to 2 feet tall and wide; leaves light green, fine-textured; flowers—pinkish, foxtail-like whisks—on nodding stems above foliage

PROPAGATION seed

NOTES Foxtail barley is short-lived but reestablishes readily from self-sown seeds, so much so that it can readily outcompete other desirable species. It tolerates a wide range of soil conditions, including salt. Cultivated barley (*H. vulgare*) is a related, but nonnative, species.

NATURAL RANGE Newfoundland to Alaska, south to Delaware, Illinois, Missouri, Texas, and California

Juncus effusus

SOFTRUSH
CYPERACEAE

ZONES 3 to 9

SOIL moist to wet, including permanent, shallow, standing water

LIGHT sun to partial sun

ATTRIBUTES dark, evergreen, cylindrical stems in erect clumps about 3 feet high

PROPAGATION divide clumps in spring

NOTES Softrush is one of the most common, easy-to-grow herbaceous species for wetland restoration projects.

NATURAL RANGE nearly cosmopolitan, and throughout our range

Luzula acuminata

HAIRY WOOD-RUSH
JUNCACEAE

ZONES 4 to ?

SOIL moist, well drained

LIGHT partial shade

ATTRIBUTES leaves dark green, shiny, to 1/2 inch wide and 12 inches long in dense clumps

PROPAGATION seed or division

NOTES Hairy wood-rush is a good ground cover for

Juncus effusus

woodland conditions. Six other species of *Luzula* are native to this region; most are found in wooded areas or clearings. *Luzula echinata* is another attractive native wood-rush.

NATURAL RANGE Newfoundland to Saskatchewan, south to Georgia, Alabama, and Iowa

Muhlenbergia capillaris

HAIRGRASS
POACEAE

ZONES ? to 6 (or colder)

SOIL dry, rocky to wet, sandy or organic soils

LIGHT sun to partial sun

ATTRIBUTES clump-forming, to 3 feet tall in flower; leaves dark green, glossy; topped by violet-pink flowers in late summer to early fall

PROPAGATION seed or division

NOTES Most of the muhly species planted in gardens are native to the southwestern U.S. and Mexico, consequently they are heat- and drought-tolerant. Fifteen additional species of this genus are native to our region.

NATURAL RANGE West Indies, eastern Mexico, and southeastern U.S. north to Oklahoma, eastern Kansas, and south Indiana, and in the Atlantic coastal states to Massachusetts

Panicum virgatum

SWITCH GRASS
POACEAE

ZONES 5 to 9

SOIL dry to wet, including a fair amount of salinity

LIGHT sun to partial sun

ATTRIBUTES dense mound of $5/8$-inch-wide and 24-

Panicum virgatum

to 36-inch-long leaves; flowers in open, large, fine-textured clusters to 24 inches long in mid summer

PROPAGATION seed, or divide clumps in spring or autumn

NOTES Cultivars have been selected primarily for reddish foliage ('Warrior', 'Rotstrahlbusch'), although I think the metallic-blue leaves of 'Heavy Metal' and its stiff upright habit (to 4 feet high) are interesting (or maybe I just like its name). Deer tongue grass (*P. clandestinum*) has coarser, bamboo-like foliage on stems that form 3- to 4-foot-tall arching mounds; it is better suited to moist, fertile soils.

NATURAL RANGE Nova Scotia and Quebec to Manitoba and Montana, south to Arizona, Mexico, and Wisconsin

Schizachyrium scoparium

LITTLE BLUESTEM
POACEAE

ZONES 4 to 9

SOIL moist, well drained to extremely dry

LIGHT sun

ATTRIBUTES stems in loose or dense tufts 18 to 40 inches high; leaves to 12 inches long, $1/4$ inch wide, turning bronze-orange after frost

PROPAGATION seed or division

NOTES Cultivars of little bluestem promise autumn fall color in rich shades of red.

NATURAL RANGE New Brunswick and Quebec to Alberta, south to Florida and Mexico

Scirpus cyperinus

BULRUSH
CYPERACEAE

ZONES 4 to ?

SOIL moist to wet, including shallow, permanent, standing water

LIGHT sun

ATTRIBUTES upright flowering stems in dense clumps to 5 feet high; terminal flower clusters dense, woolly, and light brown at maturity

PROPAGATION seed, or divide clumps in spring or autumn

NOTES Also known as wool grass. *Scirpus cyperinus* readily self-sows, and, with its ability to withstand prolonged flooding, is an exceptional species for wetland restoration projects.

Panicum virgatum 'Warrior'

Schizachyrium scoparium

NATURAL RANGE Newfoundland to British Columbia, south to Florida and Texas

Sorghastrum nutans

    INDIAN GRASS
    POACEAE
ZONES 3 to 9
SOIL moist to dry

Scirpus cyperinus

LIGHT sun to partial sun

ATTRIBUTES stems with narrow clusters of flowers and fruit, to 6+ feet high in dense clumps

PROPAGATION seed is easy; divide clump in spring or autumn

NOTES Indian grass is a key component of our native tall-grass prairies. Cultivars include selections made for waxy blue foliage ('Osage', 'Sioux Blue').

NATURAL RANGE throughout our region, south to the Gulf of Mexico, west to Utah and Arizona

Spartina pectinata

PRAIRIE CORD-GRASS
POACEAE

ZONES 4 to 9

SOIL dry to wet

LIGHT sun

ATTRIBUTES to 7 feet tall in flower; leaves arching, 5/8 inches wide and about 24 inches long, dark green, glossy, turning bright golden yellow in autumn

PROPAGATION seed or division

NOTES Prairie cord-grass is tolerant of salt and dry soils and spreads little under these conditions. The cultivar 'Aureomarginata' (golden-edged prairie cord grass) has a narrow golden band along the entire margin of each leaf.

NATURAL RANGE Newfoundland and Quebec to Alberta and Washington, south to North Carolina and Texas

Sporobolus heterolepis

PRAIRIE DROPSEED
POACEAE

ZONES 3 to 9

SOIL well drained to dry

LIGHT sun

ATTRIBUTES dense, fine-textured, upright, arching mound to over 3 feet tall; leaves threadlike, about 1/16 inch wide, glossy, medium green

PROPAGATION seed or division

NOTES Prairie dropseed is an important component of North American prairies. Of the eleven native *Sporobolus* species in this region, another that has promise for the garden is the alkali sacaton or dropseed (*S. airoides*), which naturally occurs in wet,

Sporobolus heterolepis, with *Geum triflorum* in fruit

alkaline meadows; this species has a coarser texture than the prairie dropseed but showier flowers, and it will also tolerate drought.

NATURAL RANGE Ontario to Saskatchewan and Texas, east occasionally to Pennsylvania, Connecticut, and Quebec

Tridens flavus
PURPLETOP
POACEAE

ZONES 5 to 10

SOIL well drained to moist

LIGHT sun to partial sun

ATTRIBUTES upright, clump-former, to 4 feet tall; leaves medium green, 5/8 inch wide by about 12 inches long; drooping flower clusters, glossy, reddish purple, in late summer

PROPAGATION seed or division

NOTES Purpletop can become invasive in moist, fertile soils.

NATURAL RANGE Massachusetts to southern Ontario, southern Michigan and Nebraska, south to Florida and Texas

Typha angustifolia
NARROW-LEAF CATTAIL
TYPHACEAE

ZONES 4 to 9

SOIL moist to wet, including permanent, standing water; will tolerate moderate salinity

LIGHT sun

ATTRIBUTES plants to 6+ feet high; leaves straplike, narrow (about 1/2 inch wide); fruit a brown spike to 5/8 inch in diameter

PROPAGATION seed, or divide clumps anytime

NOTES Narrow-leaf cattail will tolerate standing water 12+ inches deep, and water that is quite alkaline and brackish. Its fine-textured foliage and interesting terminal flowers and fruit make it a fine addition to very wet soils in full sun. The broad-leaf cattail, *T. latifolia*, is also common in wetlands throughout this region; it is a more robust species with broader leaves and wider fruit, and forms denser stands, often excluding all other plant species. However, like *T. angustifolia*, it is an exceptional wetland restoration species with high wildlife value.

NATURAL RANGE throughout region

Typha angustifolia

Typha latifolia

Aconitum uncinatum

EASTERN MONKSHOOD
RANUNCULACEAE

ZONES 6 to 8

SOIL moist

LIGHT sun to partial shade

ATTRIBUTES to 36 inches tall; about $3/4$ inch long, hooded blue flowers along short flower stalk in late summer atop kidney-shaped, deeply lobed leaves up to 4 inches wide

PROPAGATION seed, cold stratify for three months

NOTES All species of *Aconitum* are very poisonous. *Aconitum noveboracense,* northern monkshood, is another of the three native monkshoods in this region, and naturally occurs along streambanks and in cold woods in the Catskills of New York, northeastern Ohio, and in and near the driftless area of Wisconsin and Iowa; it is federally listed as threatened.

NATURAL RANGE southern Pennsylvania to Ohio and southern Indiana, south to North Carolina, western South Carolina, northern and western Georgia, and central Tennessee

Actaea pachypoda

WHITE BANEBERRY
RANUNCULACEAE

ZONES 3 to 8

SOIL moist

LIGHT partial shade to partial sun

ATTRIBUTES 20 to 30 inches tall; creamy white flowers in 2- to 4-inch-long, oblong cluster in spring; open cluster of $1/4$-inch-wide ivory fruit attached to pinkish flower stalks, each fruit with distinct dark "eye," persists into autumn

PROPAGATION sow seed in cold frame or outdoor open bed in fall; division is very difficult

NOTES Also listed as *A. alba;* also known as doll's eyes. Ingested fruits, even in very small quantities, are poisonous.

NATURAL RANGE eastern Quebec to Ontario and Minnesota, south to Georgia, Louisiana, and Oklahoma

Actaea rubra

RED BANEBERRY
RANUNCULACEAE

ZONES 2 to 8

SOIL moist

LIGHT shade to partial sun

ATTRIBUTES 24 to 32 inches tall; creamy white flowers in spring; open cluster of $1/4$-inch-wide, shiny, bright red fruit on red flower stalks, persists into autumn

PROPAGATION sow fresh seed for spring germination, as per *A. pachypoda;* division is very difficult

NOTES Ingested fruits, even in very small quantities, are poisonous. Both *Actaea* species have attractive flowers and foliage and a long-lasting, unique fruit display.

NATURAL RANGE circumboreal, in America from Labrador and Newfoundland to Alaska, south to

Aconitum uncinatum

Connecticut, northern New Jersey, northern Indiana, Iowa, and Arizona

Amsonia tabernaemontana
COMMON BLUESTAR
APOCYNACEAE

ZONES 3 to 9

SOIL dry to moist

LIGHT partial shade to sun (if soil moist)

ATTRIBUTES 36 to 40 inches tall; $1/2$- to $3/4$-inch-wide, light-blue, star-shaped flowers in dense, pyramidal, terminal clusters in spring; dense foliage in shrubby habit; glossy foliage turns yellow or orange in autumn

PROPAGATION harvest seed in fall, dry, sow in outdoor cold frame or cold stratify during winter; difficult to divide plants

NOTES Nectar source for mourning cloaks and other

Actaea pachypoda

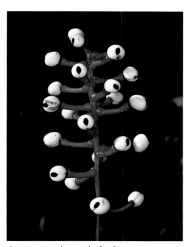

Actaea pachypoda fruit

Actaea rubra

Actaea rubra fruit

Amsonia tabernaemontana

early butterflies; var. *salicifolia* has more narrow and pointed leaves.

NATURAL RANGE coastal plain from New Jersey southward, more widespread in southern U.S., and north in the interior to southern Indiana, central Illinois, and Kansas

Anemone canadensis

CANADA ANEMONE
RANUNCULACEAE

ZONES 2 to 9

SOIL moist (for establishment) to dry

LIGHT sun to shade

ATTRIBUTES 12 to 24 inches tall; single, 1-inch-wide, white flowers held above deeply dissected, light green foliage in late spring

PROPAGATION seed, sow immediately upon ripening; divide plants during growing season

NOTES Also known as the meadow anemone. May spread aggressively by rhizomes into areas where it is not wanted.

NATURAL RANGE eastern Quebec to Alberta, south to Maryland, West Virginia, Kentucky, Missouri, New Mexico

Anemone quinquefolia

WOOD ANEMONE
RANUNCULACEAE

ZONES 3 to 8

SOIL moist

LIGHT shade to partial shade

ATTRIBUTES 3 to 6 inches tall; single, 3/4- to 1-inch-wide, white flower in early spring

PROPAGATION divide larger groups of plants

NOTES A very short, beautiful, deciduous ground cover for shaded conditions. Two other native *Anemone* species in our region for the garden are cut-leaved anemone (*A. multifida*) and pasqueflower (*A. patens*). The cut-leaved anemone is found on wet, calcareous sites or dry, rocky sites. Pasqueflower is one of the first plants to flower each spring in dry prairies and barrens of the Midwest. Closely related taxonomically to this genus, and especially to the appearance of *A. quinquefolia,* is the rue anemone (*Anemonella thalictroides*). Rue anemone occurs in dry to moist woods throughout much of our region; its flowers, which appear in early spring, are white to pale pinkish purple.

NATURAL RANGE Quebec to Manitoba, south to Maryland, Ohio, northern Indiana, and northeastern Iowa, and in the mountains to northern Georgia

Aquilegia canadensis

WILD COLUMBINE
RANUNCULACEAE

ZONES 3 to 9

SOIL well drained, circumneutral

LIGHT partial shade to sun

ATTRIBUTES 10 to 24 inches tall; numerous 1 1/2-inch-long, nodding, pale orange-red flowers in mid spring; dissected, fernlike, bluish green foliage for the remainder of the growing season

PROPAGATION easy from seed, collect when ripe and sow immediately, or let natural dispersal spread seeds into various nooks and crannies

NOTES Also known as the Canada columbine. When available, one of first native plants sought by migrating ruby-throated hummingbirds; excellent with rocks (rock gardens, patio crevices, gravel beds), especially limestone; individual plants are relatively short-lived, but abundant natural reproduction will generally maintain this species in a garden. Variety *flavescens* and the cultivar 'Corbett' have pale yellow flowers, while var. *nana* reaches only 12 inches in height.

NATURAL RANGE Nova Scotia to Saskatchewan, south to Florida and Texas

Arisaema triphyllum

JACK-IN-THE-PULPIT
ARACEAE

ZONES 3 to 9

SOIL moist, with abundant organic matter

LIGHT shade to partial shade

ATTRIBUTES 12 to 28 inches tall; unusually shaped and striped "flowers" in mid spring; clusters of brilliant red fruit in autumn

PROPAGATION collect seed in autumn when fruit are bright red, wash hands after removing covering from seed, and sow immediately in protected outside bed or store in moist peat in refrigerator and sow in spring. Relatively slow to develop from seed. Corms can be divided in autumn after leaves senesce

NOTES The flowers are actually "Jack" (or "Jill" on female plants) and are enclosed within a hooded structure called a spathe. The spathe of var. *steward-*

Anemone canadensis

Anemone quinquefolia

Aquilegia canadensis

Arisaema triphyllum

Arisaema triphyllum fruit

Arisaema triphyllum
var. *stewardsonii*

sonii, which is naturally more common in wetlands, has an especially attractive patterning of green and white stripes, developing in late spring; 'Zebrinus' has a purple spathe striped with white. Crystals of calcium oxalate exist throughout this species, making it painful to ingest.

NATURAL RANGE Nova Scotia to North Dakota, south to Florida and Texas

Aruncus dioicus

GOAT'S BEARD
ROSACEAE

ZONES 4 to 8

SOIL moist

LIGHT shade to partial sun

ATTRIBUTES 36 to 60 inches tall; large, pyramidal clusters of white flowers in early summer that are especially showy in dark locations; dense foliage, shrublike

PROPAGATION seed, will germinate without pretreatment if fresh, otherwise subject stored seeds to cold, moist stratification for one month prior to sowing; minimize propagation by division

NOTES Goat's beard will tolerate an increasing amount of sun the further north one plants it in this region; it is not for the garden with limited space. Plants are either male or female, which is relevant here because the large cluster of male flowers is more showy than the female flowers. The cultivar 'Kneiffii' is about one-half the size of the species, and var. *astilboides* reaches only 24 inches in height.

NATURAL RANGE Pennsylvania to Ohio, Indiana, and Iowa, south to North Carolina, Alabama, and Arkansas

Asarum canadense

WILD GINGER
ARISTOLOCHIACEAE

ZONES 3 to 8

SOIL moist (but will tolerate drier soils)

LIGHT shade to partial sun

ATTRIBUTES 6 to 12 inches tall; deep green, heart-shaped leaves up to 7 inches in diameter and parallel to the ground make an exceptional ground cover for very dark conditions; very unusual, deep maroon flowers that are typically hidden by leaves above

PROPAGATION readily self-sows from seed that matures in late spring; easy to divide, if moved with intact ball of soil

NOTES Under moist, shaded conditions, can really

Aruncus dioicus

Asarum canadense

Asarum canadense flower

spread; alternate food source for larvae of pipevine swallowtail butterfly; rhizomes are especially spicy-aromatic. Very closely related to wild ginger are three native heart-leaf or little brown jug species of *Hexastylis:* Virginia wild ginger (*H. virginica*), mottled wild ginger (*H. shuttleworthii*), and arrow-leaved ginger (*H. arifolia*). All three are evergreen and, while more attractive than wild ginger, are not as cold hardy.

NATURAL RANGE New Brunswick and Quebec to Ontario and Minnesota, south to North Carolina, northern Alabama, and northern Louisiana

Asclepias incarnata
SWAMP MILKWEED
ASCLEPIADACEAE

ZONES 3 to 9

SOIL moist to wet; can withstand substantial flooding even during growing season

LIGHT partial shade (especially when soils are not regularly saturated) to sun

ATTRIBUTES 24 to 48 inches tall; large, upright, flat clusters of bright, mostly pink flowers in summer

PROPAGATION very easy from seed collected in late summer as fruit capsules split. Sow in fall for spring germination, or cold stratify during winter and sow in spring

NOTES Individuals soon form multiple-stemmed clumps; cultivars with white flowers exist; larvae of the monarch butterfly eat the foliage, and many other insects feed on the nectar of the flowers.

Asclepias incarnata

NATURAL RANGE Nova Scotia to Florida, west to Saskatchewan, Utah, and New Mexico

Asclepias tuberosa
BUTTERFLY WEED
ASCLEPIADACEAE

ZONES 3 to 9

SOIL well drained (thrives in dry, sandy, even gravelly soils)

LIGHT sun

ATTRIBUTES 12 to 36 inches tall; bright orange to red-orange to even yellow flowers in upright, flat clusters in summer; foliage rich green and narrow in shape

PROPAGATION very easy from seed collected in late summer as fruit capsules split; sow in fall for spring germination, or cold stratify during winter and sow in spring

Asclepias tuberosa

NOTES Larvae of the monarch butterfly eat the foliage, and many other insects feed on the nectar of the flowers; both *Asclepias* species lag in development each spring, and it is easy to forget about them as the garden greens up. The cultivar 'Gay Butterflies' includes individuals with red and yellow flowers. Other *Asclepias* species are native to this region, but they are either too invasive (*A. syriaca,* common milkweed) or too difficult to obtain (*A. purpurascens,* purple milkweed; *A. variegata,* white milkweed).

NATURAL RANGE southern New Hampshire to Florida, west to Minnesota, South Dakota, Arizona, and Mexico

Aster divaricatus
WHITE WOOD ASTER
ASTERACEAE

ZONES 3 to 8
SOIL moist to dry
LIGHT sun to shade
ATTRIBUTES 12 to 24 inches tall; 3/4- to 1-inch-wide, white flowers (with rose center) in autumn; leaves are heart-shaped

PROPAGATION easy from seed collected and sown in fall for spring germination, or stored dry in refrigerator and sown when ready

NOTES White wood aster is very tolerant of shaded conditions. Two additional native asters well-adapted to shaded sites are the blue heart-leaved aster (*A. cordifolius*) and big-leaved aster (*A. macrophyllus*). Blue heart-leaved aster produces a showy cluster of blue-violet to rose flowers. The big-leaved aster has flowers lighter in color and much larger and coarser leaves.

NATURAL RANGE northern New Hampshire and southwest Quebec, west to the Niagara peninsula of southern Ontario, south to Washington, D.C., and southern Ohio, and in the mountain region to northern Georgia and eastern Alabama

Aster ericoides
HEATH ASTER
ASTERACEAE

ZONES 5 to 8
SOIL dry
LIGHT sun

ATTRIBUTES to 36 inches tall; clusters of 1/2-inch-wide white flowers in autumn, and lance-shaped leaves

PROPAGATION easy from seed collected and sown in fall for spring germination, or stored dry in refrigerator and sown when ready

NOTES An attractive species for dry, sunny sites; cultivars include 'Blue Star' (white flowers tinged with blue), 'Ringdove' (white tinged rose), and 'White Heather' (white with distinct yellow center). Another attractive native aster well suited to very dry sites is the prairie heart-leaved aster (*A. azureus* = *A. oolentangiensis*—I did not make up this name!). The prairie heart-leaved aster is found in prairies and dry open woods, and has blue to blue-violet flowers and much larger leaves than the heath aster. Another native aster found in prairies and other dry places is the smooth aster (*A. laevis*), which has foliage with a bluish green, waxy cast and blue or purple flowers.

NATURAL RANGE southern Maine to southeastern Manitoba, south to Delaware, northern Virginia, Tennessee, southern Illinois, Arkansas, Texas, northern Mexico, and southeastern Arizona

Aster novae-angliae
NEW ENGLAND ASTER
ASTERACEAE

ZONES 3 to 9

SOIL moist

LIGHT sun to partial sun

ATTRIBUTES 24 to 60 inches tall; 1-inch-wide, round, violet to purple or rose flowers from late summer into fall

PROPAGATION easy from seed collected and sown in fall for spring germination, or stored dry in refrigerator and sown when ready; easy to divide clumps

NOTES The many cultivars of New England aster include 'Andenken an Alma Pötschke' (bright rose flowers), 'Barr's Pink' (bright rose-pink), 'Harrington's Pink' (salmon-pink), 'Hella Lucy' (purple), 'Honeysong Pink (rich pink with bright yellow center), 'Mt. Everest' (white), 'Purple Dome' (purple flowers, smaller stature), 'September Ruby' (deep ruby-red), and 'Treasurer' (violet-blue). Dozens of *Aster* species are native to this region, found in old fields and mature forests, full sun to full shade, and

dry to wet soils, depending on the species. Much easier to grow than to identify species, so match garden conditions as much as possible to natural conditions when uncertain of species. Like the often-associated goldenrods, they would be more respected by gardeners if not so naturally abundant. Asters provide an important nectar source for insects from late summer into autumn, and many butterfly larvae eat the foliage.

NATURAL RANGE Massachusetts and Vermont to North Dakota and Wyoming, south generally to Washington, D.C., Tennessee, Arkansas, and New Mexico, and in the mountains to Virginia, North Carolina, and Alabama

Aster novi-belgii
NEW YORK ASTER
ASTERACEAE

ZONES 3 to 9

SOIL moist

LIGHT sun to partial sun

ATTRIBUTES 12 to 36 inches tall; 1-inch-wide, violet to purple, rose, or white flowers in fall

PROPAGATION easy from seed collected and sown in fall for spring germination, or stored dry in refrigerator and sown when ready; easy to divide clumps

NOTES Numerous cultivars have been selected for

Monarch butterfly on *Aster novae-angliae*

Aster novi-belgii 'Professor Anton Kippenberg'

size of plant and flower color. Dwarf cultivars (less than 15 inches tall) include 'Audrey' (lilac flowers), 'Buxton's Blue' (dark blue), 'Jenny' (red), 'Professor Anton Kippenberg' (lavender-blue semi-double) and 'Snowsprite' (white semi-double). Medium-height cultivars (less than 48 inches tall) include 'Ada Ballard' (lavender-blue double), 'Arctic' (white double), 'Ernest Ballard' (reddish pink semi-double), 'Eventide' (violet-blue semi-double), 'Patricia Ballard' (rose-pink semi-double), and 'Winston S. Churchill' (bright pink). Tall cultivars (over 48 inches) include 'Cardinal' (deep rosy red), 'Climax' (light blue), 'Fellowship' (pink semi-double), and 'White Lady' (white).

NATURAL RANGE Newfoundland to South Carolina, chiefly near coast

Aster umbellatus
FLAT-TOPPED ASTER
ASTERACEAE

ZONES 3 to 9

SOIL wet to moist

LIGHT sun to partial sun

ATTRIBUTES 36 to 72 inches tall; large, dense, flat cluster of 3/4-inch-wide, upright white flowers with yellow center

PROPAGATION easy from seed collected and sown in fall for spring germination, or stored dry in refrigerator and sown when ready; easy to divide clumps

NOTES Often a common aster in wet meadows and ditches; excellent for restoration of nonforested wetlands.

NATURAL RANGE Newfoundland to Minnesota, south generally to Virginia, Kentucky, and Illinois, and in the mountains to northern Georgia and northeastern Alabama

Baptisia australis
BLUE FALSE INDIGO
FABACEAE

ZONES 4 to 9

SOIL moist to dry (avoid soils with pH of 6.5 or higher)

LIGHT sun to partial sun

ATTRIBUTES 36 to 48 inches tall; 10- to 12-inch-long, upright stalks, 1-inch-wide, pealike, violet-blue flowers in mid to late spring, held above attractive bluish green foliage; 2- to 2 1/2-inch-long brown, turning black, pods that loosely hold large seeds

PROPAGATION collect and sow seeds in fall, or cold stratify and sow in spring; scarification improves germination

NOTES This species has a shrublike habit and long clusters of attractive bluish purple flowers.

NATURAL RANGE southern New York to North Carolina and northern Georgia, west to Nebraska and Texas

Boltonia asteroides
FALSE ASTER
ASTERACEAE

ZONES 4 to 9

SOIL wet to dry

LIGHT sun to partial sun

ATTRIBUTES 36 to 48 inches tall; large, spreading mass of numerous 3/4- to 1-inch-wide white flowers, resembling miniature daisies, in fall

PROPAGATION collect and sow seeds in fall, or cold stratify and sow in spring; to maintain desired cultivar, take stem cuttings in mid spring or divide older clumps

NOTES Occurs naturally in open wetlands; 'Snowbank', the primary form available, is more compact than the species. 'Pink Beauty' has light pink flowers and a more open habit than 'Snowbank'. A similar but much rarer species is *B. decurrens,* which occurs on floodplains along major rivers of the Midwest.
NATURAL RANGE New Jersey to Florida, west to North Dakota, Oklahoma, and Texas

Aster umbellatus

Baptisia australis

Boltonia asteroides 'Snowbank'

Calla palustris

WATER ARUM
ARACEAE

ZONES 3 to 8

SOIL wet (standing water)

LIGHT shade to partial shade

ATTRIBUTES to 12 inches tall; flower structure similar to Jack-in-the-pulpit (that is, the white, shieldlike

Calla palustris

spathe is more attractive than the flowers); leaves arrow-shaped; fruit a bright red berry, in clusters in autumn

PROPAGATION seed, sow in wet soil in autumn for spring germination; stem cuttings in summer

NOTES Water arum is an excellent plant for the shaded water garden or for shallow-water covered wetlands. The spathe of water arum is quite a sight when encountered in the shallow pools of very dark swamps, where I often see it in upstate New York in late spring.

NATURAL RANGE circumboreal, in America, south to Maryland, Indiana, and Iowa

Caltha palustris

MARSH MARIGOLD
RANUNCULACEAE

ZONES 1 to 8

SOIL moist to wet, including standing water

LIGHT sun (for best flowering) to shade

ATTRIBUTES 12 to 24 inches tall; round, upright, 1½-inch-wide, golden yellow flowers in early spring; bold, dark green, heart-shaped leaves during first half of growing season

Caltha palustris

PROPAGATION collect seeds when ripe in early summer and sow immediately or cold stratify for spring germination

NOTES Occurs naturally in wet meadows and forested wetlands of the Northeast (and Europe). The cultivar 'Flore Pleno' (= 'Monstruosa', 'Multiplex', 'Monstrosa-Plena') has double flowers; 'Alba' has white flowers.

NATURAL RANGE circumboreal, south to Virginia, West Virginia, Indiana, Illinois, and Iowa, and in the mountains to North Carolina and Tennessee

Camassia scilloides
WILD HYACINTH
LILIACEAE

ZONES 3 to 9

SOIL moist to wet

LIGHT sun to partial shade

ATTRIBUTES 12 to 16 inches tall; stalks of pale blue-violet or white flowers in mid spring

PROPAGATION difficult; slow from seed—moist, cold stratify (40°F) after collection and sow after three months

NOTES Will tolerate very wet and shaded conditions, where very few plants from bulbs do well.

NATURAL RANGE western Pennsylvania and southern Ontario to southern Wisconsin and eastern Kansas, south to Georgia and Texas

Campanula rotundifolia
HAREBELL
CAMPANULACEAE

ZONES 3 to 8

SOIL dry to moist, well drained

LIGHT partial sun to sun

ATTRIBUTES generally about 12 inches tall; basal leaves rounded, leaves of flowering stems wiry; flowers blue, bell-shaped, nodding, in summer

PROPAGATION seed, no pretreatment required if fresh

NOTES Harebell occurs on thin soils, including cliff faces in full sun.

NATURAL RANGE circumboreal, south in America to New Jersey, Indiana, Iowa, and Mexico

Cardamine concatenata
CUT-LEAF TOOTHWORT
BRASSICACEAE

ZONES 3 to 8

SOIL rich, moist, well drained

LIGHT partial shade to shade

ATTRIBUTES flowering individuals have a pair of very narrow, fingerlike leaves, above which a cluster of pinkish white flowers emerge in early spring; total plant height about 8 inches

PROPAGATION division of clumps

NOTES Also listed as *Dentaria laciniata*. Broad-leaf toothwort (*C. diphylla* = *D. diphylla*) often occurs on

Camassia scilloides

Campanula rotundifolia

Cardamine concatenata

the same rich, moist, deeply shaded sites as cut-leaf toothwort. Both are common associates of some of our region's showiest spring woodland wildflowers, including white trillium (*Trillium grandiflorum*).

NATURAL RANGE Maine and southern Quebec to Minnesota, south to Florida, Louisiana, and Oklahoma

Caulophyllum thalictroides
BLUE COHOSH
BERBERIDACEAE

ZONES 3 to 8

SOIL moist, circumneutral

LIGHT shade

ATTRIBUTES 24 to 36 inches tall; rather inconspicuous 1/2-inch-wide greenish yellow flowers in early spring as leaves unfurl, but attractive bluish green foliage during the growing season, topped by clusters of erect, dark blue, round fruit from late summer into autumn

PROPAGATION seed, but only after multiple periods of cold and warm stratification

NOTES The fine, bluish green foliage alone is reason enough to grow blue cohosh, although the dark blue fruit are interesting in autumn.

NATURAL RANGE New Brunswick to Ontario and Manitoba, south to South Carolina, Alabama, and Missouri

Chamaelirium luteum
DEVIL'S BIT
LILIACEAE

ZONES 4 to 9

SOIL moist to wet

LIGHT sun to partial shade

ATTRIBUTES 8 to 14 inches tall; long stalk (resembling a wand) of numerous small white flowers in late spring to early summer emerge from long, lance-shaped basal leaves

PROPAGATION since this species is dioecious, look for seeds only on female specimens; collect seeds in fall and sow immediately in cold frame, or moist stratify in refrigerator for spring germination

NOTES Also known as fairy wand. The long, narrow flower clusters of this species are quite showy in mid spring.

NATURAL RANGE Massachusetts to Florida, west to southern Ontario, Ohio, southern Indiana, southern Illinois, Arkansas, and Louisiana

Chelone glabra
TURTLEHEAD
SCROPHULARIACEAE

ZONES 3 to 9

SOIL wet to moist

LIGHT sun if wet, otherwise partial shade

ATTRIBUTES 36+ inches tall; terminal cluster of rather flattened and somewhat closed white flowers (resembling a turtle's head) tinged with pink from

Caulophyllum thalictroides

Chamaelirium luteum

late summer into autumn; leaves lance-shaped, dark green, and in pairs, opposite one another along stem
PROPAGATION spreads readily via rhizomes, otherwise collect seeds in late summer and early fall, and scatter in moist to wet areas
NOTES Turtlehead is often a common plant in open or closed canopy wetlands in this region; it is one of the key larval food plants for the Baltimore checkerspot.
NATURAL RANGE Newfoundland to Minnesota, south to Georgia and Alabama

Chimaphila maculata
SPOTTED WINTERGREEN
PYROLACEAE
ZONES 3 to 8
SOIL dry, sandy, acidic
LIGHT partial sun to shade
ATTRIBUTES lance-shaped evergreen leaves striped with white along midvein; flowers white, with five waxy, widely spreading petals; fruit a capsule
PROPAGATION cuttings
NOTES Both the foliage and flowers of spotted

wintergreen are quite attractive. Prince's pine or pipsissewa (*C. umbellata*) occurs on similar sites but has dark green, nonmottled foliage and a much greater geographical range. Both species are legally protected in some states to discourage collecting for Christmas garlands and wreaths.
NATURAL RANGE Maine and New Hampshire to Michigan, south to South Carolina, Georgia, and Alabama

Chrysogonum virginianum
GOLD-STAR
ASTERACEAE
ZONES (4) 5 to 9
SOIL moist to dry
LIGHT partial shade to sun
ATTRIBUTES 6 to 12 inches tall; 1-inch-wide, golden yellow flowers in spring through early summer; 1- to 2-inch-long, toothed, triangular, and dark green leaves
PROPAGATION moist stratify seeds for three months in refrigerator; spreads by stolons or rhizomes
NOTES Also known as golden star. An excellent

Chelone glabra

Chrysogonum virginianum

ground cover for a very wide range of growing conditions (moist soil in full sun to dry soil in shade); var. *virginianum* has rhizomes, relatively tall flowering stems, and a denser habit, whereas var. *australe* spreads by stolons and has shorter flowering stems. Cultivars include 'Allen Bush' (rapid grower), 'Mark Viette' (glaucous leaves), and 'Piccadilly' (more prostrate form).

NATURAL RANGE southern Pennsylvania and southeastern Ohio to Florida and Mississippi

Chrysopsis falcata

SICKLE-LEAVED GOLDEN ASTER
ASTERACEAE

ZONES 5 to 9

SOIL sandy, dry

LIGHT partial sun to sun

ATTRIBUTES narrow leaves along stem to about 12 inches tall; flowers golden yellow, 1 inch in diameter, in summer

PROPAGATION seed

NOTES Two other native golden aster species that tolerate dry sandy soils and full sun are shaggy golden aster (*C. mariana*) and hairy golden aster (*C. villosa*). Of the three mentioned here, shaggy golden aster will tolerate the most shade.

NATURAL RANGE Massachusetts to New Jersey, mostly near the coast

Cimicifuga racemosa

BLACK COHOSH
RANUNCULACEAE

ZONES 3 to 9

SOIL moist

LIGHT shade to partial sun

ATTRIBUTES 36 to 60 inches tall; 12- to 24-inch-long, upright bottlebrushlike clusters of white flowers held above dark green, compound foliage in summer

PROPAGATION seed, will require warm, moist stratification for a few months, followed by cold stratification for two months

NOTES The long white flower spikes of black cohosh are a striking contrast in summer to the otherwise very dark growing conditions under which this species thrives; an excellent nectar species for insects. Variety *cordifolia* has heart-shaped leaves. American

bugbane (*C. americana*) is shorter than black cohosh (reaches "only" 4 feet in height) and has more finely dissected foliage. It too is very shade-tolerant.

NATURAL RANGE Massachusetts to New York, Ohio, Indiana, and Missouri, south to South Carolina, Virginia, and Tennessee

Clintonia umbellulata

SPECKLED WOOD LILY
LILIACEAE

ZONES 4 to 9

SOIL moist

LIGHT partial shade to shade

ATTRIBUTES to 18 inches tall; large (to 10 inches long), straplike, dark green basal leaves from which a stalk of fragrant white flowers in a rounded cluster emerge in late spring to early summer; fruit a dark blue, round berry

PROPAGATION sow seed in autumn for spring germination

Cimicifuga racemosa

NOTES *C. borealis,* the blue bead lily, has yellow, drooping flowers in a more open head and is more suited to shaded gardens in the northern portions of our region, where it is native.

NATURAL RANGE central New York and eastern Ohio to North Carolina, Tennessee, and northern Georgia

Clintonia umbellulata

Clintonia borealis

Coreopsis lanceolata

TICKSEED
ASTERACEAE

ZONES 3 to 9

SOIL moist to dry

LIGHT sun to partial sun

ATTRIBUTES 18 to 30 inches; 2-inch-wide, golden yellow flowers in early to mid summer

PROPAGATION naturalizes readily from seed, which germinates with or without cold, moist stratification; also easy by stem cuttings

NOTES Also known as the lance-leaved coreopsis. Native to dry sandy prairies and lakeshores; cultivars include 'Brown Eyes' (yellow flowers with maroon ring near center), 'Sunburst' (yellow semidouble), and 'Sterntaler' (gold with brown ring near center). Lobed tickseed (*C. auriculata*) occurs in woods in the central to southern portions of our region; its var. *nana* (= 'Nana') develops into a low-growing mound of attractive foliage from which rich yellow flowers emerge in spring.

NATURAL RANGE Michigan and the northern shore of Lake Superior to Florida and New Mexico

Coreopsis rosea

PINK COREOPSIS
ASTERACEAE

ZONES 4 to 8

SOIL moist to wet

LIGHT sun to partial sun

ATTRIBUTES 12 inches tall; 3/4- to 1-inch-wide pink

Coreopsis rosea

flowers with yellow center, held above very open, fine-textured foliage in summer

PROPAGATION easy to divide

NOTES Naturally found along pond and lake shores but grows fine on better-drained soils, too.

NATURAL RANGE Nova Scotia and Massachusetts to Georgia, mainly on coastal plain

Coreopsis verticillata 'Zagreb'

Cypripedium parviflorum

Coreopsis verticillata

THREADLEAF TICKSEED
ASTERACEAE

ZONES 4 to 9

SOIL moist to moderately dry

LIGHT sun to partial sun

ATTRIBUTES 12 to 26 inches tall; 1-inch-wide golden yellow flowers, held above fine-textured foliage in summer

PROPAGATION easy to divide

NOTES The cultivars 'Zagreb' (deep yellow flowers) and 'Golden Showers' (bright yellow) are widely available, as is the hybrid 'Moonbeam', which has a much lighter flower color than the straight species or its cultivars.

NATURAL RANGE Maryland and Washington, D.C., to South Carolina, mainly on coastal plain

Cypripedium parviflorum

YELLOW LADYSLIPPER
ORCHIDACEAE

ZONES 4 to 8

SOIL moist, circumneutral, with lots of organic matter

LIGHT partial shade for best flowering

ATTRIBUTES var. *parviflorum,* 10 to 14 inches tall; var. *pubescens,* 12 to 18 inches; both with yellow, pouchlike sac and twisted greenish yellow sepals in mid spring

PROPAGATION divide clumps after flowering; best propagated via tissue culture

NOTES Also listed as *C. calceolus.* Variety *parviflorum* is the small yellow ladyslipper, var. *pubescens* the large. These and other ladyslipper species are some of the most beautiful, and threatened, native plants in North America. The yellow ladyslipper is relatively easy to grow. Native orchids should not be dug from the wild, unless a natural population is imminently threatened by development; most require very exacting soil conditions, probably to sustain the symbiotic fungus that each species requires to germinate and grow. A similar species but with much larger pouch and more midwestern geographical range is Kentucky ladyslipper (*C. kentuckiense*). Other native species in this region are the pink ladyslipper (*C. acaule*), showy ladyslipper (*C. reginae*) and ram's head ladyslipper (*C. arietinum*). Pink ladyslipper thrives in open, acidic woods, especially below pines; however, it is exceedingly difficult to cultivate. The showy ladyslipper is often regarded as the "queen" of North American wildflowers because of its striking beauty and size. It occurs in sunnier areas of wetlands that receive discharge of cold, calcareous groundwater. Although the smallest of the native ladyslippers, flowers of the ram's head ladyslipper are perhaps the most exquisite; this very rare species is found in northern portions of our range on dry and wet, calcareous sites, often in very dense shade, which provides the perfect setting for its strongly angled pouches of bright white infused with violet-red.

NATURAL RANGE circumboreal, south in America to South Carolina, Louisiana, and New Mexico

Delphinium tricorne

DWARF LARKSPUR
RANUNCULACEAE

ZONES 4 to 9

SOIL moist to wet

LIGHT partial shade to sun

ATTRIBUTES 8 to 14 inches tall; terminal spikes of light to deep purple, pink, or white flowers in early spring

PROPAGATION seed, cold stratify for three months (or overwinter in a cold frame), then subject to 70°F

NOTES Among my fondest memories of spring wildflowers in central Kentucky are the sweeps of dwarf larkspur, and the great natural variation in flower color among individuals at a site.

NATURAL RANGE Pennsylvania to southern Minnesota, south to North Carolina, Georgia, Alabama, and Oklahoma

Dicentra canadensis

SQUIRREL CORN
FUMARIACEAE

ZONES 3 to 8

SOIL moist

LIGHT shade to partial sun

ATTRIBUTES 3 to 5 inches tall; arching stalks hold white, heart-shaped flowers in early spring above the foliage; foliage bluish green and highly dissected

PROPAGATION sow fresh seed immediately; divide clumps

NOTES The bulblet of squirrel corn resembles a kernel of dried corn.

NATURAL RANGE southern Maine and southern Quebec to southern Minnesota, south to North Carolina, Tennessee, and Missouri

Dicentra cucullaria

DUTCHMAN'S BREECHES
FUMARIACEAE

ZONES 3 to 8

SOIL moist

LIGHT shade to partial sun

ATTRIBUTES 3 to 6 inches tall; arching stalks hold

Delphinium tricorne

Dicentra canadensis

Dicentra cucullaria

white, pants-shaped flowers in early spring above the foliage; foliage bluish green and highly dissected

PROPAGATION sow fresh seed immediately; divide clumps

NOTES The bulblet of Dutchman's breeches is white. All native *Dicentra* species have beautiful, highly dissected, bluish green foliage.

NATURAL RANGE Nova Scotia and eastern Quebec to northern Minnesota, south to Georgia, Arkansas, and Kansas; disjunct in Washington, Oregon, and Idaho

Dicentra eximia

BLEEDING HEART

FUMARIACEAE

ZONES 4 to 9

SOIL moist

LIGHT shade to sun

ATTRIBUTES 12 to 18 inches tall; arching stalks hold 1-inch-long, rosy-pink, heart-shaped flowers in late spring and sporadically into autumn; foliage highly dissected

PROPAGATION sow fresh seed immediately; spreads readily by seed

NOTES Cultivars include white ('Alba', 'Silversmith') and reddish ('Stuart Boothman') flowering types. Our native bleeding heart is crossed with the Pacific bleeding heart (*D. formosa*) to produce 'Luxuriant' and other very popular hybrids.

NATURAL RANGE chiefly southern Appalachians, from North Carolina and Tennessee to West Virginia, Pennsylvania, New Jersey, and southern and western New York

Diphylleia cymosa

UMBRELLA LEAF

BERBERIDACEAE

ZONES 4 to 8

SOIL rich, moist to wet

LIGHT partial shade to shade

ATTRIBUTES sharp-lobed leaves to 20 inches in diameter and 24 inches tall; flowers white, small, in flat cluster in late spring; fruit blue, on red stalks

PROPAGATION seed

NOTES Patches of umbrella leaf are striking. Its flowers and fruit further add to its ornamental value for shaded sites and rich, moist soils that never dry out.

NATURAL RANGE southern Appalachian mountains

Dodecatheon meadia

SHOOTING STAR

PRIMULACEAE

ZONES 4 to 9

SOIL moist

LIGHT partial shade to sun

ATTRIBUTES 8 to 14 inches tall; clusters of terminal, white to pink pendent flowers with reflexed petals in mid spring, held above clumps of long, narrow basal leaves

PROPAGATION seed, will require moist, cold stratification for three months; it is easy to produce new plants from root cuttings taken before growth initiates in the spring

NOTES When, as a horticulture student, I first saw hundreds of shooting stars blooming on ledges along limestone cliffs in central Kentucky, I was amazed I had never heard of or seen this species. Like many of our native plants, this plant is relatively small but well worth bending over for. The taxonomic nomenclature for eastern U.S. *Dodecatheon* species is inconsistent among texts. According to Gleason and Cronquist (1991), most of what occurs in this region is var. *meadia;* var. *frenchii* is native to western Kentucky and southern Illinois. The amethyst shooting star, *D. pulchellum* (= *D. radicatum, D. amethystinum*), generally has dark pink flowers and is also native to much of this region, especially in moist prairies and meadows.

NATURAL RANGE Maryland to Georgia and Alabama, west to southern Wisconsin, southeastern Minnesota, Iowa, Oklahoma, and Texas

Echinacea purpurea

PURPLE CONEFLOWER

ASTERACEAE

ZONES 3 to 9

SOIL moist

LIGHT sun to partial shade

ATTRIBUTES 26 to 36 inches tall; 3- to 4-inch-wide, dark rose flowers above leaves in summer

PROPAGATION easy from seed, sow in fall or spring

NOTES Excellent nectar species for many butterflies; goldfinches eat seeds from late summer into fall. Cultivars include 'Alba' (cream-white flowers), 'Bravado' (larger, rose-colored flowers), 'Bright Star' (rose), 'Crimson Star' (crimson-red), 'Magnus' (rose, petals droop less than species), 'Robert Bloom'

Dicentra eximia

Dodecatheon meadia

Diphylleia cymosa

Diphylleia cymosa in fruit

Echinacea purpurea

(purple-rose), 'The King' (rose-red), 'White Lustre' (white), and 'White Swan' (white). Many otherwise "Latin-challenged" readers will recognize the genus as that of the tea—here's the source of echinacea leaves for home brew. Prairie coneflower (*E. pallida*) is similar in size but has strongly reflexed petals. It occurs in dry prairies of the Midwest.
NATURAL RANGE chiefly in Ozarks and Midwest, from Illinois and southern Iowa to eastern Oklahoma, extreme northeastern Texas, and central Louisiana, east irregularly to southern Michigan, Kentucky, Tennessee, and Georgia, and less commonly to Virginia and North Carolina

Erigeron pulchellus
ROBIN'S PLANTAIN
ASTERACEAE
ZONES 3 to 8
SOIL rich, moist to wet
LIGHT partial sun to sun
ATTRIBUTES to about 18 inches tall; flowers lavender-blue to white with yellow center, about 1 inch in diameter, in spring

PROPAGATION seed
NOTES A number of better-known (as fleabanes) but weedier species of this genus are widespread in our region.
NATURAL RANGE Maine to Ontario and east-central Minnesota, south to Georgia, Mississippi, and eastern Texas

Erythronium americanum
YELLOW TROUT LILY
LILIACEAE
ZONES 3 to 9
SOIL moist
LIGHT shade
ATTRIBUTES 3 to 6 inches tall; in early spring, 1- to 2-inch-wide, nodding flowers of yellow, reflexed petals on stalks separate and above highly mottled, strap-like leaves in basal clusters; leaves senesce by mid summer
PROPAGATION easiest by dividing larger colonies
NOTES A colleague of mine won't think about fly fishing for trout until the yellow trout lily blooms. The white trout lily, *E. albidum*, is also native to this

Erythronium americanum

Eupatorium coelestinum

Erythronium albidum

region and is similar to the yellow trout lily except for its white flowers.

NATURAL RANGE Nova Scotia and western Ontario to Minnesota, south to Florida and Alabama, more common eastward

Eupatorium coelestinum
HARDY AGERATUM
ASTERACEAE

ZONES 4 to 9

SOIL moist to wet

LIGHT partial shade to sun

ATTRIBUTES 24 to 36 inches tall; terminal flat clusters of up to seventy $1/2$-inch-wide, fuzzy, blue to violet flowers in summer

PROPAGATION easy from seed or divisions

NOTES Also known as mist flower. May become too successful in sunny, moist soils, and crowd out less vigorous species. I planted a small, single-stemmed plant and the following year had more than fifty stems covering over 1 square foot. Cultivars include 'Album' (white flowers) and 'Wayside' (compact and shorter than the species). An excellent nectar species.

NATURAL RANGE New York to Illinois and Kansas, south to Florida, Texas, and West Indies

Eupatorium maculatum
SPOTTED JOE-PYE WEED
ASTERACEAE

ZONES 3 to 9

SOIL moist to wet

LIGHT sun to partial sun

ATTRIBUTES 36 to 96 inches tall; very large, rather flat-topped clusters of small, pink, fuzzy flowers in late summer above whorls of leaves

PROPAGATION easy from seed

Eupatorium fistulosum

Eupatorium maculatum

Eupatorium rugosum

Eupatorium rugosum 'Chocolate'

Eupatorium perfoliatum

NOTES Other similar species of this region are also well suited for moist garden settings and wetland restoration projects, including *E. purpureum* (purple Joe-pye weed) and *E. fistulosum* (hollow-stemmed Joe-pye weed); *E. purpureum* reportedly is better suited for shady locations. Cultivars of Joe-pye weed are also available—for example, *E. m.* 'Gateway' and *E. p.* 'Big Umbrella'. The Joe-pye weeds are very good nectar species and attract especially large, showy butterflies like the monarch and swallowtails.

NATURAL RANGE Newfoundland to British Columbia, south to Maryland, West Virginia, Illinois, Nebraska, New Mexico, and Utah, and along the higher mountains to North Carolina and Tennessee

Eupatorium rugosum
WHITE SNAKEROOT
ASTERACEAE

ZONES 4 to 9

SOIL moist

LIGHT sun to partial shade

ATTRIBUTES 24 to 36 inches tall; large, flat, terminal, 3- to 4-inch-wide clusters of twelve to twenty-four 1/4-inch-wide, white, fuzzy flowers from late summer into autumn

PROPAGATION easy from seed or division

NOTES The cultivar 'Chocolate' has burgundy-colored leaves in full sun, which provide an interesting background for the white flowers. Another native *Eupatorium* species with white flowers, but common in wetlands, is *E. perfoliatum* (boneset).

NATURAL RANGE Nova Scotia to Saskatchewan, south to Georgia and Texas

Filipendula rubra
QUEEN OF THE PRAIRIE
ROSACEAE

ZONES 3 to 8

SOIL moist

LIGHT sun to partial shade

ATTRIBUTES 72 to 96 inches tall; large (up to 9 inches wide) clusters of soft-pink flowers in mid summer above deeply cut leaves

PROPAGATION divide in spring

NOTES The cultivar 'Venusta' (= 'Magnifica') has deep pink flowers and is more vigorous. Queen of the prairie does very poorly under hot, dry conditions.

Filipendula rubra

Galax aphylla

NATURAL RANGE New York to Minnesota, south to North Carolina and Kentucky

Galax aphylla
WANDFLOWER
DIAPENSIACEAE

ZONES 4 to 8
SOIL moist to dry
LIGHT sun to shade
ATTRIBUTES round, shiny, dark green, evergreen leaves to 8 inches long, above which dense spikes of white flowers emerge in late spring to early summer
PROPAGATION seed, sow on surface of peat that is maintained evenly moist; divide clumps
NOTES I spent a number of summers walking on thick carpets of this plant in the mountains of western North Carolina, and marveled at its ability to tolerate hot, relatively dry, sunny sites as well as cool, shady conditions. The foliage alone is worthy of cultivation—it and the flowers make this an outstanding native species.
NATURAL RANGE chiefly in mountains of western

Maryland to Kentucky, south to Georgia and Alabama, and extending to coastal plain of North Carolina and southern Virginia

Gentiana clausa
CLOSED GENTIAN
GENTIANACEAE

ZONES 3 to 9
SOIL moist
LIGHT partial sun to sun
ATTRIBUTES narrow foliage along stems to about 2 feet tall, above which clusters of narrow, elliptical, closed blue flowers emerge in summer
PROPAGATION seed, cold stratify for three months
NOTES Also known as the bottle gentian. Of the dozen native gentian species in our region, prairie gentian (*G. puberulenta*) and soapwort gentian (*G. saponaria*) are also especially worthy of garden consideration. Most gentians occur on moist to wet soils except the prairie gentian, which will tolerate dry conditions. A closely related genus is fringed gentian, *Gentianopsis,* which includes two native species,

Gentiana clausa

Geranium maculatum

fringed gentian (*G. crinita*) and lesser fringed gentian (*G. procera*). Both tend to occur in calcareous, open wetlands.

NATURAL RANGE Maine and adjacent Quebec to Maryland and Ohio, and south in the mountains to North Carolina and Tennessee

Geranium maculatum
WILD GERANIUM
GERANIACEAE

ZONES 3 to 9
SOIL moist to moderately dry
LIGHT sun to partial shade
ATTRIBUTES 14 to 18 inches tall; in mid to late spring produces terminal, 1-inch-wide, pink flowers held above mounds of palmately lobed leaves
PROPAGATION will naturalize in garden via seed
NOTES Also known as cranesbill, wild geranium can smother shorter plants with its extensive rhizomes and dense foliage.
NATURAL RANGE Maine to South Carolina and northern Georgia, west to Manitoba, Nebraska, and northeastern Oklahoma

Geum rivale
WATER AVENS
ROSACEAE

ZONES 2 to 7
SOIL moist to wet
LIGHT sun to partial shade

Geum rivale

ATTRIBUTES 16 to 24 inches tall; nodding, purple-red flowers in late spring
PROPAGATION moist stratify the seed in refrigerator for three months or more before sowing
NOTES Native to open and closed canopy wetlands of the Northeast (and Europe). Cultivars include 'Leonard's Variety' (coppery rose flowers), 'Leonard's Double' (similar but double-flowered), and 'Album' (white); these may be hybrids with *G. urbanum* (wood avens), possibly resulting from natural crosses of these species where both occur in Europe. Prairie smoke, *G. triflorum*, is native to dry woods and prairies of this region; it has attractive

Geum triflorum

foliage and an interesting flower and fruit display, and is well adapted to dry soils in full sun.

NATURAL RANGE Newfoundland and Quebec to Alberta, south to New Jersey, Pennsylvania, Indiana, Michigan, and California

Hedyotis caerulea

BLUETS
RUBIACEAE

ZONES 3 to 9

SOIL wet to dry

LIGHT partial sun to sun

ATTRIBUTES small opposite leaves on slender stems above which emerge a carpet of distinctly four-petaled flowers that are blue toward the outside, then white then deep yellow in the center

PROPAGATION seed or division

NOTES Also listed as *Houstonia caerulea*. Of the ten native species of *Hedyotis* in our region, two others noteworthy for the garden are longleaf bluets (*H. longifolia*) and purple bluets (*H. purpurea*). Rarely does one notice these species until they are in bloom. They are well suited to rock gardens and along rock paths.

NATURAL RANGE Nova Scotia and Quebec to Wisconsin, south to Georgia and Arkansas

Helenium autumnale

SNEEZEWEED
ASTERACEAE

ZONES 3 to 8

SOIL moist to wet

LIGHT sun to partial shade

ATTRIBUTES 36 to 60 inches tall; terminal, 2- to 3-inch-wide yellow flowers with brown or black center in mid to late summer; main stems of plant are winged

PROPAGATION seed or division

NOTES Cultivars include 'Riverton Beauty' (yellow with purply black eye), 'Riverton Gem' (yellow with mahogany eye), and 'Rubrum' (bronze-red).

NATURAL RANGE Quebec to Florida, west to British Columbia and Arizona

Helianthus angustifolius

NARROW-LEAVED SUNFLOWER
ASTERACEAE

ZONES 5 to 9

SOIL moist to wet

LIGHT sun to partial sun

ATTRIBUTES 60 to 120 inches tall; 2- to 3-inch-wide bright yellow flowers with purple center; leaves dark green, glossy, long and narrow

PROPAGATION easy from seed or cuttings

NOTES Also known swamp sunflower. Some other native *Helianthus* species for large, brightly lit locations include *H. divaricatus* (woodland sunflower), *H. giganteus* (swamp or giant sunflower), and *H. tuberosus* (Jerusalem artichoke).

NATURAL RANGE Long Island to Florida and Texas, chiefly near the coast, but inland to southern Ohio, southern Indiana, and southern Missouri

Heliopsis helianthoides

OXEYE
ASTERACEAE

ZONES 3 to 9

SOIL moist to dry

LIGHT sun to partial sun

ATTRIBUTES 36 to 60 inches tall; pale yellow to golden orange flowers, 2 to 3 inches in diameter, throughout a bushy habit, during the summer; leaves dark green

PROPAGATION easy from seed, stem cuttings, or divisions

NOTES This species includes the subspecies or variety *scabra* (referring to sandpapery, or scabrous, leaves and stems). Cultivars include 'Gigantea' (golden semi-double flowers), 'Golden Plume'

Helenium autumnale

Helianthus divaricatus

Heliopsis helianthoides var. *scabra* 'Sommersonne'

Helianthus tuberosus

(golden double), 'Goldgrünherz' (= Goldgreenheart; golden petals surrounding greenish center), 'Incomparabilis' (golden yellow semi-double), 'Karat' (bright yellow), and 'Sommersonne' (= Summer Sun; 4-inch-wide bright yellow flowers on a 2- to 3-foot-tall plant).

NATURAL RANGE Quebec to British Columbia, south to Georgia and New Mexico

Helonias bullata
SWAMP PINK
LILIACEAE

ZONES 5 to 9

SOIL moist to wet, typically acidic and organic

LIGHT partial sun to sun

ATTRIBUTES bright green, long, shiny straplike, evergreen leaves to 12 inches long; flowers bright pink in tight mass at end of thick stalk about 12 inches tall, early spring

PROPAGATION seed, sow on surface and keep evenly moist; division

NOTES Swamp pink is a striking, spring-blooming species that, although quite rare naturally, is not too difficult to grow if planted in rich, moist to wet organic soil.

NATURAL RANGE southern New York and New Jersey to southeastern Virginia on coastal plain; also in mountains of Virginia, North Carolina, and Georgia

Hepatica acutiloba
SHARP-LOBED HEPATICA
RANUNCULACEAE

ZONES 3 to 8

SOIL moist, circumneutral

LIGHT partial shade to partial sun

ATTRIBUTES 6 to 12 inches tall; 1-inch-wide, white, purple, pink, or bluish flowers on long, slender stalks in early spring above unfurling leaves; mature leaves have three pointed lobes and are in dense mounds

PROPAGATION seed, will need a few months of moist, warm stratification, followed by cold stratification

NOTES One of the first wildflowers to emerge each spring. Its flowers provide a wonderful range of pastel colors; foliage is very attractive the remainder of the growing season.

NATURAL RANGE Quebec to Minnesota, south to Georgia, Alabama, and Missouri

Hepatica americana
ROUND-LOBED HEPATICA
RANUNCULACEAE

ZONES 3 to 8

SOIL moist

LIGHT partial shade to partial sun

ATTRIBUTES 6 to 10 inches tall; approximately 1-inch-wide flowers that are usually dark violet-blue in early spring above unfurling leaves; mature leaves have three rounded lobes and are in dense mounds

PROPAGATION seed, will need a few months of moist, warm stratification, followed by cold stratification

NOTES Both native *Hepatica* species are listed in some places as varieties of the European *H. nobilis.*

NATURAL RANGE Quebec and Nova Scotia to Minnesota and Manitoba, south to Georgia, Tennessee, and Missouri

Heuchera americana
ALUMROOT
SAXIFRAGACEAE

ZONES 3 to 9

SOIL moist to dry

LIGHT sun to partial shade

ATTRIBUTES 12 to 24 inches tall; many small yellow-green flowers widely scattered along long stalk held high above the dark green leaves

PROPAGATION seed, some will germinate without moist, cold stratification, which promotes further germination

NOTES Cultivars include 'Sunset' (purple venation in leaves). The maple-leaved alumroot, *H. villosa,* is also native to much of this region.

NATURAL RANGE Connecticut to Georgia, west to southern Ontario, southern Michigan, Indiana, southern Illinois, and eastern Oklahoma

Hibiscus moscheutos
ROSE MALLOW
MALVACEAE

ZONES 4 to 9

SOIL moist to wet

LIGHT sun

Helonias bullata

Hepatica acutiloba

Hepatica americana

Heuchera americana

Heuchera americana flowers

Hibiscus moscheutos

Hibiscus moscheutos var. *palustris*

ATTRIBUTES 48 to 84 inches tall; very large (6 to 8 inches in diameter), satiny white flowers with darker center in late summer

PROPAGATION fresh seed will germinate, or stratify under moist, cold conditions; softwood cuttings in early summer

NOTES var. *palustris* has pink flowers. Rose mallow has the stature of a robust tropical shrub, and its flowers are spectacular—an exceptionally showy herbaceous species for a sunny, wet site.

NATURAL RANGE Massachusetts and New York to Ohio, southern Wisconsin, and Missouri, south to the Gulf of Mexico; disjunct in California

Hydrastis canadensis

Hydrastis canadensis fruit

Hydrastis canadensis
GOLDENSEAL
RANUNCULACEAE

ZONES 4 to 8

SOIL rich, moist, well drained

LIGHT shade to partial sun

ATTRIBUTES 12 to 16 inches tall (half this height at peak flowering); white, feathery flowers about 1/2 inch in diameter and lacking petals in early spring, followed by bright then dark red, raspberrylike fruit in late summer; dark green leaves are paired at top of plant and resemble maple leaves; typically in dense clumps, spreading by rhizomes

PROPAGATION seed, will require multiple periods of warm and cold stratification; clumps easy to divide

NOTES Goldenseal is increasingly rare; it is over-collected for various medicinal purposes and has lost habitat as land is cleared for development. It is legally protected in some states.

NATURAL RANGE Vermont to Michigan and Minnesota, south to North Carolina, Tennessee, and Arkansas

Hydrophyllum canadense
MAPLE-LEAVED WATERLEAF
HYDROPHYLLACEAE

ZONES 3 to 8

SOIL rich, moist

LIGHT partial shade to shade

ATTRIBUTES plants to about 15 inches in height; leaves very large (to 10 inches long and wide), shaped like a maple leaf; flowers bell-shaped, pendent, white to pink-purple, about 1/2 inch long

PROPAGATION seed, cold stratify for three months

NOTES Three additional native species are biennial waterleaf (*H. appendiculatum*), hairy waterleaf (*H. macrophyllum*), and eastern waterleaf (*H. virginianum*). All waterleafs have very large leaves that contrast nicely with many of their daintier associates in rich, shaded, moist woodlands. Hairy waterleaf and eastern waterleaf have deeply cut foliage. Leaves of eastern waterleaf are typically mottled, appearing water-stained. Their flowers, which range from white to pink-purple to purple, are a bonus.

NATURAL RANGE southern Ontario to southern Minnesota, south to Pennsylvania, Tennessee, Missouri, and eastern Kansas

Iris cristata

CRESTED IRIS
IRIDACEAE

ZONES 4 to 9

SOIL moist

LIGHT partial shade

ATTRIBUTES 4 to 8 inches tall; approximately 3-inch-wide violet flowers in spring from near the tips of short, swordlike leaves

PROPAGATION easy to divide

NOTES An excellent ground cover; var. *alba* has white flowers; cultivars include 'Shenandoah Sky' (light blue), 'Summer Storm' (dark blue), and 'Vein Mountain' (very pale blue flowers with orange crests outlined in deep purple). Another similar, native upland iris is dwarf iris (*I. verna*), which tolerates sunnier and drier conditions.

NATURAL RANGE Maryland to Oklahoma and Georgia

Iris prismatica

SLENDER BLUE FLAG
IRIDACEAE

ZONES 3 to 9

SOIL wet to moist

LIGHT sun to partial shade

ATTRIBUTES 12 to 24 inches tall; large violet to rose flowers in early summer

PROPAGATION seed, sow in fall or cold, moist stratify for spring germination; easy to divide

NOTES An excellent plant with strong vertical lines for planting near or in shallow water.

NATURAL RANGE near the coast from Nova Scotia to Georgia, and in the southern Appalachians

Iris versicolor

NORTHERN BLUE FLAG
IRIDACEAE

ZONES 4 to 9

SOIL wet to moist

LIGHT sun to partial shade

Iris prismatica

Iris cristata

Iris versicolor

ATTRIBUTES 24 to 36 inches tall; blue-violet to purple flowers in late spring

PROPAGATION seed, sow in fall or cold, moist stratify for spring germination; easy to divide

NOTES The northern blue flag thrives in shallow standing water. The natural variation in flower characteristics I have seen suggests there are opportunities to make horticultural selections of this species. Additional native irises of wetlands in our region include dwarf lake iris (*I. lacustris*), copper iris (*I. fulva*), southern blue flag (*I. virginica*), and arctic blue flag (*I. setosa*). Flowers of all native irises are some shade of blue or purple, except for the copper iris, which has copper to brown-orange or reddish brown flowers.

NATURAL RANGE Newfoundland and Labrador to Manitoba, south to Virginia and Minnesota

Jeffersonia diphylla
TWINLEAF
BERBERIDACEAE

ZONES 4 to 9

SOIL moist, circumneutral

LIGHT shade to partial sun

ATTRIBUTES 12 to 18 inches tall; 1-inch-wide white flowers that each live only a few days in early spring; foliage in two distinct parts, resembling butterfly wings

PROPAGATION difficult to germinate as seeds need multiple periods of warm and cold stratification, but easily spreads in a garden if one does not care when and where plants germinate

NOTES I wait every spring for the flowers to emerge on my twinleaf plants at home. Unless I stay home all day on blooming days, I rarely ever see a flower that is fully opened, as they generally seem to last only a few hours. Nevertheless, twinleaf is an outstanding ground cover for shaded conditions, and I enjoy searching for new germinants each year.

NATURAL RANGE western New York and southern Ontario to southeastern Minnesota, south to Maryland and Alabama

Liatris spicata
BLAZING STAR
ASTERACEAE

ZONES 3 to 9

SOIL moist to wet

LIGHT sun to partial sun

ATTRIBUTES 24 to 48 inches tall; long, densely packed 6- to 15-inch-long spikes of pinkish purple flowers during the summer above many bright green, very narrow leaves

PROPAGATION easy from seed

NOTES Also known as gayfeather. Cultivars include 'August Glory' (purple-blue), 'Floristan White' (creamy white), 'Kobold' (bluish purple flowers on plants usually 30 inches tall or shorter), and 'Silver Tip' (lavender). Other native blazing stars that function well in gardens of this region include the rough

Jeffersonia diphylla

Jeffersonia diphylla

gayfeather (*L. aspera*), dotted blazing star (*L. punctata*), prairie blazing star (*L. pycnostachya*), and northern blazing star (*L. scariosa*); *L. aspera, L. punctata,* and *L. pycnostachya* are the best species for dry soils. All *Liatris* species are excellent nectar plants for butterflies; birds eat the seeds.

NATURAL RANGE New York to Michigan and southeastern Wisconsin, south to Florida and Louisiana, and occasionally west to Wyoming and New Mexico

Lilium canadense

CANADA LILY
LILIACEAE

ZONES 3 to 8

SOIL moist to wet, acidic

LIGHT sun to partial shade

ATTRIBUTES 36 to 60 inches tall; approximately 3-inch-wide, yellow, yellow-orange, to red-orange pendent, rather flat flowers in summer

PROPAGATION seed, cold stratify for three months, germinants are very slow to develop; bulb scale division possible

NOTES I have seen Canada lily in many open and forested wetlands of upstate New York, where its flowers exhibit a wide range of orange, red, and yellow color intensities.

NATURAL RANGE Quebec and Maine to Maryland and in the mountains to Virginia, west to Ohio, Kentucky, southern Indiana, and Alabama

Lilium philadelphicum

WOOD LILY
LILIACEAE

ZONES 3 to 9

SOIL moist to dry, well drained

LIGHT sun to partial sun

ATTRIBUTES 12 to 24 inches tall; red to orange-red upright flowers, about 4 inches in diameter, in summer

PROPAGATION seed, cold stratify for three months, germinants are very slow to develop; bulb scale division possible

NOTES Wood lily is better suited to drier conditions than the other native lilies mentioned here. Two varieties are recognized, var. *philadelphicum* (leaves mostly whorled) and var. *andinum* (leaves mostly alternate).

Liatris spicata

Lilium canadense

Lilium philadelphicum

NATURAL RANGE var. *philadelphicum* occurs from New Hampshire to North Carolina and Kentucky; var. *andinum* occurs from Ohio to Minnesota, British Columbia, and New Mexico

Lilium superbum
TURK'S CAP
LILIACEAE

ZONES 4 to 9

SOIL moist to wet

LIGHT sun to partial sun

ATTRIBUTES 36 to 96 inches tall; up to forty (usually twenty) 2^1/$_2$- to 3^1/$_2$-inch-wide orange to red-orange flowers along a tall stalk in summer

PROPAGATION seed, cold stratify for three months, germinants are very slow to develop; bulb scale division possible

NOTES Turk's cap is a truly spectacular native lily and—with its dozens of large, bright flowers held on very tall flower stalks—worthy of its species name. Another, but smaller, species of high elevations in the southern Appalachians is Gray's lily (*L. grayi*). Michigan lily (*L. michiganense*) is similar to Turk's cap except for minor differences in leaf margin and anther length. Michigan lily, like Turk's cap, grows best on moist to wet soils.

NATURAL RANGE Massachusetts and southeastern New Hampshire to Georgia and Alabama

Lobelia cardinalis
CARDINAL FLOWER
CAMPANULACEAE

ZONES 3 to 9

SOIL moist to wet

LIGHT sun to partial shade

ATTRIBUTES 24 to 48 inches tall; up to fifty 1^1/$_2$-inch-long, crimson flowers along a 12- to 24-inch-long stalk in late summer

PROPAGATION easy from seed, naturalizes freely in the garden where there is very moist soil and lots of light, especially on bare substrates

NOTES Like many wetland species, cardinal flower attains it greatest stature on saturated soils in full sun; incredible color in mass, especially when ruby-throated hummingbirds are visiting for nectar. Cardinal flower hybridizes with the next species, *L. siphilitica*, to produce flowers that are pink, purple, and magenta. There are forms of *L. cardinalis* with white ('Alba') and pink ('Rosea') flowers, and cultivars include 'Angel Song' (salmon and cream flowers), 'Arabella's Vision' (brilliant red), and 'Heather Pink' (soft pink). Many of the cardinal flowers sold ('Bees Flame', 'Queen Victoria') are actually hybrids of our native species with *L. splendens* (native to Mexico), or cultivars of *L.* ×*speciosa* (parents include *L. cardinalis, L. siphilitica*, and *L. splendens*)—for example, 'Oakes Ames', 'Robert Landon', and 'Wisely'.

NATURAL RANGE New Brunswick to Minnesota, south to the Gulf of Mexico

Lobelia siphilitica
GREAT BLUE LOBELIA
CAMPANULACEAE

ZONES 3 to 9

SOIL moist to wet

LIGHT sun to partial sun

ATTRIBUTES 24 to 36 inches tall; many 1-inch-long, blue flowers along stalk in late summer

PROPAGATION easy from seed, naturalizes freely in the garden where there is very moist soil and lots of light, especially on bare substrates

NOTES At least in my garden, much easier to maintain than the cardinal flower. The cultivar 'Blue Peter' has light blue flowers; 'Alba' has white flowers, and 'Nana' is smaller in stature.

Lilium superbum

Lobelia siphilitica

Lobelia cardinalis

NATURAL RANGE Maine to Manitoba and Colorado, south to North Carolina and Texas

Lupinus perennis
  BLUE LUPINE
  FABACEAE

ZONES 3 to 9

SOIL well drained (naturally thrives on acidic, infertile soils)

LIGHT sun to partial sun

ATTRIBUTES 14 to 30 inches tall; spike of many blue-violet (rarely red-violet, even white) flowers held above compact mounds of bluish green, lobed leaves

PROPAGATION some fresh seed germinate without pretreatment, while other seed will benefit from some kind of scarification, mechanical (with a file or sandpaper) or otherwise; subject stored seed to cold, moist stratification for three months

NOTES Although blue lupine thrives on excessively drained, sandy, acidic infertile soils in full sun, it has done very well in moist, circumneutral loamy soil in the partial shade of my garden. But it is hard to think of a showier native perennial for dry, acidic

Lupinus perennis

soils in full sun. I have been studying blue lupine in relation to its importance as the exclusive food plant for the federally-listed Karner blue butterfly. The flower color is variable enough over its range in eastern New York to warrant some careful horticultural selections to broaden the color range currently available commercially. The famous lupines of coastal Maine are of European origin and are not native. All lupines are nitrogen fixers, enriching the soil with nitrogen.

NATURAL RANGE southeastern Maine to Florida, west to Minnesota and Indiana

Maianthemum canadense
CANADA MAYFLOWER
LILIACEAE
ZONES 3 to 8
SOIL wet to dry
LIGHT partial sun to shade
ATTRIBUTES 2 to 4 inches tall; narrow, columnar cluster of small, white flowers in mid spring; leaves are heart-shaped, glossy, deep green, an attractive backdrop for the small red fruit that mature in late summer
PROPAGATION slow from seed, sow outdoors in the fall in a cold frame; easy to divide
NOTES Like many of our most common native plants, Canada mayflower would be more highly sought-after if not so common; an excellent ground cover for the shadiest location in the garden.
NATURAL RANGE Labrador and Newfoundland to Mackenzie, south to Maryland, South Dakota, and in the mountains to Kentucky and North Carolina

Menyanthes trifoliata
BOG BUCKBEAN
RUBIACEAE
ZONES 2 to 7
SOIL wet, organic
LIGHT partial sun to sun
ATTRIBUTES flowering stems have a pair of three-parted leaves; flowers white, highly fringed, in showy, compact, and broad terminal cluster in late spring

Menyanthes trifoliata, with *Equisetum fluviatile* and *Thelypteris palustris*

PROPAGATION seed

NOTES As its common name suggests, bog buck-bean commonly occurs in bogs, but it also is common in calcareous wetlands (fens). It is occasionally sold for pond gardens.

NATURAL RANGE circumboreal, south to New Jersey, Virginia, Ohio, Indiana, Missouri and California

Mertensia virginica
VIRGINIA BLUEBELLS
BORAGINACEAE

ZONES 3 to 9

SOIL moist in spring; will tolerate drier soils during the summer

LIGHT partial sun to shade

ATTRIBUTES 14 to 20 inches tall; terminal clusters of

Mertensia virginica

five to twenty, 1-inch-long, bell-shaped, light blue flowers in early spring; soft bluish green foliage

PROPAGATION freely naturalizes from seed

NOTES The "Virginia" part of the common name, like many other common names that begin with a state name, is a little misleading, as this species is common in many other eastern states. It is protected in some states because it is exploitably vulnerable to overcollecting. Cultivars include 'Alba' (white flowers) and 'Rubra' (pink flowers).

NATURAL RANGE New York to Michigan, Wisconsin, Iowa, and eastern Kansas, south to Alabama and Missouri

Mitella diphylla
MITERWORT
SAXIFRAGACEAE

ZONES ?, certainly suited to shaded sites throughout its natural range

SOIL moist to dry

LIGHT partial sun to partial shade

ATTRIBUTES 8 to 12 inches tall; very small white flowers, with petals that resemble a snowflake, along slender stalk held above two leaves in mid spring

PROPAGATION fresh seed should germinate immediately, or sow in cold frame for germination the following spring

NOTES One will never appreciate the miterwort unless on hands and knees, but at that level, there is no more exquisite flower.

NATURAL RANGE Quebec to Minnesota, south to Virginia, Georgia, and Missouri

Monarda didyma
OSWEGO TEA
LAMIACEAE

ZONES 3 to 9

SOIL moist

LIGHT partial sun to partial shade

ATTRIBUTES 36 to 48 inches tall; rather flat, terminal clusters of crimson to scarlet flowers in mid summer on strongly angled stems

PROPAGATION easy from seed and easy to divide (more difficult to keep in bounds on moist soil)

NOTES Another unfortunate common name because no one would guess a patch of something called Oswego tea in full bloom in mid summer looks like a small fireworks display. Also known as

bee balm, this species can take over less robust plants on moist soils. In my garden the tall meadow rue, ostrich fern, and culver's root are worthy competitors. Flowers are important nectar sources for hummingbirds and butterflies (especially fritillaries). Cultivars have been selected with a range of pink, red, and purplish flower colors. Some may be hybrids with the next native species, *M. fistulosa*.

NATURAL RANGE Maine to Michigan, south to New Jersey, West Virginia, and Ohio, and along the mountains to northern Georgia

Monarda fistulosa
WILD BERGAMOT
LAMIACEAE

ZONES 3 to 9

SOIL moist

LIGHT sun to partial shade

ATTRIBUTES 36 to 48 inches tall; rather flat, terminal clusters of violet flowers in mid summer; foliage sweetly aromatic

PROPAGATION easy from seed and easy to divide

NOTES Wild bergamot naturally occurs in more open, drier settings than Oswego tea.

NATURAL RANGE Quebec to Manitoba and British Columbia, south to Georgia, Louisiana, and Arizona

Oenothera fruticosa
SUNDROPS
ONAGRACEAE

ZONES 4 to 9

SOIL moist to dry

LIGHT sun

ATTRIBUTES 16 to 30 inches tall; 1- to 2-inch-wide, terminal, bright yellow flowers in summer

PROPAGATION easy from seed

NOTES Cultivars include 'Lady Brookborough' (more, but smaller, flowers), 'Sonnenwende' (pink buds, large yellow flowers), and 'Yellow River' (many medium-size flowers). *Oenothera tetragona,* the northern sundrops, has similar traits but is native further into northeastern North America; cultivars include 'Fireworks' (2- to 3-inch-wide bright yellow flowers on reddish stems), 'Highlights', and 'Yellow River' (deep yellow flowers). There is considerable overlap in characteristics between *O. fruticosa* and *O. tetragona,* and uncertainty as to which species some cultivars really belong. Missouri evening

Mitella diphylla

Monarda fistulosa

Oenothera fruticosa

Monarda didyma

primrose or Ozark sundrops (*O. macrocarpa* = *O. missouriensis*) has a much larger yellow flower and occurs in dry, calcareous rocky barrens and prairies. White evening primrose (*O. speciosa*) has a large white flower and occurs in similar, but not necessarily calcareous, soils.

NATURAL RANGE Massachusetts to Florida, west to Indiana, Missouri, Oklahoma, and Louisiana

Opuntia humifusa
EASTERN PRICKLY PEAR
CACTACEAE

ZONES 4 to 9

SOIL dry, sandy

LIGHT sun

ATTRIBUTES 8 to 14 inches tall; 2- to 3-inch-wide, bright yellow, satiny flowers (often with reddish center) emerge from top of very prickly, flat, elliptical, padlike leaf in early summer; fruit is dark red, 1 inch long, oblong

PROPAGATION easy (technically, but be careful of prickles) from cuttings; detached "pads" root readily

NOTES One needs to be very careful handling this species because of the small, reddish brown, sharp hairs that occur in scattered patches over the otherwise smooth leaf surface. Of all the plants in my central New York garden, visitors are most surprised to see this species thriving, especially after record cold temperatures and nearly 200 inches of snow in recent winters. The eastern prickly pear is related to *O. tuna*, the fruit of which is available in stores and markets.

NATURAL RANGE eastern Massachusetts to southern Ontario and southern Minnesota, south to Florida and eastern Texas

Oxalis violacea
VIOLET WOOD-SORREL
OXALIDACEAE

ZONES 4 to 8

SOIL dry

LIGHT partial sun to sun

ATTRIBUTES shamrock-shaped foliage that is mottled; flowers rose-violet in spring

PROPAGATION seed

NOTES While the violet wood-sorrel occurs as scattered plants in dry woods and prairies, the northern wood-sorrel (*O. acetosella*) often forms dense carpets in rich, moist, heavily shaded, cool woods further north. Northern wood-sorrel also has mottled foliage and generally white flowers with pink to red-violet veins. I am still trying to figure out why this species is so disregarded by gardeners.

NATURAL RANGE Massachusetts to North Dakota, south to Florida and Texas

Pachysandra procumbens
ALLEGHENY SPURGE
BUXACEAE

ZONES 4 to 9

SOIL moist

LIGHT shade

ATTRIBUTES 6 to 10 inches tall; bottlebrushlike clusters of whitish flowers in spring above subtly mottled, dark blue-gray leaves

PROPAGATION seed, cold stratify for three months; divide clumps

Opuntia humifusa

Oxalis violacea

NOTES Allegheny spurge is an excellent native ground cover for very shaded sites.

NATURAL RANGE Kentucky, West Virginia, and western North Carolina to northwestern Florida and southern Louisiana

Panax quinquefolius

GINSENG
ARALIACEAE

ZONES 3 to 9

SOIL rich, moist, well drained

LIGHT partial shade to shade

ATTRIBUTES a pair of two dark green leaves that consist of five leaflets each, reaching about 12 inches in height; flowers white, in tight cluster between and just above height of leaves in summer; fruit, bright red, shiny, in a cluster

Pachysandra procumbens

Panax quinquefolius

PROPAGATION seed, cold stratify for three months

NOTES Ginseng has become quite rare because of its putative medicinal qualities and the very high price paid for its roots. It is legally protected throughout our region and is cultivated for its roots. Aside from its medicinal value, it has beautiful foliage, interesting flowers, and attractive fruit. Another native, dwarf ginseng (*P. trifolius*), is a smaller plant but with nice flowers in early spring. Dwarf ginseng does not apparently have the medicinal value of ginseng and is more common, especially in moist to wet soils.

NATURAL RANGE Quebec to Minnesota and South Dakota, south to Georgia, Louisiana, and Oklahoma

Penstemon digitalis

TALL WHITE BEARDTONGUE
SCROPHULARIACEAE

ZONES 3 to 9

SOIL moist

LIGHT sun to partial shade

ATTRIBUTES 24 to 48 inches tall; terminal clusters of white snapdragonlike flowers in late spring

Penstemon digitalis

PROPAGATION easy from seed, sow on bare substrate where plants are eventually wanted or subject to three months of moist, cold stratification; selections from soft or semihard cuttings

NOTES 'Husker Red' is a superior, burgundy-leaved selection.

NATURAL RANGE Nova Scotia and Maine to Minnesota and South Dakota, south to Virginia, Alabama, and Texas

Penstemon hirsutus
HAIRY BEARDTONGUE
SCROPHULARIACEAE

ZONES 3 to 9

SOIL moist to dry

LIGHT sun to partial sun

ATTRIBUTES 12 to 18 inches tall; terminal clusters of violet to pale rose, snapdragonlike flowers in late spring

PROPAGATION easy from seed, sow on bare substrate where plants are eventually wanted or subject to three months of moist, cold stratification

NOTES Hairy beardtongue is much more tolerant of open, dry conditions than the tall white beardtongue. 'Pygmaeus' is 5 inches tall in flower.

NATURAL RANGE Quebec and Maine to Michigan and Wisconsin, south to Virginia and Kentucky

Phlox divaricata
WILD BLUE PHLOX
POLEMONIACEAE

ZONES 3 to 9

SOIL moist

LIGHT partial sun to shade

ATTRIBUTES 12 to 14 inches tall; terminal, spreading clusters of 1 1/2-inch-wide violet or lavender-blue flowers in spring

PROPAGATION easy from seed if maintaining cultivar is not important; sow in cold frame and let germinate when ready; softwood cuttings from nonflowering shoots

NOTES var. *laphamii* has deep blue flowers and reaches 10 inches in height. Cultivars include 'Clouds of Perfume' (pale blue), 'Dirigo Ice' (pale blue); 'Fuller's White' (dwarf habit and clear, white flowers), and 'Louisiana Blue' (purple-blue with magenta eye). *Phlox pilosa,* prairie phlox, is native to much of this region and resembles *P. divaricata* but occurs on drier sites, including prairies. The cultivar 'Chattahoochee' (lavender-blue with dark purple

Penstemon hirsutus

Phlox divaricata

Phlox maculata 'Miss Lingard'

Phlox paniculata

center) resulted from a cross between *P. divaricata* and *P. pilosa.*

NATURAL RANGE northwestern Vermont and adjacent Quebec to Minnesota, south to Georgia and Texas

Phlox maculata
WILD SWEET WILLIAM
POLEMONIACEAE

ZONES 3 to 9

SOIL moist

LIGHT sun to partial sun

ATTRIBUTES 24 to 30 inches tall; terminal, short pyramidal clusters of bright pink to lavender flowers in summer; leaves dark glossy green, linear to lance-shaped

PROPAGATION easy from seed, sow in cold frame and let germinate when ready; softwood cuttings from nonflowering shoots

NOTES Excellent for moist soils in full sun; mildew resistant. Cultivars include 'Alpha' (rose-pink flowers), 'Miss Lingard' (sometimes listed as a cultivar of *P. carolina*), 'Omega' (white with small lilac eye), 'Reine du Jour' (clear white with red eye), and 'Rosalinde' (dark pink). Smooth phlox (*P. glaberrima*) occurs in wet woods and open prairies of our region, and is similar to wild sweet William, although can reach over 3 feet in height.

NATURAL RANGE southern Quebec to Virginia and in the mountains to Georgia, west to southern Minnesota, Iowa, and Missouri

Phlox paniculata
SUMMER PHLOX
POLEMONIACEAE

ZONES 3 to 9

SOIL moist

LIGHT sun to partial sun

ATTRIBUTES 36 to 60 inches tall; terminal, pyramidal clusters, up to 8 inches across, of pink, lavender, or white flowers, each about 1 inch in diameter, in summer

PROPAGATION easy from seed if maintaining cultivar not important; sow in cold frame and let germinate when ready; softwood cuttings from nonflowering shoots

NOTES Excellent for moist soils in full sun. There

are so many cultivars that only relatively few can be included here: 'Amethyst' (violet), 'Blue Boy' (lavender), 'Bright Eyes' (pale pink with deep purplish red eye), 'David' (white), 'Eva Cullum' (clear pink with dark red eye, shorter stature), 'Fairest One' (rose with darker red eye), 'Franz Schubert' (lilac with star-shaped darker eye), 'Mt. Fuji' (white), 'Norah Leigh' (variegated leaves, pink to lavender flowers), 'Orange Perfection' (salmon-orange), 'Prime Minister' (white with red eye), 'Red Eyes' (light pink with red eye), 'Robert Poore' (rich purple), 'Starfire' (electric cherry-red—perhaps my favorite as I cannot think of any other flower, native or not, with this particular intensity of red), 'Thunderbolt' (bright scarlet), and 'White Admiral' (white).

NATURAL RANGE southern New York to northern Georgia, west to Illinois, Missouri and Arkansas

Phlox stolonifera
CREEPING PHLOX
POLEMONIACEAE

ZONES 4 to 9

SOIL moist

LIGHT partial sun to shade

ATTRIBUTES 6 to 10 inches tall; approximately 3/4-inch-wide, violet-blue, lavender, or white flowers held above evergreen foliage in mid spring

PROPAGATION easy from seed if maintaining cultivar not important; sow in cold frame and let germinate when ready; softwood cuttings from nonflowering shoots

NOTES Cultivars include 'Alba' (white), 'Blue Ridge' (blue-lilac), 'Bruce's White' (white with yellow eye), 'Home Fires' (pink), 'Sherwood Purple' (medium purple), and 'Variegata' (variegated foliage).

NATURAL RANGE chiefly in the Appalachians, also on the Piedmont; Pennsylvania and southern Ohio to Georgia

Phlox subulata
MOSS-PINK
POLEMONIACEAE

ZONES 3 to 9

SOIL well drained

LIGHT sun

ATTRIBUTES 2 to 6 inches tall; 1/2- to 3/4-inch-wide,

pink blooms above mosslike, bright green foliage in early spring

PROPAGATION by division or layering, or cuttings in late fall

NOTES An excellent low mat with colorful blooms for the rock garden because one often finds it on rock naturally. Cultivars cover the colors of blue or purple (var. *atropurpurea*, 'Benita', 'Blue Hills', 'Bluets', 'Cushion Blue', 'Emerald Blue', 'Oakington Blue'), pink ('Alexander's Surprise', 'Brightness', 'Coral Eye', 'Cushion Pink', 'Emerald Pink', 'Maiden's Blush', 'Marjory'), red ('Crimson Beauty', 'Red Wings', 'Scarlet Flame', 'Starglow'), white (var. *alba*, 'Profusion' [with red eye], 'Snowflake', 'White Delight'), and variegated ('Candy Stripe' [white and pink]).

NATURAL RANGE southern New York to southern Michigan, south to the mountains of North Carolina and Tennessee

Physostegia virginiana
FALSE DRAGONHEAD
SCROPHULARIACEAE

ZONES 3 to 9

SOIL moderately dry to wet

LIGHT sun to partial sun

ATTRIBUTES 24 to 60 inches tall; dozens of 1-inch-long, light to dark pink snapdragonlike flowers along 12- to 18-inch-long terminal spike in late summer; foliage long, narrow, shiny

PROPAGATION easy from seed, cuttings, and division

NOTES Also known as the obedient plant. Under full sun and moist to wet soils, the false dragonhead aggressively spreads. Cultivars include var. *alba* (white flowers that bloom a few weeks before species), var. *grandiflora* (larger flowers and stature), var. *nana* (less than 24 inches tall), 'Pink Bouquet' (bright pink), 'Rose Bouquet' (lilac-pink), 'Rosy Spire' (rosy crimson), 'Summer Snow' (clean white), 'Variegata' (variegated foliage and less aggressive), and 'Vivid' (darker pink). Of all the perennials in my garden, the plant that the most people inquire about when not in flower (besides the eastern prickly pear and hosta cultivars) is *P. v.* 'Variegata' because the foliage is so striking, both in terms of its strong green and white contrasts, as well as its arrangement along the stiff, upright stems.

Phlox stolonifera 'Home Fires'

Phlox subulata

Physostegia virginiana

NATURAL RANGE Maine and Quebec to Manitoba and North Dakota, south to Florida and northern Mexico

Podophyllum peltatum

MAYAPPLE
BERBERIDACEAE

ZONES 3 to 9

SOIL wet to dry

LIGHT partial sun to partial shade

ATTRIBUTES 8 to 16 inches tall; a single white, waxy, 1 1/2- to 2-inch-wide flower borne below and only in axils of two very large, palmately lobed leaves (each up to 12 inches in diameter); fruit ovoid, 2 inches long

PROPAGATION easy to divide

NOTES One has to look under the pair of large, glossy, umbrellalike leaves to see the showy white flowers of mayapple. The fruit is edible but only after it is ripe (i.e., soft, yellow) and in small quanti-

Podophyllum peltatum

Polemonium reptans

ties. This species can be quite invasive, outcompeting many of its companions in my garden, including smaller hostas.

NATURAL RANGE Quebec to Minnesota, south to Florida and Texas

Polemonium reptans
JACOB'S LADDER
POLEMONIACEAE

ZONES 3 to 8

SOIL moist

LIGHT partial sun to partial shade

ATTRIBUTES 10 to 16 inches tall; terminal, loose, drooping clusters of 1/2-inch-wide light blue flowers in spring above dissected foliage

PROPAGATION seed, warm stratify for three months then cold stratify for three months

NOTES Cultivars include var. *alba* (white flowers) and 'Blue Pearl' (bright blue). A showier and much rarer species is Appalachian Jacob's ladder (*P. vanbruntiae*), which has stamens exserted way beyond the corolla and a richer flower color overall. Appalachian Jacob's ladder grows on wet, partially shaded sites.

NATURAL RANGE New York to Minnesota, south to

Virginia, Alabama, and eastern Oklahoma, most abundant west of the mountains

Polygonatum commutatum
SOLOMON'S SEAL
LILIACEAE

ZONES 3 to 9

SOIL moist

LIGHT shade to partial sun

ATTRIBUTES to 84 inches tall; long, arching stalks holding dozens of 3/4-inch-long, bell-shaped flowers, three to eight per leaf axil; bluish green, 3- to 7-inch-long alternate leaves; fruit resembles a small dark blue marble, in pairs at each leaf axil

PROPAGATION easy to divide

NOTES Much more vigorous than the false Solomon's seal (*Smilacina racemosa*). There are two other native Solomon's seals in this region, *P. biflorum* and *P. pubescens,* which are very similar to *P. commutatum* except are much smaller (generally 12 to 30 inches tall). Gleason and Cronquist (1991) consider *P. commutatum* a synonym of *P. pubescens.*

NATURAL RANGE Massachusetts and southern New Hampshire to Minnesota, Manitoba, and North Dakota, south to Florida and northern Mexico

Porteranthus trifoliatus
INDIAN PHYSIC
ROSACEAE

ZONES 4 to 9

SOIL moist to dry

Polygonatum commutatum

Porteranthus trifoliatus

LIGHT sun to partial shade

ATTRIBUTES 24 to 36 inches tall; terminal, 1-inch-wide, white, star-shaped flowers in late spring and early summer on wiry, reddish stems; foliage rich dark green and three-parted

PROPAGATION easy from seed

NOTES Also listed as *Gillenia trifoliata*. Medium texture in foliage, very light texture in flower, most effective in mass; its flowers remind me of little white doves.

NATURAL RANGE southern Ontario to Delaware, North Carolina and Georgia, west to eastern Ohio, eastern Kentucky, and Alabama, and irregularly to southern Michigan, southern Illinois, and southern Missouri

Potentilla tridentata

THREE-TOOTHED CINQUEFOIL
ROSACEAE

ZONES 2 to 9

SOIL well drained, acidic

LIGHT sun to partial shade

ATTRIBUTES 2 to 4 inches tall; 1/4-inch-wide white blooms in summer above glossy, dark green, palmately lobed foliage, which turns dark red in autumn

PROPAGATION easy from seed or division

NOTES An excellent ground cover and rock garden plant, especially on acidic soils; the cultivar 'Minima' reaches only 3 inches tall.

NATURAL RANGE Greenland to Mackenzie, south to Connecticut, Michigan, Iowa, and in the mountains to Georgia

Ratibida pinnata

PRAIRIE CONEFLOWER
ASTERACEAE

ZONES 3 to 9

SOIL dry to moist (but well drained)

LIGHT sun

ATTRIBUTES 24 to 48 inches tall; light yellow flowers, about 3 inches in diameter, with drooping petals and a greenish center that changes to brown in summer

PROPAGATION easy from seed; cold, moist stratification for three months improves germination but is not necessary

NOTES Also known as the gray-headed coneflower. Common in mesic to dry prairies.

NATURAL RANGE southern Ontario to Minnesota and South Dakota, south to Tennessee, Georgia, western Florida, Louisiana, and Oklahoma

Ratibida pinnata

Potentilla tridentata

Rudbeckia fulgida

Rudbeckia fulgida

EASTERN CONEFLOWER
ASTERACEAE

ZONES 3 to 9

SOIL moist

LIGHT sun to partial sun

ATTRIBUTES 20 to 30 inches tall; 2- to 2^1/$_2$-inch-wide, rather flat bright golden yellow flowers with dark brown center in mid summer

PROPAGATION easy from seed or division

NOTES Good nectar species for butterflies and other insects. 'Goldsturm' generally is most available form of the eastern coneflower, selected for its putative smaller, more compact stature. Three natural varieties, which differ primarily in size of flower and shape of leaves, are recognized. *Rudbeckia triloba* (three-lobed coneflower) is similar to *R. fulgida* except some of its leaves are deeply three-lobed and its flowers are a bit smaller; its natural range is Connecticut to Michigan, Iowa, and Nebraska, south to Florida and Texas.

NATURAL RANGE Pennsylvania to Michigan, Illinois, and southern Missouri, south to Florida and Texas

Rudbeckia hirta

Rudbeckia hirta

BLACK-EYED SUSAN
ASTERACEAE

ZONES 3 to 9

SOIL moist to dry

LIGHT sun to partial shade

ATTRIBUTES 24 to 36 inches tall; 3-inch-wide, rather flat golden yellow flowers with dark brown center in mid summer

PROPAGATION easy from seed or division

NOTES Two varieties are widely recognized, var. *hirta*, which is found in relatively undisturbed habitats, and var. *pulcherrima*, which is more common in disturbed habitats. Furthermore, leaves on var. *hirta* are coarsely toothed, and those on var. *pulcherrima* are finely toothed or entire.

NATURAL RANGE Newfoundland to Florida, west to British Columbia and Mexico

Rudbeckia laciniata

CUTLEAF CONEFLOWER
ASTERACEAE

ZONES 3 to 9

SOIL moist

LIGHT sun to partial shade

ATTRIBUTES 36 to 72 inches tall; 2- to 3^1/$_2$-inch-wide, light yellow flowers with drooping petals and green center in summer; leaves deeply dissected

PROPAGATION easy from seed or division

NOTES Three natural varieties are generally recognized, differing primarily in stature and flower size. Of cultivars available, 'Gold Drop' has double flowers and much smaller stature (to 36 inches tall), 'Golden Glow' has double light yellow flowers and vigorous growth, and 'Goldquelle' carries double yellow flowers on plants 36 to 48 inches tall.

NATURAL RANGE Quebec to Florida, west to Montana and Arizona

Rudbeckia laciniata

Sanguinaria canadensis

Sanguinaria canadensis

BLOODROOT
PAPAVERACEAE

ZONES 3 to 9

SOIL moist, well drained

LIGHT partial sun to shade

ATTRIBUTES 5 to 12 inches tall; 3-inch-wide white flowers with yellow centers in early spring, flowers lasting for very short period; foliage nearly round and to 12 inches in diameter, bluish to bright green and deeply lobed

PROPAGATION sow seed in appropriate garden setting or divide plants

NOTES 'Multiplex' has double and much longer-lasting flowers and is striking in bloom; 'Plena' is another double-flowering form. True, that the foliage becomes less attractive later during the growing season, but it is quite showy until then.

NATURAL RANGE Nova Scotia to Ontario and Manitoba, south to Florida and Oklahoma

Sanguisorba canadensis

AMERICAN BURNET
ROSACEAE

ZONES 4 to 8

SOIL moist

LIGHT sun to partial sun

ATTRIBUTES 48 to 72 inches tall; terminal, 6- to 8-inch-long, cylindrical spikes of many white flowers from late summer into autumn; leaves dissected

PROPAGATION fresh seed should germinate in three to four weeks at 70°F; cold stratify older seeds for four weeks; divide in spring

NOTES One of last showy native herbaceous plant species not in the aster family to bloom each growing season.

NATURAL RANGE Newfoundland and Labrador to Manitoba, south to New Jersey, Pennsylvania, Ohio, and Indiana, and in the mountains to West Virginia, Kentucky, and North Carolina

Sedum ternatum

WILD STONECROP
CRASSULACEAE

ZONES 4 to 9

SOIL moist, well drained

LIGHT sun to shade

ATTRIBUTES 4 to 8 inches tall; small white flowers along spreading, branched stalk in late spring; leaves evergreen, dark green, rounded, succulent, in whorls of three

PROPAGATION easy from cuttings and division

NOTES Wild stonecrop is very well suited to the rock garden, in full sun to shade. The cultivar 'Minus' is smaller in all respects.

NATURAL RANGE New Jersey to northern Georgia, west to Iowa and Arkansas

Senecio aureus

GOLDEN RAGWORT
ASTERACEAE

ZONES 5 to 8

SOIL moist to wet soils

LIGHT sun to shade

ATTRIBUTES 12 to 24 inches tall; terminal, $1/2$- to 1-inch-wide, bright golden yellow flowers in mid spring; leaves dark green and glossy

PROPAGATION seeds freely about the garden if soil is moist to wet

NOTES Listed in relatively few gardening books on perennials, the golden ragwort produces many miniature sunflowers in mid spring, especially in very moist to wet soils. One of first native species in the aster family to bloom each year.

NATURAL RANGE Labrador to Minnesota, south to North Carolina, northern Georgia, and central Arkansas

Sanguisorba canadensis

Sedum ternatum

Senecio aureus

Silene virginica

FIRE PINK

CARYOPHYLLACEAE

ZONES 4 to 9

SOIL moist, well drained

LIGHT sun to partial shade

ATTRIBUTES 8 to 14 inches tall; crimson or scarlet, five-petaled flowers each about 2 inches in diameter in mid spring

PROPAGATION easy from seed or cuttings

NOTES "Pink" because this species is in the pink family, certainly not a reference to flower color; rather short-lived unless it self-sows. Of the many other native *Silene* species in this region, *S. regia* (wild pink or royal catchfly) is especially showy. *Silene regia*, with its crimson petals in mid summer, is outstanding in flower but, with its large leaves and very large stature (to 5 feet tall), quite coarse most of the growing season. The natural range of *S. regia* is

Silene virginica

Ohio to eastern Missouri, south to Alabama and Georgia.

NATURAL RANGE New Jersey and western New York to southern Ontario and southeastern Michigan, south to Georgia and Oklahoma

Silene regia

Silphium laciniatum

Silphium laciniatum

COMPASS PLANT
ASTERACEAE

ZONES 3 to 9

SOIL moist to dry

LIGHT sun

ATTRIBUTES 36 to 96 inches tall; clusters of up to 5-inch-wide yellow flowers above very large (at base of plant, to 18 inches long) and divided leaves

PROPAGATION easy from seed

NOTES The common name refers to the habit of the basal leaves, which tend to orient themselves in a north-south direction.

NATURAL RANGE Ohio to Minnesota and South Dakota, south to Alabama and Texas

Silphium terebinthinaceum

PRAIRIE DOCK
ASTERACEAE

ZONES 3 to 9

SOIL moist to dry

LIGHT sun

ATTRIBUTES 48 to 96 inches tall; yellow flowers in summer above huge (to 2 feet long), paddlelike leaves

PROPAGATION easy from seed

NOTES Other *Silphium* species are native to this region and may have a role in some gardens or especially restored prairies, for example, *S. perfoliatum* (cup plant) and *S. trifoliatum* (rosin weed).

NATURAL RANGE southern Ontario and Ohio to Minnesota, south to Georgia and Mississippi

Sisyrinchium angustifolium

BLUE-EYED GRASS
IRIDACEAE

ZONES 3 to 9

SOIL moist

LIGHT partial sun to sun

ATTRIBUTES straplike foliage generally about 12 inches in height; flowers bluish purple with bright yellow center, shaped like a star, about 1/2 inch wide, in mid spring; fruit a capsule

PROPAGATION seed or division

NOTES Rarely noticed unless in flower. The cultivar 'Lucerne' has a deep bluish-purple flower about 3/4 inch in diameter. There are seven additional species native to our region; most occur in open woods,

Silphium terebinthinaceum

prairies, meadows, and some are more common on sandy soils.

NATURAL RANGE Newfoundland to Minnesota, south to Florida and Texas

Smilacina racemosa
FALSE SOLOMON'S SEAL
LILIACEAE

ZONES 3 to 8

SOIL moist

LIGHT partial sun to shade

ATTRIBUTES 12 to 36 inches tall; approximately 6-inch-long, dense, terminal clusters of white flowers in mid spring followed by grapelike clusters of green, then white, then red (at maturity) fruit; leaves bright green, with deep veins

PROPAGATION seed is difficult, sow in fall in outdoor bed; easy to divide clumps

NOTES A fine addition to the shaded garden in spring (long terminal clusters of bright, white flowers), summer (rich green foliage along arching stems), and fall (clusters of red fruit); not as invasive as the true Solomon's seal, at least in my garden.

Silphium perfoliatum

Smilacina racemosa

Smilacina racemosa fruit

Smilacina stellata

NATURAL RANGE Nova Scotia to British Columbia, south to Georgia and Arizona

Smilacina stellata
STARRY FALSE SOLOMON'S SEAL
LILIACEAE

ZONES 3 to 8

SOIL moist to wet

LIGHT sun to shade

ATTRIBUTES 12 to 30 inches tall; approximately 3-inch-long, open, terminal cluster of about six to twelve white, 1/3-inch-wide, starlike flowers followed by marblelike fruit that is deep red at maturity

PROPAGATION seed is difficult, sow in fall in outdoor bed; easy to divide

NOTES Naturally occurs in wet or dry, often sandy soils that are circumneutral or basic; individual flowers are much showier than other *Smilacina* species, but there are not as many in a cluster as *S. racemosa*. Three-leaved false Solomon's seal (*S. trifolia*) also grows in wetlands but in sunny to partially shaded acidic peatlands (bogs).

NATURAL RANGE Newfoundland to British Columbia, south to New Jersey, Virginia, Indiana, Missouri, and California

Solidago caesia

Solidago caesia
BLUE-STEMMED GOLDENROD
ASTERACEAE

ZONES 3 to 9

SOIL moist to dry

LIGHT sun to shade

ATTRIBUTES 16 to 36 inches tall; small golden yellow flowers in two rows on short spikes in autumn; foliage lance-shaped and dark bluish green

PROPAGATION easy from seed or cuttings

NOTES A fine shady, woodland goldenrod, in contrast to the many species found in sunny old fields throughout the region. Some are reluctant to plant goldenrods, believing these plants cause allergy problems. The real culprits are other, often less conspicuous plants that occur with the goldenrods, especially ragweed (*Ambrosia*) species. While many have tried to repair goldenrod's reputation for decades, too many people still have not heard this message.

NATURAL RANGE Nova Scotia and southern Quebec to Wisconsin, south to Florida and Texas

Solidago canadensis
CANADA GOLDENROD
ASTERACEAE

ZONES 3 to 9

SOIL moist to dry

LIGHT sun

ATTRIBUTES 36 to 72 inches tall; large open sprays of small golden yellow flowers in autumn

PROPAGATION easy from seed sown in autumn, or from divisions

NOTES Five natural varieties of Canada goldenrod are recognized in this region, differing primarily by stem hairiness and flower size. Before planting, be aware that Canada goldenrod is a very robust species that readily spreads via rhizomes. I think it is one of the finest for flower arrangements, because of the striking size and architecture of its flower stalk. In my garden, it is combined with numerous other native goldenrods and asters where a free-for-all for growing space takes place each year. I really enjoy the combination of various yellows, purples, and white in this patch during flowering, but visitors during most of the growing season prior to flowering must think I have forgotten to weed this area as it is very chaotic in appearance. Other especially attractive native goldenrod species include gray goldenrod (*S. nemoralis*), sweet goldenrod (*S. odora*), stiff goldenrod (*S. rigida*), and seaside goldenrod (*S. sempervirens*). All do very well, and are easier to maintain, on drier soils.

NATURAL RANGE throughout most of the U.S. and southern Canada

Solidago flexicaulis
ZIG-ZAG GOLDENROD
ASTERACEAE

ZONES 3 to 8

SOIL moist to dry

Solidago canadensis

Solidago flexicaulis 'Variegata'

LIGHT sun to shade

ATTRIBUTES 12 to 48 inches tall; small golden yellow flowers at end of stalk that has a zig-zag pattern; leaves rather egg-shaped, dark green, coarsely toothed

PROPAGATION easy from seed or cuttings

NOTES The zig-zag goldenrod is also native to woodlands and is especially well suited to shade; the cultivar 'Variegata' has variegated green and yellowish leaves. Elm-leaved goldenrod (*S. ulmifolia*) is another native woodland species.

NATURAL RANGE Nova Scotia and New Brunswick to North Dakota, south to Virginia, Kentucky, and Arkansas, and in the mountains to Georgia

Solidago rugosa
ROUGH-STEMMED GOLDENROD
ASTERACEAE

ZONES 3 to 9

SOIL moist to dry

LIGHT sun to partial sun

ATTRIBUTES 24 to 72 inches tall; golden yellow flowers in autumn

PROPAGATION easy from seed or cuttings

NOTES An old-field species that can easily overtake less robust plants; the cultivar 'Fireworks' is less aggressive and has long flower stalks that trail like fading fireworks. Two subspecies, one including three varieties, are recognized, indicating the large amount of natural variation in leaf, stem, and flower traits, and habitat differences.

NATURAL RANGE Newfoundland to Florida, west to Michigan, Missouri, and Texas

Solidago speciosa
SHOWY GOLDENROD
ASTERACEAE

ZONES 3 to 9

SOIL moist to dry

LIGHT sun to partial sun

ATTRIBUTES 24 to 60 inches tall; small, light yellow flowers densely packed along an unbranched stalk in autumn

PROPAGATION easy from seed or cuttings

NOTES Three varieties that differ in leaf and flower characteristics occur in this region. Many additional goldenrod species are native to this region and any might be worthy for a particular garden setting.

NATURAL RANGE Massachusetts and southern New Hampshire to Minnesota and Wyoming, south to Georgia, Arkansas, Texas, and New Mexico

Spigelia marilandica
INDIAN PINK
LOGANIACEAE

ZONES 4 to 9

SOIL moist

LIGHT partial sun to partial shade

ATTRIBUTES 12 to 18 inches tall; in summer, terminal, upright, 2-inch-long, narrow, ellipsoidal, crimson flowers that upon opening have light yellow throats

PROPAGATION seed, will require cold, moist stratification for three months prior to germination

NOTES Native to the more southern portions of this region; hummingbirds will frequent for nectar.

NATURAL RANGE North Carolina to southern Indiana, southern Missouri, and Oklahoma, south to Florida and Texas

Stylophorum diphyllum
CELANDINE POPPY
PAPAVERACEAE

ZONES 4 to 8

SOIL moist

LIGHT partial sun to shade

ATTRIBUTES 12 to 20 inches tall; 1$\frac{1}{2}$- to 2-inch-wide, bright yellow flowers from leaf axils in spring

PROPAGATION easy from seed, and will naturally seed into any garden opening

NOTES I will never forget when I first saw this species in central Kentucky about thirty years ago, blooming on slopes of rich, basic soil along with wild blue phlox (*Phlox divaricata*), dwarf larkspur (*Delphinium tricorne*), blue-eyed Mary (*Collinsia verna*), and many other spring-flowering species. The intense yellow flowers of the celandine poppy were a wonderful contrast to the many blues, purples, and other colors on these slopes.

NATURAL RANGE western Pennsylvania to southern Michigan and Wisconsin, south to Tennessee and Arkansas

Spigelia marilandica

Stylophorum diphyllum

Symplocarpus foetidus flowers in early spring

Symplocarpus foetidus in mid summer

Symplocarpus foetidus

SKUNK CABBAGE

ARACEAE

ZONES 3 to 7

SOIL wet to flooded

LIGHT sun to shade

ATTRIBUTES 18 to 36 inches tall, leaves about 24 inches long and longer when growing on saturated, organic soils in partial shade; flowers are deep maroon and open as snow is melting in this region; fruit is a conelike structure that holds many large seeds

PROPAGATION difficult from seed, subject to periods of warm and cold stratification; difficult to divide

NOTES Skunk cabbage will probably never become the hosta for wet soils, but, growing in saturated, organic soils, it is a striking plant as leaves unfurl and mature. It is especially interesting in very early spring, when its flowers produce enough heat to melt the adjacent snow. Unfortunately, the flowers smell like rotten meat, to attract the flies that pollinate them, and all plant parts, when crushed, smell like a skunk that has been aggravated.

NATURAL RANGE Quebec and Nova Scotia to North Carolina, west to Minnesota and Iowa

Thalictrum dasycarpum

PURPLE MEADOW RUE
RANUNCULACEAE

ZONES 3 to 8

SOIL moist

LIGHT sun to partial shade

ATTRIBUTES 36 to 84 inches tall; large, open plumes of pale to dark pink-purple flowers in early summer; foliage bluish green and fernlike

PROPAGATION easy from seed, subject to cold, moist stratification for three months or sow in cold frame or outdoor bed in autumn

NOTES A wonderful, tall but light-textured (especially in flower) addition to the woodland garden.

NATURAL RANGE southwestern Ontario to Alberta and Washington, south to Ohio, Indiana, Missouri, Oklahoma, and Arizona

Thalictrum dioicum

EARLY MEADOW RUE
RANUNCULACEAE

ZONES 3 to 8

SOIL moist

LIGHT partial sun to shade

ATTRIBUTES 12 to 36 inches tall; open clusters of tassel-like yellow flowers at end of dissected, bluish green foliage

PROPAGATION easy from seed, subject to cold, moist stratification for three months or sow in cold frame or outdoor bed in autumn

NOTES Early meadow rue does not have the stature of the other two *Thalictrum* species covered here, but it does have the dissected foliage that is fernlike.

NATURAL RANGE Quebec to Manitoba, south to South Carolina, Georgia, Alabama, and Missouri

Thalictrum dioicum

Thalictrum pubescens

Thalictrum pubescens

TALL MEADOW RUE
RANUNCULACEAE

ZONES 3 to 9

SOIL moist to wet

LIGHT sun to shade

ATTRIBUTES 36 to 120 inches tall; large, open plumes of white flowers in summer; foliage bluish green and fernlike

PROPAGATION easy from seed, subject to cold, moist stratification for three months or sow in cold frame or outdoor bed in autumn

NOTES Also listed as *T. polygamum*. Tall meadow rue is often a common plant in many wetlands, especially those on rich, slightly acidic or circumneutral soils; it is a fine companion with the robust Oswego tea (*Monarda didyma*) and culver's root (*Veronicastrum virginicum*), as they all bloom at the same time and thrive on moist soils in partial shade. I am amazed by how many books on plants for the garden overlook this beautiful species.

NATURAL RANGE Labrador and Quebec to Ontario, south to southern North Carolina, Tennessee, and Indiana

Tiarella cordifolia

FOAMFLOWER
SAXIFRAGACEAE

ZONES 3 to 9

SOIL moist

LIGHT sun to shade

ATTRIBUTES 3 to 10 inches tall; columnar, dense mass of star-shaped, 1/4-inch-wide, white flowers on a 3- to 4-inch-long stalk atop heart-shaped leaves in spring

PROPAGATION easy from seed or division, on moist sites spreads readily via stolons

NOTES var. *collina* (= *T. wherryi*) is native to the southern Appalachians and southern portions of this region, and is similar but does not have stolons, therefore is a more compact plant. Cultivars include var. *albiflora* (whiter flowers than species), var. *purpurea* (leaves are somewhat bronze, flowers pale pink to rose), 'Moorgrun' (smaller leaves than species), 'Oakleaf' (dark green leaves, pinkish flowers), and 'Purpurea' (purple-tinged foliage with pale pink to rose flowers).

Tiarella cordifolia

NATURAL RANGE Nova Scotia to Ontario and eastern Wisconsin, south to Georgia and Alabama

Tradescantia ohiensis

SMOOTH SPIDERWORT
COMMELINACEAE

ZONES 3 to 9

SOIL moist to dry

LIGHT sun to partial sun

ATTRIBUTES 12 to 24 inches tall; blue or rose (seldom white), 1-inch-wide flowers in spring

PROPAGATION easy from seed, cuttings, and division

NOTES Good luck finding either of the native spiderworts mentioned here, as most that are available are cultivars of hybrids from native species (see notes for next species). I have seen our native species in their natural habitats and think they are fine as they are, without the hybridization. They are easy to grow and provide a unique architectural form to the landscape.

NATURAL RANGE Massachusetts to Minnesota, south to Florida and Texas

Tradescantia virginiana

Trientalis borealis

Tradescantia virginiana
VIRGINIA SPIDERWORT
COMMELINACEAE

ZONES 3 to 9

SOIL moist

LIGHT sun to shade

ATTRIBUTES 12 to 24 inches tall; approximately 1-inch-wide, purple, blue-violet, lavender, rose and even white flowers in spring

PROPAGATION easy from seed, cuttings, and division

NOTES According to most sources, most spiderwort cultivars are hybrids (*T.* Andersoniana Group) of two or more native species (*T. ohiensis, T. subaspera,* and *T. virginiana*). If you are interested in this group, some of many include 'Bilberry Ice' (light red-violet), 'Bluestone' (blue-lavender), 'Concord Grape' (red-violet), 'Innocence' (white), 'Joy' (rose-purple), 'Pauline' (pink), 'Purewell Giant' (dark pink), 'Purple Dome' (medium purple), and 'Zwanenburg Blue' (medium purple).

NATURAL RANGE Maine to Pennsylvania, Michigan, and Minnesota, south to Georgia and Missouri

Trientalis borealis
STARFLOWER
PRIMULACEAE

ZONES 2 to 8

SOIL rich, moist to wet

LIGHT partial shade to shade

ATTRIBUTES lance-shaped leaves in one set of whorls on stem about 6 inches tall; bright white, star-shaped flowers on slender stalks 1 to 2 inches long and above the leaves in late spring and early summer

PROPAGATION seed or division

NOTES I encounter starflower often in the very dark coniferous forested wetlands I work in. When in bloom it is easy to see from far away because of its bright white flowers.

NATURAL RANGE Labrador and Newfoundland to Alberta, south to Pennsylvania, northern Ohio, northern Illinois, and Minnesota; also on the coastal plain from Massachusetts to Virginia, and irregularly in southern Appalachians

Trillium erectum
PURPLE TRILLIUM
LILIACEAE

ZONES 3 to 8

SOIL moist, slightly acidic to acidic best

LIGHT partial shade

ATTRIBUTES 6 to 20 inches tall; 2- to 3-inch-wide, deep reddish, three-petaled flowers in mid spring

PROPAGATION seed, will require alternating periods of warm and cold, moist stratification; like all trilliums, reportedly takes seven years to produce its first flowers

NOTES A greenish yellow flowering form naturally occurs in this region. Other purple trilliums occur in

Trillium erectum

Trillium erectum, greenish yellow flowering form

Trillium cuneatum

this region, including three that produce flowers lacking a stalk (i.e., they are sessile). These sessile species, all of which have green and silvery mottled foliage, are *T. cuneatum* (whippoorwill flower), *T. recurvatum* (prairie trillium), and *T. sessile* (sessile trillium). *Trillium luteum* (yellow trillium) is also native to this region and resembles *T. cuneatum* except for its lemon-scented, bright yellow flowers. All *Trillium* species generally grow best in rich, moist soils under moderate shade.

NATURAL RANGE Quebec and Ontario to Maryland and Ohio, south to the mountains of North Carolina, Georgia, and Tennessee

Trillium recurvatum

Trillium sessile

Trillium luteum

Trillium flexipes

Trillium flexipes
BENT TRILLIUM
LILIACEAE

ZONES 4 to 8?

SOIL moist, slightly alkaline best

LIGHT partial shade

ATTRIBUTES about 12 inches tall; white flower on rather long stalk that is typically below the wedge-shaped leaves

PROPAGATION seed, will require alternating periods of warm and cold, moist stratification

NOTES Similar to *T. cernuum* (nodding trillium), which is native to deeply shaded forested wetlands in the Northeast.

NATURAL RANGE Michigan to Minnesota, south to northern Arkansas, northern Alabama, and north-western Georgia

Trillium grandiflorum
WHITE TRILLIUM
LILIACEAE

ZONES 3 to 8

SOIL moist, circumneutral

LIGHT partial sun to partial shade

ATTRIBUTES 8 to 20 inches tall; 2- to 3-inch-wide,

Trillium grandiflorum

Trillium grandiflorum, green and white flowering form

Trillium grandiflorum 'Flore Pleno'

Trillium undulatum

Trollius laxus

pure white, three-petaled flowers that turn pinkish in mid spring

PROPAGATION seed, will require alternating periods of warm and cold, moist stratification

NOTES White trillium offers an outstanding spring show in the front of a lightly shaded border or en masse. Cultivars of white trillium include 'Flore Pleno' (double flowers) and var. *roseum* (pink flowers). The very small snow trillium (*T. nivale*) grows best under similar conditions but blooms weeks earlier and only reaches about 4 inches in height. Painted trillium (*T. undulatum*), sometimes common on moist, well-drained, acidic soils in this region, is my favorite, but is not readily available yet and is apparently not easy to grow. Trilliums are protected species in most states, to minimize their exploitation from the wild.

NATURAL RANGE Quebec and Maine to Minnesota, south to Pennsylvania, Ohio, and Indiana, and in the mountains to northern Georgia and northeastern Alabama

Trollius laxus
LARGE-FLOWERED BELLWORT
SPREADING GLOBEFLOWER
RANUNCULACEAE

ZONES 4 to 8

SOIL moist to wet, circumneutral; high in organic matter

LIGHT partial sun to sun (if soil is consistently saturated)

ATTRIBUTES 12 to 20 inches tall; five-"petaled" (they are actually sepals) moonlight-yellow flowers, about

1¼ inches wide, held above deeply dissected, glossy and dark green leaves in early to mid spring. Plants form dense mounds of foliage on proper sites

PROPAGATION seed, cold stratify for three months

NOTES Once a candidate for federal listing as threatened, the spreading globeflower is generally very rare over its range. I have been spoiled by viewing thousands of this species in full bloom in many of New York's fens, peatlands fed by calcium-enriched groundwater.

NATURAL RANGE Connecticut to Delaware, Pennsylvania and Ohio

Uvularia grandiflora
LARGE-FLOWERED BELLWORT
LILIACEAE

ZONES 3 to 8

SOIL moist

LIGHT partial sun to shade

ATTRIBUTES 12 to 16 inches tall; 1- to 2-inch-long, pendent, pale to rich yellow flowers in early spring; foliage bluish green

PROPAGATION seed, will require multiple cycles of warm and cold stratification

NOTES The cultivar 'Sunbonnet' has bigger, brighter flowers than the species. Two other bellworts native to this region, both with pale green flowers, are *U. perfoliata* (perfoliate bellwort) and *U. sessilifolia* (sessile bellwort). All bellworts are worthy for the garden that is deeply shaded by deciduous trees. With somewhat similar foliage and in the same family are two other native species worthy of garden at-

Uvularia grandiflora

Veratrum viride flowers

tention, fairy-bells (*Disporum maculatum*) and rosy twisted stalk (*Streptopus roseus*). Both species occur in rich, deeply shaded woods and have attractive foliage and modest flowers and fruit.

NATURAL RANGE Maine and southern Quebec to Minnesota and North Dakota, south to Connecticut, Virginia, northern Georgia, Alabama, and Oklahoma

Veratrum viride

FALSE HELLEBORE
LILIACEAE

ZONES 3 to 8

SOIL moist to wet, thriving in organic soils

LIGHT partial sun to shade

ATTRIBUTES 24 to 48 inches tall; large bright green, pleated leaves spiral along stem that ends in an 18- to 24-inch-long flower cluster of many star-shaped, yellow-green flowers

PROPAGATION seed, will require three months of cold stratification

NOTES False hellebore is a robust plant with strong architecture and large, terminal clusters of green flowers. It will thrive especially in very damp soils. A very similar genus in the lily family is *Melanthium* (bunchflower), which includes two native species in our region, *M. virginicum* and *M. hybridum*. Both, like *V. viride,* can be grown for foliage effect, which is enhanced by their greenish white flowers.

NATURAL RANGE Quebec to Ontario, south to North Carolina; Alaska to Oregon

Veronicastrum virginicum

CULVER'S ROOT
SCROPHULARIACEAE

ZONES 3 to 9

SOIL moist to wet

LIGHT sun to partial shade

ATTRIBUTES 36 to 72 inches tall; terminal, erect clusters of 6- to 9-inch-long spikes of many 1/4-inch-wide white flowers in mid summer; leaves in whorls of three to six along stems

PROPAGATION easy from seed, cuttings, or division

NOTES var. *alba* has pure white flowers; var. *rosea* has pink flowers.

NATURAL RANGE Vermont to Ontario and Manitoba, south to Georgia and Louisiana

Veronicastrum virginicum

Viola adunca var. minor

Viola rostrata

Viola adunca
HOOKSPUR VIOLET
VIOLACEAE

ZONES 2 to 9

SOIL moist to dry

LIGHT sun to partial shade

ATTRIBUTES 3 to 6 inches tall; ¾-inch-wide, violet flowers in spring atop compact, short mounds of dark green leaves

PROPAGATION easy from seed or division

NOTES This species includes var. *minor* (= *V. labradorica*), Labrador violet, which occurs in the northern portions of this region, and even further north. The Labrador violet has very dark purple-green leaves and makes an excellent ground cover.

Similar species include *V. rostrata* (long-spurred violet) and *V. conspersa* (dog violet). Dozens of other violet species are native to this region—twenty species and numerous natural hybrids are native to New York alone.

NATURAL RANGE Greenland and Labrador to Alaska, south to New York, Michigan, Minnesota, and California

Viola canadensis
CANADA VIOLET
VIOLACEAE

ZONES 3 to 8

SOIL moist

LIGHT partial sun to shade

ATTRIBUTES 10 to 16 inches tall; satiny white flowers with intense yellow and purple-streaked center in early spring, flowers turning purplish with age

PROPAGATION easy from seed

NOTES Canada violet is especially well suited to gardens that are shaded by deciduous trees.

NATURAL RANGE Newfoundland to Alaska and British Columbia, Alabama, Arkansas, and Arizona

Viola cucullata

MARSH BLUE VIOLET
VIOLACEAE

ZONES 4 to 9

SOIL moist to wet

LIGHT sun (if wet) to shade

ATTRIBUTES about 6 inches tall; approximately 3/4-inch-wide, dark lavender to pale violet flowers in spring; leaves nearly heart-shaped

PROPAGATION easy from seed

NOTES One of a number of violets that naturally occur in wetlands in this region; cultivars include 'Freckles' (pale blue with purple spots), 'Red Giant' (rose-red), 'Royal Robe' (dark violet-blue), and 'White Czar' (white with yellow eye). Dooryard violet (*V. sororia*) is similar but much more widespread, occurring in moist and wet soils, and often on disturbed sites.

NATURAL RANGE Newfoundland to Ontario and Minnesota, south to North Carolina, Georgia, Tennessee, and eastern Arkansas

Viola pedata

BIRD'S-FOOT VIOLET
VIOLACEAE

ZONES 3 to 9

SOIL well drained; sandy best

LIGHT sun to partial sun

ATTRIBUTES 3 to 5 inches tall; relatively large (about 1 inch in diameter) violet flowers in spring; leaves deeply dissected

PROPAGATION easy from seed

NOTES The bird's-foot violet naturally occurs on very open, dry sites. Cultivars include var. *alba* (white flowers), var. *bicolor* (dark purple upper petals and violet on the lower petals), var. *concolor* (violet flowers with white spot at the base of lower petal), and 'Artist's Palette'. Wood violet (*V. palmata*) is similar in appearance and affinity to drier

Viola canadensis

Viola cucullata

Viola pedata

soils in the region. Arrow-leaved violet (*V. sagittata*) and ovate-leaved violet (*V. fimbriatula*) also occur on dry soils.

NATURAL RANGE Maine to Minnesota, south to northern Florida and eastern Texas

Viola pubescens

YELLOW VIOLET
VIOLACEAE

ZONES 3 to 9

SOIL moist

LIGHT partial sun to shade

ATTRIBUTES 8 to 16 inches tall; 1/2-inch-wide bright

Viola pubescens

yellow flowers with purple streaks toward the center, in early to mid spring

PROPAGATION easy from seed

NOTES Often not far from the Canada violet, in the same woods. Both species really thrive beneath deciduous canopies that soon after flowering will create a dark shade below.

NATURAL RANGE Nova Scotia to Manitoba and North Dakota, south to South Carolina, Georgia, Louisiana, and Texas

Waldsteinia fragarioides

BARREN STRAWBERRY
ROSACEAE

ZONES 3 to 8

SOIL moist to dry

LIGHT sun to shade

ATTRIBUTES 3 to 6 inches tall; 1/2-inch-wide bright yellow, five-petaled flowers above unfolding, glossy, three-parted, initially light leaves in spring; leaves becoming dark green and glossy

PROPAGATION easy to divide

NOTES Barren strawberry is a very adaptable, excellent ground cover worthy of consideration for the glossy, deep green foliage alone; spreads via rhizomes. Highly drought-tolerant once established.

NATURAL RANGE Maine and western Quebec to Minnesota, south to Pennsylvania, Indiana, and in the mountains to Georgia and Alabama

Waldsteinia fragarioides

Zigadenus elegans

WHITE CAMAS
LILIACEAE

ZONES 3 to 9

SOIL moist

LIGHT sun

ATTRIBUTES 24 to 36 inches tall; open stalks of many white, star-shaped, 1/2-inch-wide flowers

PROPAGATION seed, cold stratify for three months

NOTES Another common name, mountain death camas (sounds more like a kid's video game), indicates that this plant is very poisonous to people. Similar in appearance until it blooms is fly-poison (*Amianthium muscaetoxicum*), which produces a compact, terminal, white mass of white flowers held high above the leaves in late spring to early summer. It occurs in open woods in the central to southern portions of our region.

NATURAL RANGE Quebec to New York, west across northern U.S. and adjacent Canada to the cordilleran region from Alaska to northern Mexico; disjunct in the southern Appalachians (Virginia to North Carolina) and in the Ozarks (Missouri and Arkansas)

Zigadenus elegans

Zizia aurea

GOLDEN ALEXANDERS
APIACEAE

ZONES 4 to 9

SOIL moist to wet

LIGHT sun to partial shade

ATTRIBUTES 12 to 36 inches tall; terminal, flat clusters (about 3 inches in diameter) of bright yellow flowers in late spring

PROPAGATION easy from seed

NOTES A similar native species, except for its heart-shaped leaves, is *Z. aptera* (heart-leaved alexanders). Both are excellent choices for open wet garden spots or wetland restoration seed mixes. These species are also the larval food plants for the black swallowtail butterfly.

NATURAL RANGE Quebec and Maine to Saskatchewan, south to Florida and Texas

Zizia aurea

VINES

Including prostrate, trailing species

Aristolochia macrophylla

DUTCHMAN'S PIPE
ARISTOLOCHIACEAE

ZONES 4 to 8

SOIL moist, well drained

LIGHT sun to partial shade

ATTRIBUTES twining vine that can reach 30+ feet in height, depending on structural support it is given; leaves simple, alternate, heart-shaped, 4 to 10 inches long, dark green; flowers shaped like a curved pipe, yellow-green, to $1^1/2$ inches long; fruit a ribbed capsule about $2^1/2$ inches long

PROPAGATION seed, cold stratify for three months; cuttings taken in July, or division of plant

NOTES Also listed as *A. durior.* Dutchman's pipe has notable foliage and is very fast-growing. As a twining, high-climbing component of dense Appalachian forests, it is also well adapted to very shaded conditions.

NATURAL RANGE Appalachian region from southern Pennsylvania to northern Georgia

Bignonia capreolata

CROSS-VINE
BIGNONIACEAE

ZONES 6 to 9

SOIL moist, well drained

LIGHT sun to partial shade

ATTRIBUTES self-clinging vine to 50+ feet; leaves opposite, consist of two leaflets, each 2 to 6 inches long, semi-evergreen or evergreen, dark green, shiny, turning reddish purple in autumn; flowers trumpet-shaped, to 2 inches long, typically reddish brown (with yellow or orange interior), in spring; fruit a slender capsule to 7 inches long

PROPAGATION seed, will germinate without pretreatment; cuttings taken in early summer

NOTES Cross-vine climbs by its small, disklike pads, adhering to any porous structure. Cultivars have

been selected that have richer shades of red or orange.

NATURAL RANGE southern Maryland to southern Ohio and southern Missouri, south to Florida and Louisiana

Campis radicans

TRUMPETCREEPER
BIGNONIACEAE

ZONES 4 to 9

SOIL any!

LIGHT sun to partial sun

ATTRIBUTES clinging (by numerous roots along stem), very fast-growing, suckering vine, to 40+ feet; leaves pinnately compound, opposite, about 12 inches long, dark green, glossy; flowers trumpet-shaped, to 3 inches long, shades of orange and scarlet, in clusters up to 12, in summer; fruit a capsule 3 to 5 inches long

Aristolochia macrophylla

Bignonia capreolata

PROPAGATION seed, cold stratify for two months; softwood cuttings root readily; root cuttings easy too
NOTES There are few such beautiful plants that will thrive under such poor conditions, including well-drained sandy, infertile soils all along the East Coast in communities immediately adjacent to the ocean (and its salt spray). However, trumpetcreeper is most difficult to control on rich, moist soils; cutting it only promotes root sprouts, which I pull out by the many dozens each year in my garden adjacent to a trumpetcreeper I planted years ago. Cultivars have been selected for specific shades of yellow, red, and orange flowers.
NATURAL RANGE New Jersey to Ohio and Iowa, south to Florida and Texas

Celastrus scandens
AMERICAN BITTERSWEET
CELASTRACEAE

ZONES 3 to 8
SOIL dry to moist
LIGHT sun to partial sun
ATTRIBUTES twining vine to 50+ feet high if structure available; leaves simple, alternate, 2 to 4 inches long, dark green, shiny, turning pale green to yellow in autumn; flowers typically dioecious, yellowish white, in 2- to 4-inch-long terminal cluster; fruit a round, three-lobed orange capsule, about 1/3 inch in diameter, which splits open, exposing shiny, scarlet seeds
PROPAGATION seed, cold stratify for two to six months; softwood cuttings root readily
NOTES Male and female specimens must be somewhat close together to get the fruit production that

Campsis radicans

Celastrus scandens

this species is so highly valued for. The somewhat similar but even more aggressive Oriental bittersweet (*C. orbiculatus*) has flowers and fruits along the stem, rather than at the end of the stem as for the American bittersweet.

NATURAL RANGE Quebec and Ontario to Manitoba and Wyoming, south to western South Carolina, northern Georgia, eastern Alabama, Louisiana, and Texas

Clematis virginiana

VIRGIN'S BOWER
RANUNCULACEAE

ZONES 4 to 8

SOIL moist

LIGHT sun to partial sun

ATTRIBUTES twining vine to 20+ feet high; leaves bright green; flowers about 3/4 inch in diameter, white, in 3- to 6-inch-long clusters along the stem throughout mid to late summer into autumn; fruit a wispy cluster

PROPAGATION seed, cold stratify for two to three months

NOTES While its flowers are not as big and brightly colored as the hybrids and many cultivars of non-native *Clematis* species, the virgin's bower is a beautiful plant for late summer bloom. Purple clematis (*C. occidentalis*) is another native clematis of this region. Purple clematis produces bluish purple flowers in spring.

NATURAL RANGE Nova Scotia and eastern Quebec to Manitoba, south to Georgia and Louisiana

Decumaria barbara

CLIMBING HYDRANGEA
HYDRANGEACEAE

ZONES 5 to 9

SOIL moist and enriched with organic matter best, to wet

LIGHT partial shade to shade

ATTRIBUTES clinging (by aerial rootlets) vine to 30+ feet; leaves simple, opposite, 3 to 5 inches long, shiny, dark green, turning pale cream-yellow in autumn, petiole 1 to 2 inches long; flowers 1/4 inch in diameter, white, fragrant, in 2- to 3-inch-long and -wide pyramidal and terminal cluster; fruit a capsule about 1/3 inch long

PROPAGATION seed, will germinate without pretreatment

NOTES Also known as wood vamp, climbing hydrangea naturally occurs in forested wetlands of the southeastern U.S.; a few cultivars with better foliage characteristics are becoming available.

NATURAL RANGE southeastern Virginia to Florida and Louisiana

Gelsemium sempervirens

CAROLINA YELLOW JESSAMINE
LOGANIACEAE

ZONES 6 to 9

SOIL moist, well drained, acidic best, but will tolerate much broader conditions

LIGHT sun to partial sun

ATTRIBUTES twining vine to 20+ feet high; leaves simple, opposite, lance-shaped, shiny, dark green, evergreen, turning yellowish or purple green in autumn; flowers funnel-shaped, five-lobed, 1 1/2 inches long, yellow, fragrant; fruit a short capsule

PROPAGATION seed, will germinate without pretreatment; cuttings root readily

NOTES A few cultivars have been selected for increased cold hardiness and flower characteristics.

NATURAL RANGE southeastern Virginia to Tennessee and Arkansas, south to Florida and Mexico

Linnaea borealis

TWINFLOWER
CAPRIFOLIACEAE

ZONES 2 to 6

SOIL rich, moist, acidic, well drained, high in organic matter

LIGHT partial sun to partial shade

ATTRIBUTES slender, trailing vine with small, oval, evergreen leaves along short, erect side branches to 4 inches tall; flowers pinkish, bell-shaped, in nodding pairs at top of 2- to 4-inch-long stalk, in late spring to summer; fruit a tiny capsule

PROPAGATION easy from cuttings

NOTES Because twinflower does produce a woody stem, it is included in this section instead of with the herbaceous wildflowers. I hardly notice it where it is naturally abundant until it blooms. Worth the effort to cultivate.

NATURAL RANGE circumpolar, south in America to

Clematis virginiana

Decumaria barbara

Gelsemium sempervirens

New Jersey, West Virginia, northern Indiana, Minnesota, and California

Lonicera dioica
GLAUCOUS HONEYSUCKLE
CAPRIFOLIACEAE

ZONES 3 to 9

SOIL moist to wet

LIGHT sun to partial shade

ATTRIBUTES twining vine; leaves simple, opposite, 2 to 4 inches long, dark green above, generally white and waxy beneath; flowers tube-shaped, to 1 inch long, yellow to purple, in summer

PROPAGATION seed, cold stratify for three months; cuttings

NOTES Four naturally occurring varieties are recognized in this region, based on the hairiness of a portion of the flower and leaves. Given the value of this species as a very cold hardy vine and its great geographical range, it has much potential for selection of improved foliage and flowers especially.

NATURAL RANGE Massachusetts, Quebec, and northern Ontario to Mackenzie and British Columbia, south to Oklahoma, Iowa, Illinois, Indiana, North Carolina and New Jersey

Lonicera sempervirens
TRUMPET HONEYSUCKLE
CAPRIFOLIACEAE

ZONES 4 to 9

SOIL moist, well drained

LIGHT sun to partial shade (as with all vines mentioned here, flower production is highest under greatest amount of sun)

ATTRIBUTES twining vine to 20+ feet; leaves simple, opposite, 1 to 3 inches long, dark bluish green above and white, waxy below; flower tube-shaped, narrow, to 2 inches long, orange-red to red (with yellow and orange inside), in summer; fruit a round, red berry, 1/4 inch in diameter

PROPAGATION seed, cold stratify for three months; cuttings

NOTES With its long, tubular, orange-red flowers, trumpet honeysuckle is an excellent source of nectar for hummingbirds. Numerous cultivars have been selected for more compact form, more brilliant or richer flowers and longer bloom period, and greater insect and disease resistance.

NATURAL RANGE Connecticut to Florida and west to Oklahoma

Menispermum canadense
MOONSEED
MENISPERMACEAE

ZONES 4 to 8

SOIL moist

LIGHT partial sun to partial shade

ATTRIBUTES slender, twining vine to about 20 feet

Lonicera dioica

Lonicera sempervirens

high; leaves alternate, dark green, nearly round or shallowly three-lobed, 4 to 10 inches in diameter; flowers greenish yellow to white in open clusters that arise from leaf axils in early summer; fruit bluish black, round, about 1/3 inch wide

PROPAGATION easy by division

NOTES This species is named after its moon-shaped seeds; rarely cultivated but deserves consideration.

NATURAL RANGE western Quebec and western New England to Manitoba, south to Georgia and Oklahoma

Mitchella repens

PARTRIDGEBERRY

RUBIACEAE

ZONES 3 to 8

SOIL rich, moist, well drained

LIGHT partial shade to shade

ATTRIBUTES prostrate vine with opposite, nearly round evergreen leaves on slender, wiry stems; flowers tubular, white, in pairs; fruit a bright red berrylike double drupe

PROPAGATION cuttings easiest

NOTES Similar to twinflower in habit but hugs ground more, partridgeberry is attractive in flower and fruit, especially against dark green, shiny foliage.

NATURAL RANGE Nova Scotia to Ontario and Minnesota, south to Florida and Texas

Parthenocissus quinquefolia

VIRGINIA CREEPER

VITACEAE

ZONES 4 to 9

SOIL any, including those subjected to urban conditions and salt spray

LIGHT sun to shade

ATTRIBUTES clinging (by adhesive disks at end of tendrils) vine to 50+ feet (whatever height of tree or other supporting structure is); leaves palmately compound, consisting of five leaflets to 4 inches long, alternate, glossy, dark green, turning intense shades of red and purple in autumn; flowers greenish white, in clusters; fruit round, 1/4 inch in diameter, bluish black with slight white waxy surface, borne on bright red stalks

PROPAGATION seed, cold stratify for one to two months; cuttings easy

NOTES Virginia creeper and poison-ivy (*Toxicodendron radicans* = *Rhus radicans*—not recommended here!) are the two most outstanding vines native to this region for fall color, often peaking in late summer for the former species, well before the trees have started to turn. A similar species in this region is *P. vitacea* (= *P. inserta*), grape-woodbine, which differs from Virginia creeper by having few branched tendrils and lacking adhesive disks.

NATURAL RANGE Maine to Ohio, Iowa, and Nebraska, south to Florida and Texas

Menispermum canadense

Parthenocissus quinquefolia foliage and fruit

Parthenocissus quinquefolia in autumn

Vitis labrusca

FOX GRAPE
VITACEAE

ZONES 4 to 8

SOIL moist, well drained

LIGHT sun

ATTRIBUTES high climbing vine (to tree tops), tendrils all along stem; leaves alternate, broad, often three-lobed, covered below with rusty hairs; fruit a cluster of dull red to purplish black grapes with sweetish or astringent taste

PROPAGATION seed, cold stratify for three months; cuttings

NOTES The fox grape is parent to some well-known cultivated grape varieties, including the Concord grape. Other native grape species in this region include the summer grape (*V. aestivalis*), frost grape (*V. riparia*), and muscadine grape (*V. rotundifolia*). Grape species cultivated for screening purposes generally need substantial pruning (in late winter) to keep in bounds and to maintain heavy fruit production. Many cultivated grape varieties come from *V. vinifera*, which is native to northwestern India and the Orient.

NATURAL RANGE Maine to southern Michigan, south to South Carolina and Tennessee

Wisteria frutescens

AMERICAN WISTERIA
FABACEAE

ZONES 5 to 9

SOIL moist to wet

LIGHT sun to partial sun

ATTRIBUTES twining vine to 30+ feet high; leaves pinnately compound (nine to fifteen leaflets), alternate, 7 to 12 inches long, bright green; flowers 3/4 inch long, blue-purple with central yellow spot, along a 4- to 6-inch-long pendulous stalk in late spring to early summer (later than more popular Asian species); fruit a 2- to 4-inch-long, hairless pod that holds rather round seeds

PROPAGATION seed, will germinate without pretreatment; cuttings root readily

NOTES Also known as the Atlantic wisteria. Another native wisteria, the Kentucky or Mississippi wisteria (*W. macrostachya* = *W. frutescens* var. *macrostachya*), is similar but has a flower cluster about twice the length of the American wisteria. These native wisterias, with flowers that rival the commonly planted species from Asia, are not nearly as vigorous. Both are very tolerant of poorly drained soils, because they naturally occur in forested wetlands. A few cultivars with even showier flower displays have been selected.

NATURAL RANGE Virginia to Florida and Texas, north in the interior to Arkansas

Vitis riparia

Wisteria frutescens

SHRUBS

Alnus incana subsp. *rugosa*

SPECKLED ALDER

BETULACEAE

ZONES 3 to 6

SOIL moist to wet, including standing water

LIGHT sun to partial sun

ATTRIBUTES typically a large, multistemmed shrub or small tree 15 to 25 feet tall; leaves are alternate, simple, nearly ovate, dark green; flowers are aments; fruit a woody, conelike structure

PROPAGATION seed, cold stratify for three to five months

NOTES Also listed as *A. rugosa.* No outstanding ornamental attributes but an exceptional species for wetland restoration projects because of its tolerance to saturated soils and its ability to fix atmospheric nitrogen. The "speckled" bark (due to numerous horizontal lenticels) of younger stems provides an interesting display during the winter months. *Alnus serrulata,* tag or hazel alder (Zones 5 to 9), is similar in most attributes but naturally occurs further south in this region. The two other alder species native to our region are the green or mountain alder (*A. viridis* subsp. *crispa* = *A. crispa*) and the seaside alder (*A. maritima*). Green alder is a nearly circumboreal species. All alder species fix atmospheric nitrogen and thrive on wet soils.

NATURAL RANGE circumboreal, south to Maryland, West Virginia, Illinois, into western North American mountains

Amelanchier stolonifera

RUNNING SERVICEBERRY

ROSACEAE

ZONES 4 to ?

SOIL moist to dry

LIGHT partial sun to sun

ATTRIBUTES thicket-forming (via stolons) small shrub with erect stems to about 5 feet tall; leaves alternate, simple; flowers white; fruit purplish black, sweet, ripening in early summer

PROPAGATION seed, cold stratify for three months; division of clumps

NOTES Also listed as *A. spicata.* With all the attention our native tree serviceberries (*A. arborea, A. canadensis, A. laevis*) receive by horticulturists, and the degree of natural hybridization that occurs in this genus, it seems that there should be opportunities to find better ornamental characteristics among the shrubby species. Others in our region are mountain serviceberry or mountain juneberry (*A. bartramiana*), bush juneberry (*A. humilis*), and roundleaf or New England serviceberry (*A. sanguinea*). The taxonomic uncertainties in this genus are amazing given the relatively small number of species recognized in most treatments.

NATURAL RANGE Quebec and Maine to Minnesota, south to New York, Michigan, Iowa and in the mountains to North Carolina

Leaf of *Alnus incana* subsp. *rugosa*

Amorpha fruticosa

INDIGOBUSH
FABACEAE

ZONES 4 to 9

SOIL dry to moist; adapted to a wide range of soil conditions, especially poor

LIGHT sun

ATTRIBUTES about 10 feet tall and wide, becoming leggy, especially on rich, moist soils; leaves are bright green, pinnately compound, alternate; flowers are deep purplish blue and borne in 3- to 6-inch-long spikes in June; fruit a persistent pod about 1/3 inch long

PROPAGATION seed, cold stratify or scarify mechanically or with acid; softwood cuttings

NOTES Also known as false indigo. Especially well adapted to very poor soils in full sun. The flower color of indigobush is very rich but so dark that flowers get lost in the mass of foliage. There are some cultivars of this species with white ('Albiflora') and pale blue ('Coerulea') flowers and variations in foliage and form.

NATURAL RANGE New Hampshire to Minnesota and south Saskatchewan, south to Florida, Texas, southern California, and northern Mexico

Arctostaphylos uva-ursi

BEARBERRY
ERICACEAE

ZONES 2 to 6

SOIL excessively drained, raw (infertile) sands or sloping rock surfaces

LIGHT sun to partial sun

ATTRIBUTES about 9 inches tall with a 3-foot-plus spread; glossy, thick, evergreen, small, simple, alternate leaves that become bronze to reddish in autumn; flowers small, urn-shaped, white with pink margin; fruit bright red, to 1/3 inch in diameter, matures in late summer and persists

PROPAGATION seed is difficult, acid scarify for thirty to sixty minutes, followed by cold stratification for three to five months; hardwood cuttings taken in late fall through winter require high concentration of rooting hormone

NOTES Also known as kinnikinick. Stems root along the surface, allowing bearberry to cover very large areas. Bearberry is especially adapted to thriving and spreading on acidic, infertile, sandy soils. There are numerous cultivars selected for more compact form and growth habit and variations in leaf and fruit color and size. Only recently have this species and varieties become more readily available.

NATURAL RANGE circumboreal, in North America from Labrador to Alaska, south to Virginia, northern Indiana, Illinois, New Mexico, and California

Amorpha fruticosa

Arctostaphylos uva-ursi

Aronia arbutifolia

Aronia melanocarpa

Aronia arbutifolia

RED CHOKEBERRY
ROSACEAE

ZONES 4 to 9

SOIL dry to moist, even wet, soil

LIGHT sun to partial sun

ATTRIBUTES about 8 feet tall and 4 feet wide although can spread more through root suckers; leaves alternate, simple, dark, glossy green, turning various shades of red, orange, and purple in autumn; flowers round, white, 1/3 inch wide, in clusters up to twenty; fruit, 1/4 inch in diameter, glossy, bright red in autumn into winter; very astringent taste

PROPAGATION seed, cold stratify for three months; softwood cuttings easy to root; division

NOTES 'Brilliantissima' is the most widely available cultivar, selected for its more reliably brilliant fall color and more abundant and showier flowers and fruits. Native shrubs like red chokeberry make one wonder why so many, so much less attractive non-native shrubs are continually planted instead.

NATURAL RANGE Newfoundland to Florida and Texas, southward especially on and near coastal plain but also in mountains, extending to Kentucky and West Virginia

Aronia melanocarpa

BLACK CHOKEBERRY
ROSACEAE

ZONES 3 to 8

SOIL dry to moist, even wet, soil

LIGHT sun to partial sun

ATTRIBUTES about 8 feet tall and 3 feet wide although can spread more through root suckers; leaves alternate, simple, dark, glossy green, turning various shades of red, orange, and purple in autumn; flowers round, white, 1/3 inch wide, in clusters up to twenty; fruit, 1/4 inch in diameter, glossy, purplish black in autumn into winter; very astringent taste

PROPAGATION seed, cold stratify for three months; softwood cuttings easy to root; division

NOTES Some varieties are more compact ('Autumn Magic', Iroquois Beauty™, 'Viking') and offer outstanding foliage, flower, and fruit characteristics. I see this species often while working in acidic peatlands, some of the most difficult growing conditions available. Black chokeberry is a very good choice for wetland restoration projects, as well as typical home landscape settings. Purple chokeberry (*A.* ×*prunifolia*), with purple fruit, is a natural hybrid between red and black chokeberry.

NATURAL RANGE Newfoundland and southern Labrador to northern Georgia and Alabama, west to eastern Minnesota, northeastern Iowa, and southeastern Missouri

Betula pumila
BOG BIRCH
BETULACEAE

ZONES 2 to 6

SOIL moist to wet

LIGHT sun

ATTRIBUTES upright stems that form dense shrub to 10 feet tall; leaves nearly round in outline and with rounded teeth along margin, dark green on top; flowers in upright, columnar structure (catkin); fruit an upright ament

PROPAGATION seed, cold stratify for three months

NOTES Bog birch is a very cold hardy shrub for wet, especially organic soils. I like it primarily because few other woody species have leaves that look like those of bog birch, and because it occurs in some of the finest calcareous wetlands (fens) I have visited, where so many beautiful native orchids like the showy ladyslipper (*Cypripedium reginae*) and dragon's mouth (*Arethusa bulbosa*) also occur.

NATURAL RANGE Newfoundland and Quebec to southern Ontario and Michigan, south to New Jersey, Maryland, central Ohio, and northern Indiana

Callicarpa americana
AMERICAN BEAUTYBERRY
VERBENACEAE

ZONES 6 to 11

SOIL moist

LIGHT sun to partial sun

ATTRIBUTES open, arching habit to 8 feet tall; leaves opposite, hairy, about 6 inches long; flowers light lavender-pink; fruit 1/4 inch in diameter, violet to magenta, in dense clusters

PROPAGATION seed, cold stratify for three months, although seeds collected in December may germi-

Betula pumila

Callicarpa americana

nate without pretreatment; softwood cuttings root easily

NOTES var. *lactea* has white flowers and fruit.

NATURAL RANGE southwest Maryland to North Carolina and Arkansas, south to Mexico and the West Indies

Calycanthus floridus

SWEETSHRUB
CALYCANTHACEAE

ZONES 4 to 9

SOIL rich, moist, well drained

LIGHT sun to shade

ATTRIBUTES dense habit, about 8 feet high and wide, more straggly as shade increases; leaves opposite, simple, to 5 inches long, dark green; flowers dark reddish brown to nearly red, about 2 inches in diameter, can be very fragrant (fruity), mostly in May; fruit, urn-shaped, leathery, wrinkled, to 3 inches long; stems very aromatic when crushed

PROPAGATION seed, cold stratify for three months

NOTES Also known as Carolina allspice. Varieties are available with more lustrous leaves, stronger flower fragrance, and richer flower color.

NATURAL RANGE southern Pennsylvania and southern Ohio to Georgia, northwest Florida and southeast Mississippi

Ceanothus americanus

NEW JERSEY TEA
RHAMNACEAE

ZONES 4 to 8

SOIL dry and sandy best, otherwise well drained

LIGHT sun or partial sun

ATTRIBUTES dense habit, about 3 feet high and wide; leaves alternate, simple, dark green; flowers white, very small but borne on masses of terminal 1- to 2-inch-long stalks in June and July; fruit a dry capsule

PROPAGATION seed, cold stratify for three months; softwood cuttings easy to root

NOTES Also known as redroot. An exceptional, compact shrub with beautiful white masses of summer flowers for very dry and sunny sites; this species fixes atmospheric nitrogen, so is especially valuable for land restoration under these conditions. Another *Ceanothus* in our region is prairie-redroot (*C. herbaceus*), which is similar except that

it has narrower leaves and its flower clusters are mostly terminal, rather than arising from leaf axils along the stem.

NATURAL RANGE Quebec to Minnesota, south to Florida and Texas

Cephalanthus occidentalis

BUTTONBUSH
RUBIACEAE

ZONES 5 to 11

SOIL moist to permanently (and somewhat deeply) flooded

LIGHT sun

ATTRIBUTES open habit about 9 feet high and wide; leaves opposite or whorled, simple, bright to dark green, glossy, to 6 inches long; flowers creamy white, in dense, round mass about 1 inch in diameter during the summer; fruit a small, round, hard mass of nutlets that persist through winter

PROPAGATION seed, will germinate without pretreatment; softwood and hardwood cuttings also easy

NOTES Few woody plants native to this region tolerate such prolonged, deep flooding as buttonbush—perhaps such relatively inaccessible habitats are the reason why so few people have seen the very showy flowers of this species.

NATURAL RANGE Nova Scotia, New Brunswick and Quebec to Minnesota, south to Mexico and West Indies

Chamaedaphne calyculata

LEATHERLEAF
ERICACEAE

ZONES 2 to 7

SOIL wet, acidic, organic (i.e., peat)

LIGHT partial sun to sun

ATTRIBUTES arching stems to about 30 inches tall; leaves leathery, elliptical, about 1 inch long; flowers urn-shaped, white, pendent, in long terminal clusters; fruit a capsule

PROPAGATION seed, sow on moist peat; cuttings

NOTES The first time I ever saw leatherleaf was many years ago, in northern Wisconsin in mid May. Despite the snow and ice throughout the area, leatherleaf was in full bloom in a bog. It is one of the most common bog species, and is actually growing too rapidly in a pool that I filled with peat moss and

Calycanthus floridus

Cephalanthus occidentalis flowers

Ceanothus americanus

Cephalanthus occidentalis, with (nonnative) *Iris pseudacorus*

Chamaedaphne calyculata

Ledum groenlandicum

keep rather saturated with a number of its common associates, including Labrador tea (*Ledum groenlandicum*). Labrador tea leaves are leathery, dark green on top, and densely brown hairy on the bottom; its bright white flowers are in terminal, rounded clusters and open about one month later.

NATURAL RANGE circumboreal, south to New Jersey, Ohio, northern Indiana, northern Illinois, and in the mountains to North Carolina

Chionanthus virginicus
FRINGETREE
OLEACEAE

ZONES 4 to 9

SOIL dry to wet, best growth on rich, moist, well-drained site

LIGHT sun to partial sun

ATTRIBUTES multiple-stemmed large shrub to 25 feet high and wide, or small tree; leaves opposite, simple, about 6 inches long, dark green, becoming yellowish green to bright or golden yellow in autumn; flowers white, in fleecy clusters about 8 inches long in June; fruit is a dark blue, waxy, egg-shaped fruit about 1/2 inch in diameter

PROPAGATION seed, will require warm, then cold stratification; cuttings not much easier

NOTES I have seen fringetree emerging from crevices in granite domes near Atlanta, in floodplains of the North Carolina Piedmont, and in gardens of central New York. Although it is a coarse-textured plant, especially relative to its foliage and moderately stout stems, when it is in flower I imagine what it would be like to stand next to a soft, billowy cloud.

NATURAL RANGE New Jersey to Florida, west irregularly to southern Ohio, southern Missouri, eastern Oklahoma, and eastern Texas

Clethra acuminata
CINNAMON CLETHRA
CLETHRACEAE

ZONES 5 to 8

SOIL rich, moist, well drained

LIGHT partial shade to shade

ATTRIBUTES sparsely stemmed shrub or small tree to about 15 feet high; leaves alternate, simple, dark green about 6 inches long, turning yellow in autumn; flowers white, fragrant, five-petaled, borne along terminal, 6-inch-long raceme in July and August; fruit a dry, small capsule; bark a beautiful, exfoliating cinnamon-brown with polished appearance below

PROPAGATION seed, will germinate without pretreatment; softwood cuttings root readily

NOTES An excellent shrub to attract butterflies.

NATURAL RANGE southwest Pennsylvania to eastern Kentucky and western Virginia, south to Tennessee and northeast Georgia

Clethra alnifolia
SUMMERSWEET CLETHRA
CLETHRACEAE

ZONES 4 to 9

SOIL moist to wet, acidic best, but grows fine in circumneutral soils of central New York

LIGHT partial shade to sun

ATTRIBUTES columnar-shaped habit to about 8 feet high and 6 feet wide; leaves alternate, simple, dark

Chionanthus virginicus

Clethra acuminata

Clethra alnifolia

green, pale yellow to golden brown in autumn; flowers white, fragrant, five-petaled, borne in 6-inch-long raceme in July and August; fruit a small, dry capsule

PROPAGATION seed, no pretreatment for germination required; cuttings taken in summer root readily

NOTES Summersweet clethra is a fine small shrub with summer blooms, especially for wet, shaded sites. Many cultivars are available that generally improve on form and foliage and flower characteristics, including 'Hummingbird', which has dark green leaves, very compact form, and a profusion of flowers; additional cultivars, including 'Rosea' and 'Ruby Spice', have pink flowers.

NATURAL RANGE mostly near the coast from Nova Scotia and Maine to Florida and Texas

Comptonia peregrina
SWEETFERN
MYRICACEAE

ZONES 2 to 6

SOIL dry, sandy or gravelly, infertile, acidic soil

LIGHT sun to partial sun

ATTRIBUTES single plant to 4 feet high and wide but spreads widely by root suckers; leaves alternate, dark green, resemble a fern; flowers yellow-green, in catkins in early to mid spring; fruit a small nutlet borne in clusters

Comptonia peregrina

Comptonia peregrina flowers

Cornus amomum

Cornus amomum in autumn

PROPAGATION root pieces dug during dormant season probably most likely to succeed

NOTES Few such attractive plants, native or otherwise, thrive like sweetfern in full sun and dry, infertile, acidic soils. Fixes atmospheric nitrogen.

NATURAL RANGE New York to North Carolina, western South Carolina, and northern Georgia, west to Saskatchewan, Minnesota, Illinois and Tennessee

Cornus amomum
SILKY DOGWOOD
CORNACEAE

ZONES 4 to 8

SOIL moist to wet

LIGHT partial sun to sun

ATTRIBUTES ultimately about 10 feet high and wide; leaves opposite, simple, to 4 inches long, turning shades of purple and red in autumn; flowers white, very small but carried in an approximately 2-inch-wide, flat-topped cluster in June; fruit round, porcelain-blue, 1/4 inch wide, in clusters

PROPAGATION seed, cold stratify for three to four months; softwood cuttings

NOTES An excellent shrub with a nice flower and fruit display, and high wildlife value for poorly drained soils and wetland restoration projects. Two other native dogwood shrub species of wetlands in our region are the rough-leaved dogwood (*C. drummondii*) and southern swamp dogwood (*C. stricta*); like all dogwood species, they have attractive flowers, fruit, and fall color.

NATURAL RANGE Maine and Quebec to Minnesota, south to Georgia, Arkansas, and Oklahoma

Cornus canadensis
BUNCHBERRY
CORNACEAE

ZONES 2 to 6

SOIL moist, acidic, high in organic matter best

LIGHT shade to sun

ATTRIBUTES carpet-forming ground cover to about 6 inches high; leaves simple, about 2 inches long, in whorl-like arrangement of four to six, dark green in summer, shades of red and purple in autumn; flowers very small and not attractive but surrounded by four large, white bracts similar to flowering dogwood (*C. florida*), making a very showy display in late spring into summer; fruit a scarlet drupe 1/4 inch in diameter and persisting through fall

PROPAGATION seed, will require warm then cold stratification periods; division of clumps easiest

NOTES When rather exacting site conditions exist,

Cornus canadensis

Cornus canadensis in fruit

will spread by rhizomes; an excellent companion to taller shrubs and trees which thrives on partially shaded, acidic, moist, well-drained sites.

NATURAL RANGE Greenland to Alaska and eastern Asia, south to New Jersey, Pennsylvania, Indiana, and Minnesota, and in the mountains to Maryland, West Virginia, Virginia, and California

Cornus racemosa
GRAY DOGWOOD
CORNACEAE

ZONES 3 to 8

SOIL dry to wet

LIGHT shade to sun

ATTRIBUTES single stems can reach 10 feet high but are typically surrounded by a profusion of root sprouts that result in a very wide spread and shape that is domed; leaves simple, opposite, about 3 inches long, turning shades of purple and red in autumn; flowers small, white, in 2-inch-wide, abundant clusters in June; fruit round, white, 1/4 inch in diameter, borne on bright red stalks

PROPAGATION seed, will require warm then cold stratification periods; softwood cuttings will root with hormone treatment; division of clumps

NOTES Flowers, fruit, and fall color of gray dogwood are very attractive, and fruit are favored by many bird species; an old-field species, like staghorn sumac (*Rhus typhina*) and goldenrods (*Solidago* spp.), that would be more appreciated if not so common naturally.

NATURAL RANGE Maine and southern Quebec to southern Manitoba, south to Virginia, southern Illinois, and Missouri

Cornus rugosa
ROUNDLEAF DOGWOOD
CORNACEAE

ZONES 3 to 7

SOIL moist to dry, circumneutral to alkaline

LIGHT sun to shade

ATTRIBUTES open, wide-spreading branches that reach about 10 feet high and wide, occasionally a small tree; leaves simple, opposite, nearly round, about 4 inches long, turning shades of purple and red in fall; flowers small, white, in clusters about 2 inches in diameter in June; fruit light blue, borne on pinkish stalks; stems green during the growing season but turning pinkish with black streaks during the winter when exposed to sunlight

Cornus racemosa in autumn

Cornus racemosa

Cornus rugosa

PROPAGATION seed, will require warm then cold stratification periods; softwood cuttings will root with hormone treatment

NOTES Of the dogwood species listed here, I have seen this one most regularly on the driest sites, often emerging from crevices in limestone bedrock throughout central New York.

NATURAL RANGE Quebec to northern Ontario and Manitoba, south to New Jersey, Pennsylvania, northern Ohio, northern Indiana, and Iowa, and in mountains to Virginia

Cornus rugosa fruit

Cornus sericea
RED-OSIER DOGWOOD
CORNACEAE

ZONES 2 to 7

SOIL moist to wet, even tolerating standing water for prolonged periods

LIGHT sun to partial sun

ATTRIBUTES reaching about 9 feet high and wide; leaves simple, opposite, about 4 inches long, with shades of purple and red in autumn; flowers small, white, in an approximately 2-inch-wide, flat cluster in June; fruit round, white, 1/3 inch in diameter, borne on red stalks; stems relatively stout (among dogwood species), green when shaded but turning bright or blood red in winter

Cornus sericea fruit

Cornus sericea in autumn

PROPAGATION seed, cold stratify for two to three months; softwood and hardwood cuttings easy

NOTES Also listed as *C. stolonifera*. Of the dogwood species listed here, has the most stout and red stems, and is best suited to the wettest soils. An excellent shrub for the winter garden, especially in areas blanketed by snow, which provides a striking contrast to its red stems. Numerous cultivars of this species have been selected for better red stem color ('Cardinal', 'Cheyenne'), yellow stems ('Flaviramea'), variegated leaves ('Silver and Gold', 'Sunshine'), and more compact habit ('Allemans', 'Isanti', 'Kelseyi').

NATURAL RANGE Newfoundland to Alaska, south to Pennsylvania, Indiana, Illinois, and northern Mexico

Corylus americana
AMERICAN HAZELNUT
BETULACEAE

ZONES 4 to 9

SOIL dry to moist, but well drained

LIGHT sun to partial sun

ATTRIBUTES very dense stems, to 10 feet high and wider; leaves simple, alternate, about 4 inches long; flowers are catkins in early spring; fruit a husk that covers the 1/2-inch-wide, rather flattened nut

PROPAGATION seed, cold stratify for three months

NOTES Also known as the American filbert, American hazelnut suckers freely. The beaked hazelnut, *C. cornuta*, also occurs naturally in this region and has many similar features except it tends to be smaller in stature and has a much longer fruit husk.

NATURAL RANGE Maine to Saskatchewan, south to Georgia, Louisiana, and Oklahoma

Diervilla lonicera
BUSH-HONEYSUCKLE
CAPRIFOLIACEAE

ZONES 3 to 7

SOIL dry to moist, well drained

LIGHT sun to shade

ATTRIBUTES arching stems to about 3 1/2 feet high; leaves simple, opposite, bright to dark green; flowers about 3/4 inch long, tubular, yellow, in terminal cluster during the summer; fruit a capsule

PROPAGATION seed, sow on surface of media then cold stratify for three months; softwood cuttings root readily

Corylus americana fruit

Corylus cornuta fruit

NOTES Bush-honeysuckle is quite restrained in habit compared to most species of honeysuckle in the genus *Lonicera,* especially the Eurasian species that are becoming such a problem throughout this region. The true honeysuckles have a round berry-like fruit that is usually red, orange, or yellow (black for *L. japonica*), whereas the fruit of bush-honey-suckle is a dry, inconspicuous capsule.

NATURAL RANGE Newfoundland to Saskatchewan, south to North Carolina, Tennessee, Indiana, and Iowa

Dirca palustris
LEATHERWOOD
THYMELAEACEAE

ZONES 4 to 9

SOIL moist to wet, including standing water

LIGHT sun to shade (best leaf color in partial shade to shade)

ATTRIBUTES about 6 feet high and wide; leaves simple, alternate, to 3 inches long, turning yellow in autumn; flowers bell-shaped, yellow, about 1/3 inch long, in small clusters, in very early spring; fruit oval, 1/3 inch long, pale green to reddish

PROPAGATION seed, cold stratify for three months

NOTES Living stems can literally be tied into knots.

NATURAL RANGE Nova Scotia and southern Quebec to Minnesota, south to Florida, Alabama, Arkansas, and Oklahoma

Diervilla lonicera

Dirca palustris

Epigaea repens

TRAILING ARBUTUS
ERICACEAE

ZONES 3 to 9

SOIL moist, well drained, acidic, high in sand or gravel and organic matter

LIGHT partial sun to sun

ATTRIBUTES dense, prostrate habit to 6 inches tall; leaves leathery, evergreen, oval, alternate, 1 to 3 inches long; flowers tubular, white to pink, in clusters of four to six, highly fragrant

PROPAGATION cuttings or division of existing clumps

NOTES Trailing arbutus is legally protected in some states to keep this species from being overcollected and becoming more rare. It is indeed one of our most beautiful, although small, native plants. When encountered, it is typically in large patches. Cultivating such displays is very difficult.

NATURAL RANGE Newfoundland and Quebec to Saskatchewan, south to Florida, Mississippi, and Iowa

Euonymus atropurpureus

EASTERN WAHOO
CELASTRACEAE

ZONES 4 to 9

SOIL moist, well drained

LIGHT sun to shade

ATTRIBUTES erect shrub or small tree to about 20 feet tall; leaves simple, opposite, about 4 inches long, dark green, turning pale yellow in autumn; flowers small, brownish purple, with four petals; fruit red, smooth, holding a bright red, covered seed

PROPAGATION seed, warm stratify for two months then cold stratify for at least three months

NOTES *E. americanus,* American euonymus or strawberry-bush, also occurs in this region and differs from eastern wahoo by having a smaller stature, five-petaled flowers, and fruit with a very bumpy surface. Another native species in this genus, but with a prostrate habit, is the running strawberry-bush (*E. obovatus*). Running strawberry-bush can reach a height of about 1 foot and would make a nice ground cover in shade.

NATURAL RANGE New York to North Dakota, south to Florida and Texas

Fothergilla gardenii

DWARF FOTHERGILLA
HAMAMELIDACEAE

ZONES 5 to 8

SOIL acidic, moist, organic best, but grows fine in circumneutral, loamy soils of central New York

LIGHT sun to shade

ATTRIBUTES to 6 feet tall and wide, spreading further by root suckers; leaves simple, alternate, about 2 1/2 inches long, dark green to blue green, developing intense yellow, orange, red shades in autumn; flowers white, borne in 1 1/2-inch-long spikes before the leaves expand in early spring; fruit a capsule

PROPAGATION seed is difficult, will require warm then cold stratification; cuttings; division of suckering clumps

NOTES Quite variable in many traits; a number of cultivars have been selected for more bluish green foliage ('Blue Mist', for example) and other orna-

Epigaea repens

Euonymus atropurpureus

mental features. One of the finest native shrubs for flowers, summer foliage, and fall color, growing well in shade or sun, if the site is not too dry. Although naturally found on acidic, organic soils, it has been doing fine on the circumneutral, mineral soils of upstate New York.

NATURAL RANGE North Carolina to southern Alabama and panhandle of Florida

Fothergilla major

LARGE FOTHERGILLA
HAMAMELIDACEAE

ZONES 4 to 8

SOIL moist, well drained, acidic

LIGHT partial sun to shade

ATTRIBUTES rounded habit to 10 feet tall and wide; leaves simple, alternate, dark green, developing shades of yellow, orange, or red in autumn; flowers white, in 2-inch-long spikes as leaves expand in spring; fruit a capsule

PROPAGATION seed is difficult, will require warm then cold stratification; cuttings

NOTES Cultivars have been selected to favor various ornamental features, especially flowers and fall color ('Mt. Airy').

NATURAL RANGE northern North Carolina and Tennessee to northern Alabama

Gaultheria procumbens

TEABERRY
ERICACEAE

ZONES 3 to 5

SOIL acidic, dry to moist; organic or sandy

LIGHT sun to shade

ATTRIBUTES forms open clumps to 6 inches high; leaves simple, crowded near top of plant, dark green, leathery, evergreen, turning reddish in fall and winter, with wintergreen taste when chewed; flowers pinkish white, barrel-shaped, about 1/3 inch long, in summer; fruit round, bright red, 1/3 inch wide, very fragrant when crushed

PROPAGATION seed, cold stratify for one to three months; division of clumps

NOTES Also known as wintergreen. Perhaps one of the more challenging native ground covers to cultivate, along with bunchberry (*Cornus canadensis*), but worth the effort, as this little plant is beautiful

Fothergilla gardenii

Fothergilla major

Gaultheria procumbens flowers

Gaultheria procumbens

in both flower and fruit. The only other native *Gaultheria* species in this region, creeping snowberry (*G. hispidula*), is much less known among gardeners. Creeping snowberry has a prostrate habit, very small, dark green, evergreen leaf, and white fruit; it requires moist, organic soil conditions, especially thriving on rotting tree stumps and logs in shade.

NATURAL RANGE Newfoundland to Manitoba, south to Virginia, Kentucky, northern Indiana, Minnesota, and in the mountains to Georgia and Alabama

Gaylussacia baccata
BLACK HUCKLEBERRY
ERICACEAE

ZONES 4 to 9
SOIL wet to dry
LIGHT sun to shade
ATTRIBUTES to about $3^1/2$ feet tall and often wider; leaves simple, alternate, to 2 inches long, turning various shades of red and purple in autumn; flowers urn-shaped, yellowish green in late spring; fruit black, round

PROPAGATION seed, cold stratify for three months; softwood cuttings treated with rooting hormone
NOTES Another native shrub, like black chokeberry (*Aronia melanocarpa*) that I have seen thriving in acidic peatlands (i.e., wet, organic soil) as well as dry uplands. Two other native *Gaylussacia* species, dangleberry (*G. frondosa*) and dwarf huckleberry (*G. dumosa*), grow especially well on moist to wet sandy soils. Dangleberry will reach about 6 feet in height, whereas the dwarf huckleberry is about 2 feet tall at maturity but spreads laterally by rhizomes.
NATURAL RANGE Newfoundland and Quebec to Ontario and Manitoba, south to Georgia, Alabama, and Missouri

Gaylussacia brachycera
BOX HUCKLEBERRY
ERICACEAE

ZONES 5 to 7
SOIL moist, well drained, acidic, organic
LIGHT partial shade
ATTRIBUTES spreading profusely and forming dense mounds reaching $1^1/2$ feet high; leaves simple, alter-

Gaylussacia brachycera

Gaylussacia baccata

nate, to 1 inch long, dark green, glossy, evergreen, turning deep bronze to reddish purple in late autumn into winter; flowers urn-shaped, 1/4 inch long, white or pinkish, in late spring; fruit dark blue, round

PROPAGATION seed, warm then cold stratification; cuttings treated with rooting hormone

NOTES Box huckleberry is a dwarf, dense, broadleaf evergreen that would quickly become very popular if more readily available.

NATURAL RANGE Maryland and Delaware to Pennsylvania, Kentucky, and eastern Tennessee

Hamamelis vernalis

VERNAL WITCH-HAZEL
HAMAMELIDACEAE

ZONES 4 to 8

SOIL moist to wet soils, including those with occasional standing water

LIGHT sun to partial shade

ATTRIBUTES to about 10 feet high and wide, with a rather vase-shaped branching habit; leaves simple, alternate, about 4 inches long, turning shades of yel-

Hamamelis vernalis

low in autumn; flowers have four straplike, yellow to red petals, fragrant, in winter to early spring; fruit a woody capsule

PROPAGATION seed is difficult; softwood cuttings treated with rooting hormone

NOTES As one can see from its natural range, this species requires me to stretch the geographical limits of this book in order to include it—an advantage of authoring a book! Vernal witch-hazel is a very unusual plant in that it flowers in the winter and early spring, and tolerates wet soils and a very broad range of soil pH. Cultivars with consistently good fall and flower colors are available ('Autumn Embers', for example).

NATURAL RANGE Missouri to Louisiana and Oklahoma

Hamamelis virginiana

WITCH-HAZEL
HAMAMELIDACEAE

ZONES 3 to 8

SOIL moist

LIGHT shade to sun

ATTRIBUTES several large crooked stems to about 20 feet high and wide; leaves simple, alternate, about 5 inches long, turning shades of yellow in autumn; flowers have four straplike, yellow petals opening in mid to late autumn before or after leaf drop; fruit a capsule

PROPAGATION seed and cuttings difficult

NOTES Sometimes in bloom in upstate New York

Hamamelis virginiana

when our first real snowfall occurs; it would be valuable to find selections that bloom earliest and latest, providing flowers throughout the fall.

NATURAL RANGE Quebec and Nova Scotia to northern Michigan and Minnesota, south to Florida and Texas

Hydrangea arborescens

SMOOTH HYDRANGEA
HYDRANGEACEAE

ZONES 4 to 9

SOIL dry to moist

LIGHT shade to sun

ATTRIBUTES straggling shrub to about 5 feet high and wider, spreading by root suckers; leaves simple, opposite, about 6 inches long; flowers white, in 4- to 6-inch-wide, rather flat clusters in summer; fruit a capsule; bark on older stems exfoliates

PROPAGATION seed, will germinate without pretreatment; softwood cuttings

NOTES Every natural occurrence in which I have seen this species has very steep slopes and is very shaded; if planted in full sun, may need occasional watering during dry periods; cultivars are available with much larger flower clusters, for example, 'Annabelle' (flowers to 1 foot across) and 'Grandiflora' ("Hills of Snow").

Hydrangea arborescens

NATURAL RANGE southern New York to Ohio, Missouri, and Oklahoma, south to Georgia, Louisiana, and Arkansas

Hydrangea quercifolia

OAKLEAF HYDRANGEA
HYDRANGEACEAE

ZONES 5 to 9

SOIL moist, well drained

LIGHT partial shade to sun

ATTRIBUTES about 10 feet tall and at least as wide; leaves simple, opposite, to 8 inches long, resemble an oak leaf, turn various shades of purple and red in autumn; flowers initially white then purplish pink then brown, in pyramidal clusters to 12 inches long in early to mid summer; fruit a capsule; bark cinnamon-brown, exfoliating

PROPAGATION seed, will germinate without pretreatment; root suckers can be dug and transplanted

NOTES As for the vernal witch-hazel (*Hamamelis vernalis*), I am stretching the geographic scope of this book a bit because this species is native to the eastern U.S. and is such a fine shrub for shaded sites, where it does best. Just as one has to occasionally travel further south for great examples of some food and drink, some truly southern plant species are worth including here, and will thrive, in more northern gardens. Many cultivars are available with improved flower characteristics, fall color, and form; 'Snow Queen' is especially nice.

NATURAL RANGE Georgia, Florida, Alabama, and Mississippi

Hypericum frondosum

GOLDEN ST. JOHN'S WORT
CLUSIACEAE

ZONES 5 to 8

SOIL dry to moist

Hydrangea quercifolia

Hydrangea quercifolia in autumn

Hypericum frondosum 'Sunburst'

LIGHT sun

ATTRIBUTES rounded mound to 4 feet tall; leaves opposite, simple, about 2 inches long, rich bluish green; flowers bright yellow, 1 to 2 inches in diameter in early to mid summer; fruit a capsule

PROPAGATION seed, will germinate without pretreatment; cuttings taken in mid to late summer

NOTES Golden St. John's wort naturally occurs in cedar barrens and rock outcrops. The cultivar 'Sunburst' grows 3 feet high and 4 feet wide and has an outstanding flower display in summer.

NATURAL RANGE Tennessee and Kentucky to southern Indiana, southern Georgia, and eastern Texas

Hypericum kalmianum

Hypericum kalmianum
KALM'S ST. JOHN'S WORT
CLUSIACEAE

ZONES 4 to 7

SOIL dry to moist

LIGHT shade to sun

ATTRIBUTES to 3 feet tall; leaves simple, opposite, about 1 1/2 inches long, bluish green above and whitish below; flowers bright yellow, about 1 inch wide, in July; fruit a capsule

PROPAGATION seed, will germinate without pretreatment; cuttings taken in mid to late summer

NOTES Kalm's St. John's wort occurs in rocky conditions similar to those that suit the golden St. John's wort but has a much more northern natural distribution, and is cold hardier.

NATURAL RANGE about Lakes Erie, Huron, and Michigan, inland in central Wisconsin and along the Ottawa River in Quebec

Hypericum prolificum
SHRUBBY ST. JOHN'S WORT
CLUSIACEAE

ZONES 4 to 8

SOIL dry, rocky to moist

LIGHT sun to partial shade

ATTRIBUTES dense branching to 5 feet high and

Hypericum prolificum

wide; leaves simple, opposite, dark green; flowers bright yellow, to 1 inch in diameter, in early to mid summer; fruit a capsule; bark exfoliates

PROPAGATION seed, will germinate without pretreatment; softwood cuttings

NOTES Of the native St. John's worts covered here, this species is the tallest and naturally occurs over the greatest range of soil conditions. Dense hypericum (*H. densiflorum*) is another native shrubby *Hypericum* species in our region; it has smaller flowers and leaves than *H. prolificum* but is of similar stature and has a tolerance to a great range of sites.

NATURAL RANGE New York to southern Michigan and Minnesota, south to Georgia and Louisiana

Ilex decidua

Ilex decidua
POSSUM HAW
AQUIFOLIACEAE

ZONES 5 to 9

SOIL moist to wet

LIGHT sun to shade

ATTRIBUTES to about 20 feet high and slightly less spread; leaves simple, alternate, glossy, dark green; flowers white, very small; fruit round, orange to scarlet, solitary or in small clusters

PROPAGATION seed is difficult, will require multiple cycles of warm and cold stratification

NOTES Possum haw naturally occurs in wetlands so is an excellent choice for saturated soils. Cultivars with better form and fruit color are available ('Warren's Red', for example).

NATURAL RANGE Washington, D.C., to Florida and Texas, north in the interior to southern Indiana, southern Illinois, and southern Missouri

Ilex glabra
INKBERRY
AQUIFOLIACEAE

ZONES 5 to 9

SOIL moist to wet, acidic

LIGHT sun to partial shade

ATTRIBUTES about 8 feet high and a little wider,

Ilex glabra

Ilex glabra fruit

spreading by root suckers; leaves simple, alternate, glossy, dark green, evergreen, about 1^1/$_2$ inches long; flowers dioecious, small, creamy white, early summer; fruit black, round, to ^{1}/$_3$ inch in diameter

PROPAGATION seed is difficult, will require multiple cycles of warm and cold stratification; cuttings treated with rooting hormone, relatively easy

NOTES Somewhat resembles a more open version of the nonnative, common boxwood (*Buxus sempervirens*). Like the other native holly shrub species covered here, inkberry is well adapted to saturated soils. Numerous cultivars of inkberry are available that improve on foliage characteristics (darker green) and form (more compact), for example, 'Compacta', Nordic®, 'Nova Scotia', and 'Shamrock'.

NATURAL RANGE Nova Scotia to Florida and Louisiana

Ilex verticillata
WINTERBERRY
AQUIFOLIACEAE

ZONES 3 to 9

SOIL moist to wet, including prolonged standing water; best in organic soils that are acidic but has grown well for nearly two decades in my garden in the well-drained, circumneutral, mineral soils of central New York

LIGHT sun to shade (as for most species, fruiting increases with increasing sun)

ATTRIBUTES about 10 feet high and wide, spreading by root suckers; leaves simple, alternate, dark green, about 2^1/$_2$ inches long; flowers dioecious, small, creamy white; fruit bright red, round, about ^{1}/$_3$ inch wide, often in small clusters, persisting into winter

PROPAGATION seed is difficult, will require multiple cycles of warm and cold stratification; softwood cuttings root readily

NOTES One of the many rewards for being out in the swamps of the Northeast in autumn is the opportunity to see winterberry when the fruit display (on female individuals only) is quite striking. Many cultivars are available that have more compact form, darker foliage, bigger and brighter (including yellow) fruits, and greater production of pollen; if a cultivar is desired and there is room for only one (plus a male pollinator), 'Winter Red' is the best choice. Another good cultivar, but more compact, is 'Red Sprite'. Additionally, there are numerous cultivars from crosses between *I. verticillata* and *I. serrata* (finetooth holly, native to Japan and China). Smooth winterberry (*I. laevigata*) is also native to our region, in wetlands east of the Appalachians. It is quite similar to *I. verticillata* except the fruit of smooth winterberry is borne singly along the twig and is slightly larger.

NATURAL RANGE Newfoundland and Quebec to Ontario and Michigan, south to Georgia and Mississippi

Itea virginica
VIRGINIA SWEET SPIRE
GROSSULARIACEAE

ZONES 5 to 9

SOIL moist to wet, including prolonged standing water; will tolerate occasional drought

LIGHT sun to shade

ATTRIBUTES about 8 feet tall and wide; leaves simple, alternate, about 3 inches long, turning shades of purple, red, orange, and yellow in autumn, evergreen in the South; flowers fragrant, white, to ^{1}/$_2$ inch wide, borne in upright raceme to 6 inches long in very showy display in early summer; fruit a capsule

PROPAGATION seed require no pregermination treatment; softwood cuttings root readily

NOTES Also known as Virginia willow. I first saw Virginia sweet spire about twenty-five years ago in the Pine Barrens of central and southern New Jersey, one of my favorite places to see so many beautiful,

Ilex verticillata

Itea virginica 'Henry's Garnet'

Itea virginica 'Sprich'

Juniperus communis

Juniperus horizontalis

interesting native plants in the eastern U.S. I had never been exposed to this species in any horticulture courses and thought at the time that this plant (even without knowing of its fall color display) would be an outstanding addition to the landscape—looks like others made the same discovery, as this species, primarily in the form of some fine cultivars, is now readily available. 'Henry's Garnet' has an excellent flower display as well as reddish purple fall color; 'Sprich' (Little Henry™) is similar but more compact.

NATURAL RANGE southern New Jersey and eastern Pennsylvania to Florida and Louisiana, north in the Mississippi Valley to southern Illinois

Juniperus communis

COMMON JUNIPER
CUPRESSACEAE

ZONES 2 to 6

SOIL dry to excessively drained, sandy or rocky, any pH

LIGHT sun

ATTRIBUTES quite variable in form from prostrate and only a few feet tall (but very wide) to 10 feet tall and wide, to pyramidal; leaves awl-shaped, sharply pointed, bluish green on one side, waxy white on other side, in whorls of three; flowers dioecious; fruit berrylike, round, bluish to black and waxy white at maturity, smells like gin when crushed (actually, gin smells like common juniper, as gin's distinctive flavoring comes from the oil of the "berries" from this species); bark fibrous, reddish brown

PROPAGATION seed, will require two to three months of warm stratification followed by at least three months of cold stratification; cuttings treated with rooting hormone

NOTES There are many cultivars of common juniper that promise specific forms or foliage color (including yellow). Few, if any, species can better tolerate cold, barren soils and full sun.

NATURAL RANGE circumboreal, south in America to Pennsylvania, Wisconsin, Minnesota, the Rocky Mountain states, and irregularly to South Carolina and southern Indiana

Juniperus horizontalis

HORIZONTAL JUNIPER
CUPRESSACEAE

ZONES 4 to 9

SOIL rocky, sandy, marly; dry especially, but even tolerating wet soils

LIGHT sun

ATTRIBUTES prostrate, rarely more than 1 foot above the ground, rooting along its way; foliage either scale- or awl-like, green, turning purplish in winter; fruit a round berrylike cone to 1/3 inch wide, bluish at maturity

PROPAGATION seed, will require two to three months of warm stratification followed by at least three months of cold stratification; cuttings treated with rooting hormone

NOTES Also known as creeping juniper. Could any native shrub species be better known by the general public? Yet few who know it realize this species is native to the Northeast. Dozens of readily available cultivars have distinct forms (generally less than 18 inches high, but some only 6 inches high), foliage (mostly shades of green, blue, gray, silver; a few yellow or golden), and autumn color (generally shades of purple). While it is no challenge to locate and buy many of these cultivars, good luck finding the straight species: although I have seen it in the wild, I have never found it for sale. I have always been impressed by the hot, dry, sunny sites on which this species will thrive but am equally amazed by seeing it thrive at its only natural site in New York, growing in permanently saturated marl with a pH over 8.

NATURAL RANGE nearly transcontinental in Canada, from Newfoundland, Labrador, and Quebec to the Yukon and northern British Columbia and disjunct in Alaska, more scattered south to Maine, New Hampshire, New York, Michigan, Wisconsin, Minnesota, and Wyoming

Kalmia latifolia

MOUNTAIN-LAUREL
ERICACEAE

ZONES 4 to 9

SOIL moist, well drained, acidic; under natural occurrences, sandy or rocky, but best growth on soils high in organic matter

LIGHT sun to shade

ATTRIBUTES about 10 feet tall and a bit narrower at maturity, much more open habit in shade than in sun, stems becoming crooked with age; leaves

Kalmia latifolia

simple, usually alternate, 2 to 5 inches long, dark green, shiny, leathery, evergreen; flowers nearly round, about 1 inch in diameter, mostly white or pink with additional reddish purple markings, in late spring, very attractive in bud before flowers fully develop; fruit a capsule

PROPAGATION seed, will germinate without pretreatment if sown on surface of media; cuttings very difficult; tissue culture used for commercial production

NOTES Of the three *Kalmia* species native to this region, this is by far the most valuable for most landscape uses, although its requirements are somewhat exacting; because of its very fine, fibrous, and shallow root system, mountain-laurel growth is favored by mulching around the base of the plant. There has been great horticultural interest in this shrub since I learned about it nearly thirty years ago. Many cultivars are available that have unique bud colors (reds and pinks), flower colors (pure white, pink, deep purple-pink, coral, cinnamon-red), and compact forms. The other two native *Kalmia* species, bog-laurel (*K. polifolia*) and sheep-laurel (*K. angustifolia*), are much shorter in stature and have a more northern geographical distribution. Bog-laurel is naturally restricted to saturated, acidic soils of bogs, whereas sheep-laurel occurs on dry to wet acidic soils that are high in sand or organic matter. I have seen much variation in flower size and color in sheep-laurel and

believe it has much potential for cultivation under a very wide range of site conditions as a shorter, more cold hardy version of *K. latifolia*. Bog-rosemary (*Andromeda glaucophylla*) is similar to bog-laurel and often grows beside it in bogs. Bog-rosemary has urn-shaped, mostly white flowers and alternate leaves (that resemble the herb rosemary), whereas the bog-laurel has wheel-like, pink flowers and opposite leaves. Bog-rosemary is becoming widely available for purchase but like all members of the heath family, requires exacting soil conditions: acidic, organic, and moist.

NATURAL RANGE southeastern Maine to Georgia, west to southern Ohio, southern Indiana, Mississippi, western Florida, and southeast Louisiana

Leucothoe fontanesiana
DROOPING LEUCOTHOE
ERICACEAE

ZONES 5 to 8

SOIL moist, well drained, acidic soil high in organic matter

LIGHT partial sun to shade

ATTRIBUTES a 5-foot-high and -wide mound of arching branches; leaves simple, alternate, 2 to 5 inches long, dark green, shiny, leathery, evergreen, turning bronze to purplish in winter; flowers white, fragrant, urn-shaped, to $1/3$ inch long, borne along a 2- to 3-inch-long raceme, mid to late spring; fruit a capsule

Kalmia angustifolia

Leucothoe fontanesiana

PROPAGATION seed, sow on surface of media; cuttings

NOTES Also listed as *L. walteri;* also known as fetter-bush. A fine, broadleaf evergreen with graceful, arching stems, especially for deeply shaded conditions. The other native species of this genus in our region is the swamp dog-laurel or dog-hobble (*L. axillaris*), which is very similar in appearance to *L. fontanesiana.*

NATURAL RANGE Virginia to North Carolina, Tennessee, Georgia, and Alabama (and outlying station in Baltimore County, Maryland)

Lindera benzoin

SPICEBUSH
LAURACEAE

ZONES 4 to 9

SOIL moist best, but will grow in drier and wetter conditions

LIGHT sun to shade

ATTRIBUTES about 10 feet high and wide; leaves simple, alternate, about 4 inches long, turning yellow to bronze in autumn; flowers dioecious, yellow, very small but in numerous clusters along slender stems, in very early spring; fruit oval, about 1/3 inch long, bright scarlet, very fragrant when crushed (as are all parts of this plant)

PROPAGATION seed, warm stratify for one month then cold stratify for three months; cuttings difficult

NOTES One of the very first native shrubs to bloom each spring (along with leatherwood, *Dirca palustris*). Although its individual flowers are not particularly showy, many are packed along its stems, creating a most welcome, bright sight each spring.

NATURAL RANGE southern Maine to Michigan, south to Florida and Texas

Lyonia mariana

STAGGER-BUSH
ERICACEAE

ZONES 5 to 9

SOIL moist, well drained, sandy, acidic

LIGHT partial sun to sun

ATTRIBUTES to about 6 feet tall; leaves simple, alternate, to 3 inches long, dark green, turning reddish in fall; flowers tubular, white or pinkish, about 1/2 inch long, in late spring to early summer; fruit a capsule

PROPAGATION seed, plant on surface of moist peat; cuttings

NOTES All three *Lyonia* species native to our region have very attractive flower displays and good fall color. Fetterbush lyonia (*L. lucida*) reaches a height similar to that of stagger-bush, is evergreen, and is found on wetter sites. Maleberry (*L. ligustrina*) can reach 12 feet in height, is deciduous, and is found on

Lindera benzoin

Lindera benzoin fruit

Lyonia ligustrina

wet sites, including deeply and permanently flooded soils.

NATURAL RANGE Rhode Island to eastern Pennsylvania, Tennessee, southern Missouri, Texas, and Florida

Myrica pensylvanica

Myrica gale

Myrica pensylvanica

NORTHERN BAYBERRY
MYRICACEAE

ZONES 3 to 6

SOIL dry to wet

LIGHT sun to partial shade

ATTRIBUTES about 8 feet high and wider as it spreads by root suckers; leaves simple, alternate, about 3 inches long, deep green, aromatic when crushed; flowers mostly dioecious, catkins; fruit numerous, round, $1/5$ inch wide, gray, waxy-coated, aromatic when crushed, persists into winter

PROPAGATION seed, remove wax and cold stratify for three months; cuttings require rooting hormone

NOTES Occurs naturally along sandy seashores as well as marly wetlands of the Northeast; an important restoration species because of its tolerance to a wide range of site conditions (including salt spray) and its nitrogen-fixing ability. A similar native species, but with a more southern range overall, larger stature, and evergreen leaves, is the southern or swamp bayberry (*M. heterophylla*). Another native, but smaller, *Myrica* species that is widespread in the more northern half of this region is sweetgale (*M. gale*). Sweetgale has dark bluish green leaves that are highly aromatic when crushed, and reaches about 4 feet tall. It is often found in much deeper standing water, and rarely on dry sites, compared to northern bayberry. All *Myrica* species fix atmospheric nitrogen.

NATURAL RANGE Newfoundland to North Carolina, less commonly inland to Ohio and southern Ontario

Nemopanthus mucronatus

MOUNTAIN-HOLLY
AQUIFOLIACEAE

ZONES 4 to 6

SOIL moist to wet

LIGHT sun to shade

ATTRIBUTES can form dense thickets about 8 feet high and wider, by root sprouting; leaves simple, alternate or appearing whorled on spur shoots, about $1^1/2$ inches long; flowers mostly dioecious, small, inconspicuous; fruit nearly round, about $1/3$ inch wide, vermilion-red to scarlet-purple on long stalk

PROPAGATION seed, will require warm

Nemopanthus mucronatus

Paxistima canbyi

stratification for five months followed by cold stratification for three months

NOTES I have walked through what seems like miles of dense mountain-holly thickets in the wetlands of upstate New York, and doing so is just as much fun as walking through mountain-laurel and rhododendron thickets in the southern Appalachians. But, when fruiting in late summer and autumn, mountain-holly rivals most species of deciduous hollies, native or otherwise. Someone should be searching for an individual specimen that holds its fruit later into the autumn and winter, when leaves are absent.

NATURAL RANGE Newfoundland and Quebec to Minnesota, south to West Virginia and Indiana

Paxistima canbyi
MOUNTAIN LOVER
CELASTRACEAE

ZONES 3 to 7

SOIL dry to moist

LIGHT sun to partial shade

ATTRIBUTES evergreen mound rarely over 1 foot high; leaves simple, opposite, about $^1\!/_2$ inch long, shiny, dark green, evergreen; flowers very small ($^1\!/_5$ inch across), greenish or reddish, in mid spring; fruit an inconspicuous capsule

PROPAGATION divide plants or root cuttings taken in mid summer

NOTES Also known as cliff green. Found naturally on rocky, calcareous conditions, this species is well suited to dry, circumneutral soils but will grow well on a wider range of sites; an excellent compact (when grown in full sun), dwarf evergreen, which can also be trimmed into a very short hedge.

NATURAL RANGE West Virginia to southern Ontario and eastern Kentucky

Philadelphus inodorus
MOCK-ORANGE
HYDRANGEACEAE

ZONES 6 to 8

SOIL moist

LIGHT sun to partial shade

ATTRIBUTES dense, arching stems to about 10 feet high; leaves simple, opposite, to 4 inches long; flowers cup-shaped, about 2 inches in diameter, in late spring; fruit a capsule

PROPAGATION seed, will germinate without pretreatment; softwood cuttings

NOTES Mock-orange flowers have a light fragrance of orange blossoms.

NATURAL RANGE eastern Pennsylvania, Virginia, Tennessee, Georgia, and Alabama

Physocarpus opulifolius

EASTERN NINEBARK
ROSACEAE

ZONES 2 to 7

SOIL dry to wet, sandy or rocky

LIGHT sun to partial shade

ATTRIBUTES somewhat arching stems to about 8 feet high and wide; leaves simple, alternate, about 2 inches long, yellow to bronze in autumn; flowers white or pinkish, each about 1/3 inch wide and in round heads about 2 inches in diameter all along the stem in late spring to early summer; fruit about 1/4 inch long, reddish brown at maturity; bark on older stems exfoliates

PROPAGATION seed, will germinate without pre-treatment; softwood cuttings easy

NOTES Why are ten thousand (or more!) *Spiraea* ×*vanhouttei* planted in the eastern U.S. for each eastern ninebark? This species is not much larger than *Forsythia*, yet blooms during the time of year when its flowers are not competing with numerous spring bulbs. A few cultivars of eastern ninebark have more compact habit or more interesting foliage color; for example, the foliage of 'Diablo' is a very rich reddish purple to dark green.

NATURAL RANGE Quebec to North Dakota and Colorado, south to North Carolina, Tennessee, and Arkansas

Pieris floribunda

MOUNTAIN-ANDROMEDA
ERICACEAE

ZONES 4 to 6

SOIL moist

LIGHT sun to partial shade

ATTRIBUTES to about 5 feet high and wide; leaves simple, alternate, about 2 inches long, glossy, dark, evergreen; flowers white, urn-shaped, 1/4 inch long, borne along 2- to 4-inch-long, upright, stalk; fruit a capsule

PROPAGATION seed, will germinate without pre-treatment; cuttings difficult

NOTES Found primarily at high elevations in the southern Appalachians, I have long wondered why this species is so hard to purchase while its Japanese cousin (*P. japonica*, Japanese pieris) is sold nearly everywhere.

NATURAL RANGE Virginia and West Virginia, south to Florida and Louisiana

Physocarpus opulifolius

Pieris floribunda

Potentilla fruticosa

SHRUBBY CINQUEFOIL
ROSACEAE

ZONES 2 to 6

SOIL dry to wet

LIGHT sun to partial sun

ATTRIBUTES very dense branching, to about $3^{1}/2$ feet high and wide; leaves pinnately compound, alternate, to 1 inch long, silky gray-green; flowers about 1 inch in diameter, round, bright yellow throughout summer until frost; fruit a capsule

PROPAGATION seed, will germinate without pretreatment; cuttings treated with rooting hormone root readily

NOTES One develops a greater appreciation for this species when it is seen in the calcareous, groundwater-fed peatlands (fens) of the Northeast, which, although beautiful, do not offer easy conditions under which to grow. Too many cultivars to mention even a few here, but they generally offer flower colors different from the species, including shades of yellow, orange, red, pink, and white. Some cultivars have foliage of various green shades and more compact form. Additional cultivars have been selected from hybrids with other nonnative, woody *Potentilla* species.

NATURAL RANGE circumboreal, south to New Jersey, northern Illinois, South Dakota, and Arizona

Potentilla fruticosa

Prunus virginiana

CHOKECHERRY
ROSACEAE

ZONES 2 to 6

SOIL moist, well drained, but will tolerate much drier conditions

LIGHT sun to partial shade

ATTRIBUTES dense shrub, due to root suckering, or small tree to over 20 feet high; leaves simple, alternate, about 4 inches long, dark green, often with shades of red and orange in autumn; flowers white, round, about $1/3$ inch wide, packed along a 3- to 6-inch-long stalk; fruit round, $1/3$ inch wide, initially red, turning dark purple, astringent

PROPAGATION seed, cold stratify for three months; division of clumps

NOTES A few cultivars of chokecherry are available, including 'Canada Red' (rounded crown, reddish

Prunus virginiana

Prunus pumila

Prunus virginiana fruit

leaves) and 'Schubert' (pyramidal habit and reddish purple foliage). Two additional shrubby *Prunus* species native to our region are beach plum (*P. maritima*) and sand cherry (*P. pumila*). Both species have attractive flowers and fruit displays, form dense thickets (beach plum to 6 feet tall, sand cherry about half as tall), and are excellent stabilizers especially of dry, sandy soils. Both also tolerate rocky soils, salt spray, and alkaline conditions. I have seen sand cherries only a few times in the fall, but their fire-red color was outstanding, especially against the light brown sand dunes that they carpeted.

NATURAL RANGE Newfoundland to British Columbia, south to North Carolina, Texas, and California

Quercus ilicifolia

Quercus prinoides

Rhododendron arborescens

Quercus ilicifolia

SCRUB OAK
FAGACEAE

ZONES 4 to 7

SOIL dry, infertile, sandy or rocky, acidic

LIGHT sun to partial sun

ATTRIBUTES dense shrub or tree to about 20 feet high; leaves simple, alternate, about 4 inches long; flowers in aments; fruit a small acorn

PROPAGATION seed, cold stratify for three months

NOTES Scrub oak has yet to be "discovered" by horticulturists, yet few plants thrive under such dry, sunny, infertile conditions. The glossy, leathery foliage of scrub oak is very attractive. Scrub oak is one of over two dozen oak species native to this region but one of only two here with shrub habit, the other being dwarf chestnut oak, *Q. prinoides*. Dwarf chestnut oak often naturally occurs with scrub oak on the same difficult sites.

NATURAL RANGE southern Maine to central New York, Ohio, West Virginia, and North Carolina

Rhododendron arborescens

SWEET AZALEA
ERICACEAE

ZONES 4 to 7

SOIL moist, well drained, acidic, high in organic matter

LIGHT sun to partial shade

ATTRIBUTES about 15 feet high and wide, sometimes a small tree; leaves simple, alternate, about $2^1/_2$ inches long, shiny, dark green, often turning reddish in autumn; flowers to 2 inches wide, white to light pink, often with red and yellow, fragrant, in late spring to early summer; fruit a capsule

PROPAGATION seed, sow on surface of media

NOTES The flowers of sweet azalea, as the common name suggests, have a very strong, most pleasant fragrance.

NATURAL RANGE Pennsylvania to Kentucky, south to Georgia and Alabama

Rhododendron atlanticum

ATLANTIC AZALEA
ERICACEAE

ZONES 5 to 8

SOIL moist, well drained, acidic, sandy, high in organic matter best

LIGHT sun to partial shade
ATTRIBUTES to 5 feet high and wider because of root suckering; leaves simple, alternate, bluish green, to 2 inches long; flowers 1½ inches wide, white or flushed with red, in mid spring; fruit a capsule
PROPAGATION seed, sow on surface of media
NOTES Also known as the coast azalea, Atlantic azalea is a bit shorter in stature than many of the other native azaleas included here.
NATURAL RANGE southern New Jersey to Texas

Rhododendron calendulaceum

FLAME AZALEA
ERICACEAE

ZONES 5 to 7
SOIL moist, well drained, acidic, high in organic matter
LIGHT sun to partial shade
ATTRIBUTES to 10 feet tall; leaves simple, alternate, 2 to 4 inches long; flowers in clusters of five to fifteen, nearly 2 inches in diameter, yellow to orange to red, in mid spring; fruit a capsule
PROPAGATION seed, sow on surface of media
NOTES I think this is the first shrub in the woods that I ever really noticed—up until that time, all green woody forms in the forest understory were just blobs. The common name is most appropriate, and

is appreciated when one is hiking through the dark forests in which this species occurs and flame azalea is seen in full bloom, way off in the distance. Flower color naturally varies tremendously, but all colors are as bright and showy as any flower can be. Flame azalea has been hybridized with other native (and nonnative) *Rhododendron* species to yield some outstanding cultivars. A similarly outstanding native azalea that blooms a month or so later, after leaves fully develop, is the Cumberland azalea (*R. bakeri*).
NATURAL RANGE Pennsylvania and southern Ohio to Georgia and Alabama

Rhododendron canadense

RHODORA
ERICACEAE

ZONES 2 to 6
SOIL moist to wet, acidic, high in organic matter
LIGHT sun to partial shade
ATTRIBUTES to about 4 feet high and wide; leaves simple, alternate, gray-green, to 2 inches long; flowers rose-purple to white, about 1 inch long, before the leaves in early spring; fruit a capsule
PROPAGATION seed, sow on surface of media
NOTES A few white-flowered varieties exist, including var. *albiflorum* and var. *album,* the latter of which is also more compact in habit.
NATURAL RANGE Newfoundland to Quebec to

Rhododendron calendulaceum

Rhododendron canadense

Ontario, south to eastern Pennsylvania and northern New Jersey

Rhododendron canescens
PIEDMONT AZALEA
ERICACEAE
ZONES 5 to 9
SOIL moist, well drained, acidic, high in organic matter
LIGHT sun to partial shade
ATTRIBUTES to about 15 feet high and as wide,

Rhododendron canescens

somewhat colonial by root suckers; leaves simple, alternate; flowers pink or white in early spring; fruit a capsule
PROPAGATION seed, sow on surface of media
NOTES As with many of the native azaleas, the flowers of this species vary much in color. It does spread more vigorously than many azaleas, because of the root suckers it produces.
NATURAL RANGE Delaware to Florida and Texas

Rhododendron maximum
ROSEBAY RHODODENDRON
ERICACEAE
ZONES 3 to 7
SOIL moist to wet (occasionally occurs in swamps), acidic, high in organic matter
LIGHT sun to partial shade
ATTRIBUTES twisted branches easily can reach 20+ feet high and wide in dense thickets; leaves simple, alternate, to 8 inches long, dark green, leathery, evergreen; flowers white to pink, spotted with olive-green or orange, about $1^1/_2$ inches in diameter, early summer; fruit a capsule
PROPAGATION seed, sow on surface of media

Rhododendron maximum

NOTES Rosebay rhododendron is easily the largest of the native species covered here, and one of the largest of all native shrubs. A few cultivars, primarily with richer pink (to purple) flowers, are available. Catawba rhododendron (*R. catawbiense*) is similar in appearance but restricted to the highest elevations of the southern mountains of our region. This species is the parent for many excellent cultivars and hybrids. Also in our region but at the highest elevations in alpine communities of the northeastern mountains and much farther north is the Lappland rose-bay (*R. lapponicum*). Lappland rose-bay has very small, evergreen leaves (about 1/2 inch long) and rarely grows above 12 inches in height; its bright purple flowers open in June.

Rhododendron minus

Rhododendron periclymenoides

NATURAL RANGE Nova Scotia to southern Ontario and southern Ohio, south especially in mountains to Georgia and Alabama

Rhododendron minus
CAROLINA RHODODENDRON
ERICACEAE

ZONES 5 to 8

SOIL moist, well drained, acidic, high in organic matter

LIGHT sun to partial shade

ATTRIBUTES about 6 feet high and wide; leaves simple, alternate, about 2 1/2 inches long, dark green, evergreen; flowers pink to white, about 1 1/2 inches in diameter, in clusters of four to ten; fruit a capsule

PROPAGATION seed, sow on surface of media

NOTES Also listed as *R. carolinianum.* Variety *carolinianum* (Carolina rhododendron) is found at higher elevations in the southern Appalachians and can reach 10 feet high, whereas the maximum height of var. *minus* (Piedmont rhododendron) is at least half this height.

NATURAL RANGE mountains of North Carolina and Tennessee

Rhododendron periclymenoides
PINXTER AZALEA
ERICACEAE

ZONES 4 to 8

SOIL dry to wet (occasionally occurs in swamps; moist soil best), acidic, high in organic matter

LIGHT sun to partial shade

ATTRIBUTES to 8 feet high and wider due to root suckers; leaves simple, alternate, 2 to 4 inches long; flowers pink (sometimes white), 1 1/2 inches in diameter in mid spring, often fragrant; fruit a capsule

PROPAGATION seed, sow on surface of media

NOTES Also listed as *R. nudiflorum.* Similar to most of the native azaleas here—very showy as is and terribly underutilized—but certainly there is an opportunity to find even better selections.

NATURAL RANGE Vermont and Massachusetts to central New York, south to South Carolina and Tennessee

Rhododendron prinophyllum

ROSESHELL AZALEA
ERICACEAE

ZONES 4 to 8

SOIL dry to moist

LIGHT sun to partial shade

ATTRIBUTES to about 10 feet high; leaves simple; flowers bright pink to white, near 2 inches in diameter, five to nine per cluster, very fragrant, in mid spring; fruit a capsule

PROPAGATION seed, sow on surface of media

NOTES Also listed as *R. roseum.* Roseshell azalea is apparently more tolerant of circumneutral soils than most *Rhododendron* species.

NATURAL RANGE Maine and southern Quebec to Virginia and Kentucky, southern Illinois, southern Missouri, Arkansas, and eastern Oklahoma

Rhododendron vaseyi

PINKSHELL AZALEA
ERICACEAE

ZONES 4 to 7

SOIL moist, well drained, acidic, high in organic matter

LIGHT sun to partial shade

ATTRIBUTES to about 8 feet high and a bit narrower; leaves simple, alternate, turning reddish in autumn; flowers 1½ inches wide, rose-colored, five to eight per cluster, in mid spring; fruit a capsule

PROPAGATION seed, sow on surface of media

NOTES Perhaps the earliest blooming native azalea covered here.

NATURAL RANGE mountains of North Carolina

Rhododendron viscosum

SWAMP AZALEA
ERICACEAE

ZONES 4 to 9

SOIL moist to wet; acidic, high in organic matter

LIGHT sun to partial shade

ATTRIBUTES to 8 feet high and wide, spreading by root suckers; leaves simple, alternate, about 2 inches long; flowers white, about 1 inch wide, in clusters of four to nine, spicy-fragrant, in early summer

PROPAGATION seed, sow on surface of media

NOTES Many years ago I "discovered" this species on a typically hot and humid summer day in southern New Jersey wetlands by its strong honeysuckle-like fragrance. In fact, until I looked more closely, I thought this species was indeed a honeysuckle.

NATURAL RANGE Maine to Ohio and Florida

Rhus aromatica

FRAGRANT SUMAC
ANACARDIACEAE

ZONES 3 to 9

SOIL dry to moist, well drained

LIGHT sun to partial shade

ATTRIBUTES to about 8 feet high and wider by means of rooting along prostrate stems; leaves compound, consisting of three dark green and shiny leaflets, to 3 inches long, turning shades of red, purple, and orange in autumn; flowers (mostly dioecious) yellow in early spring; fruit a red, hairy drupe, ¼ inch in diameter, persisting into winter

PROPAGATION seed, acid scarify then cold stratify

Rhododendron prinophyllum

Rhododendron viscosum

Rhus aromatica

Rhus copallina fruit

for one to three months; softwood cuttings rather easy

NOTES Although some authors mention acidic soils, I have seen this species growing from limestone bedrock in northern New York. A few cultivars are available that have more compact form and glossier foliage. Given its tremendous geographical range, this species is another native plant that deserves much more careful examination for improved selections, especially relative to fruit display, fall color, and form.

NATURAL RANGE southwestern Quebec and western Vermont to northwestern Florida, west to Alberta, Oregon, California, and Mexico

Rhus copallina
SHINING SUMAC
ANACARDIACEAE

ZONES 4 to 9

SOIL dry, rocky or sandy, to moist but well drained

LIGHT sun to partial sun

ATTRIBUTES crooked stems to over 20 feet high and wide, sometimes a small tree that is somewhat broad at the top; spreads by root suckers; leaves pinnately compound, glossy, dark green, turning brilliant and deep shades of red and purple in autumn; flowers dioecious, small, yellow-green, in pyramidal clusters about 6 inches long in mid summer; fruit round, crimson, in pyramidal clusters about 6 inches long

PROPAGATION seed, acid scarify for one hour; root cuttings

NOTES Less coarse-textured than the next two *Rhus* species, with glossier summer foliage, but all have outstanding autumn color and fruit display.

NATURAL RANGE southern Maine to Florida, west to Indiana, southern Illinois, southeast Nebraska and Texas

Rhus glabra
SMOOTH SUMAC
ANACARDIACEAE

ZONES 3 to 9

SOIL dry to moist, well drained

LIGHT sun to partial sun

ATTRIBUTES reaches 15 feet tall and wide, spreading by root suckers; leaves pinnately compound, to 18 inches long, turning shades of red, purple, orange, and yellow in autumn; flowers dioecious, small, yellow-green, in pyramidal clusters up to 10 inches long in summer; fruit round, small, blood-red, in pyramidal clusters that persist into winter

PROPAGATION seed, acid scarify for one hour; root cuttings

NOTES The cultivar 'Laciniata' has deeply dissected leaves and bright scarlet fruits.

NATURAL RANGE New England and southern Quebec to British Columbia, south to northern Florida, Texas, and Mexico

Rhus copallina in autumn

Rhus glabra fruit

Rhus glabra flowers

Rhus typhina

STAGHORN SUMAC
ANACARDIACEAE

ZONES 4 to 8

SOIL dry to moist and well drained

LIGHT sun to partial sun

ATTRIBUTES to 25+ feet high, with equal spread by means of root suckers; leaves pinnately compound, 1 to 2 feet long, turning shades of red, purple, and orange in autumn; flowers dioecious, small, yellow-green, in pyramidal clusters to 8 inches long; fruit round, hairy, dark red, in pyramidal clusters; stems stout and densely hairy

PROPAGATION seed, acid scarify for one hour; root cuttings

NOTES Staghorn sumac and gray dogwood (*Cornus racemosa*), along with *Solidago* (goldenrod) and *Aster* species dominate many old fields throughout the Northeast. Very few woody species rival the intense autumn color of staghorn sumac. 'Dissecta' and 'Laciniata' have deeply dissected leaves, giving foli-age a very lacy appearance; both are female selections, so fruit display is a bonus.

NATURAL RANGE Nova Scotia and southern Quebec to Minnesota, south to West Virginia and Ohio, irregularly to northern Georgia, northern Alabama, and Iowa

Rhus typhina 'Laciniata'

Rhus typhina

Ribes odoratum

Robinia hispida

Ribes odoratum
CLOVE CURRANT
GROSSULARIACEAE

ZONES 4 to 6

SOIL dry to moist

LIGHT sun or partial shade

ATTRIBUTES to 8 feet tall and wider, by means of root sprouts; leaves simple, alternate, bluish green, about 2 inches long and wide; flowers dioecious, yellow, fragrant, in clusters of five to ten, in early spring; fruit black, $1/3$ inch wide in early summer

PROPAGATION seed, cold stratify for three months; softwood cuttings

NOTES Also known as the buffalo currant. This and other *Ribes* species are the alternate host for white pine blister rust, a serious fungus disease of eastern white pine (*Pinus strobus*). Other native *Ribes* species in our region include eastern black currant (*R. americanum*), skunk currant (*R. glandulosum*), wild gooseberry (*R. hirtellum*), and swamp red currant (*R. triste*). All of these grow well on moist to wet soils. Eastern black currant and wild gooseberry have the best tasting fruit of all listed here.

NATURAL RANGE Minnesota to Arkansas, west and south to South Dakota, Colorado, and Texas

Robinia hispida
BRISTLY LOCUST
FABACEAE

ZONES 5 to 8

SOIL dry, infertile, rocky or sandy

LIGHT sun

ATTRIBUTES to about 10 feet high and wider by means of root suckers; leaves pinnately compound, bluish green, to 9 inches long; flowers rose-pink to pale purple along 2- to 4-inch-long, hanging stalk, in early summer; fruit a densely hairy pod

PROPAGATION seed, acid or mechanically scarify, or soak in hot water

NOTES Includes var. *fertilis*. Fixes atmospheric nitrogen and spreads readily by root suckers, so especially valuable for land reclamation purposes.

NATURAL RANGE southwestern Virginia to North Carolina and northern Georgia

Rosa carolina
CAROLINA ROSE
ROSACEAE

ZONES 4 to 9

SOIL dry

LIGHT sun

ATTRIBUTES to about 5 feet high and wider, spreading by root suckers; leaves pinnately compound (usually five leaflets), alternate, glossy, rich

Rosa carolina

Rosa carolina, immature fruit

Rosa palustris

green, turning reddish in autumn; flowers pinkish, to 2^1/$_2$ inches in diameter, usually solitary, fragrant; fruit red, ^{1}/$_3$ inch wide, pear-shaped, persisting into winter; stems heavily armed

PROPAGATION seed, cold stratify for three to four months; softwood and hardwood cuttings not difficult

NOTES Also known as the pasture rose, Carolina rose is well suited to very dry conditions.

NATURAL RANGE Maine to Minnesota, south to Florida and Texas

Rosa virginiana
VIRGINIA ROSE
ROSACEAE

ZONES 3 to 7

SOIL dry to moist, well drained

LIGHT sun

ATTRIBUTES dense mound to 6 feet high; leaves pinnately compound (seven to nine leaflets), dark green, glossy, turning shades of purple, red, orange, and yellow in autumn; flowers pink, fragrant, to 2^1/$_2$ inches in diameter, typically solitary, early summer; fruit bright red, nearly round, about ^{1}/$_2$ inch in diameter, persisting into winter; stems generally with paired thorns

PROPAGATION seed, cold stratify for three to four months; softwood and hardwood cuttings not difficult

NOTES Virginia rose is quite attractive (glossy foliage, pink flowers, persistent scarlet fruit, maroon fall color) throughout much of the year and is very drought-tolerant. Other native roses of our region include bristly rose (*R. acicularis*), smooth rose (*R. blanda*), swamp rose (*R. palustris*), and climbing prairie rose (*R. setigera*). Bristly rose and smooth rose have pink flowers, bright red fruit, and reach about 5 feet in height. Swamp rose has similar flowers and orange-red fruit and often grows in deep standing water. Of all our native roses, the climbing prairie rose is best suited for trellises and lattice work because of its very long stems. It has rosy-pink flowers that fade to white, and red fruit.

NATURAL RANGE Newfoundland to Pennsylvania and Virginia, and inland irregularly to Missouri

Rubus odoratus

FLOWERING RASPBERRY
ROSACEAE

ZONES 4 to 6

SOIL moist, well drained

LIGHT sun to shade

ATTRIBUTES arching stems to about 5 feet high, in open colonies; leaves simple, alternate, palmately lobed and resembling a maple; flowers round, rose-purple, about 1 inch in diameter in summer; fruit a dry (usually), dark red berry about 1/2 inch wide; stems have exfoliating bark and are thornless

PROPAGATION seed, cold stratify for three months; cuttings easy

NOTES Flowering raspberry is another native plant that has been totally neglected, and I cannot understand why, given its beautiful flowers, interesting exfoliating stems, arching habit, and tolerance to substantial shade. A similar native species is thimbleberry (*R. parviflorus*) except it has large white flowers. Many of the best raspberry and blackberry cultivars grown for fruit production are selections of our native species—*R. allegheniensis* (blackberry), *R. idaeus* (red raspberry), and *R. occidentalis* (black raspberry), for example.

NATURAL RANGE Nova Scotia and Maine to Michigan, south to North Carolina and Tennessee

Salix candida

HOARY WILLOW
SALICACEAE

ZONES 2 to 6

SOIL moist to wet, especially on those high in calcium

LIGHT sun

ATTRIBUTES upright stems to about 5 feet in height; leaves simple, alternate, narrowly lance-shaped, dark green on top, densely white hairy beneath

PROPAGATION seed, will germinate without pretreatment (but must be fresh); cuttings

NOTES Also known as the sage-leaved willow, hoary willow is often abundant in calcareous peatlands (fens). There are dozens of native willow species, mostly shrubs, in our region. Other shrubby (sometimes small-tree) native willow species I especially like are dune willow (*S. cordata*), diamond willow (*S. eriocephala*), sandbar willow (*S. exigua*), shining

Rubus odoratus

Salix candida

Salix uva-ursi

willow (*S. lucida*), satiny willow (*S. pellita*), silky willow (*S. sericea*), and autumn willow (*S. serissima*). Most are found naturally in wetlands although the dune willow thrives on some dunes of the Great Lakes basin. Two others are especially well suited to the alpine rock garden, bearberry willow (*S. uva-ursi*) and herb-like willow (*S. herbacea*). Both have a prostrate habit, very small leaves, and are found in alpine communities of northeastern North America.

NATURAL RANGE Labrador to Alaska, south to New Jersey, Pennsylvania, Ohio, Indiana, Illinois, Iowa, and Colorado

Sambucus canadensis

BLACK ELDERBERRY
CAPRIFOLIACEAE

ZONES 4 to 9

SOIL dry to wet

LIGHT sun to partial sun

ATTRIBUTES dense, arching stems in thickets to about 10 feet high and wider, spreading by stolons; leaves pinnately compound, alternate, to 6 inches long; flowers white, very small, in flat-topped clusters up to 10 inches wide, in summer; fruit purple-black, 1/4 inch in diameter

PROPAGATION seed, warm stratify for two months then cold stratify for at least three months; softwood cuttings

NOTES Also known as the American elder. Naturally occurs in open canopy wetlands; black elderberry fruit can be made into jams, jellies, wine, and is favored by many bird species. A few cultivars are available, with finer foliage texture, larger flowers and fruit, and red fruit. The other native *Sambucus* in this region is *S. racemosa,* the red elderberry or red-berried elder, which is sometimes common on rich, moist, shaded sites. The red elderberry flowers in early spring and has beautiful, bright red fruit that matures about the time black elderberry flowers. The fruit of red elderberry is either edible or poisonous, depending on the reference. Both elderberry species get very large very quickly.

NATURAL RANGE Nova Scotia and Quebec to Manitoba and South Dakota, south to Mexico and the West Indies

Shepherdia canadensis

BUFFALO BERRY
ELAEAGNACEAE

ZONES 2 to 6

SOIL dry

LIGHT sun

ATTRIBUTES about 8 feet high and wide; leaves simple, opposite, to 2 inches long, grayish dark green; flowers dioecious, small, yellowish, in mid spring; fruit yellowish red, to 1/4 inch long; stems covered with scaly pubescence

PROPAGATION seed, cold stratify for two to three months

Sambucus canadensis

Sambucus racemosa

NOTES Also known as rabbit-berry. Fixes atmospheric nitrogen, and will tolerate very dry, alkaline soils in full sun, as well as salt spray.
NATURAL RANGE Newfoundland to Alaska, south to New York, northern Indiana, South Dakota, and Arizona

Spiraea alba
MEADOWSWEET
ROSACEAE
ZONES 3 to 5
SOIL dry to wet
LIGHT sun

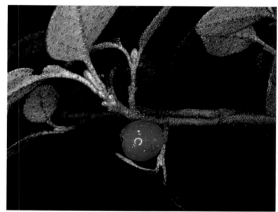

Shepherdia canadensis

Karner blue butterfly on *Spiraea alba*

ATTRIBUTES to about 6 feet high and wider; leaves simple, alternate, bluish green, about 2 inches long; flowers 1/4 inch in diameter, white (sometimes pink), in pyramidal, terminal clusters to about 6 inches long, in summer; fruit small, dry, brown
PROPAGATION seed, will germinate without pretreatment; softwood cuttings root readily
NOTES Meadowsweet, which includes *S. latifolia*, tolerates a tremendous range in soil moisture conditions, from dry to occasional standing water, whereas *S. tomentosa* is not as tolerant of the drier conditions.
NATURAL RANGE Newfoundland and Quebec to Alberta, south to North Carolina, Missouri, and South Dakota

Spiraea tomentosa
HARDHACK
ROSACEAE
ZONES 4 to 6
SOIL moist to wet
LIGHT sun
ATTRIBUTES to about 4 feet high and wider; leaves simple, alternate, velvety rusty hairy below; flowers

Spiraea tomentosa

deep rose (sometimes white), about 1/6 inch wide, in narrow pyramidal, terminal clusters to 8 inches long, in summer; fruit small, dry, brown

PROPAGATION seed, will germinate without pretreatment; softwood cuttings root readily

NOTES Both *Spiraea* species strongly attract butterflies and other nectar-feeding insects in the summer.

NATURAL RANGE Nova Scotia and New Brunswick to Quebec and Minnesota, south to North Carolina, Tennessee, and Arkansas

Staphylea trifolia

BLADDERNUT
STAPHYLEACEAE

ZONES 4 to 8

SOIL moist, well drained

LIGHT sun to partial shade

ATTRIBUTES erect, somewhat arching branches to 15 feet high, occasionally a small tree; leaves pinnately compound, opposite, to 4 inches long, dark green; flowers white, bell-shaped, 1/3 inch long in drooping cluster about 2 inches long, in mid spring; fruit inflated, three-parted, to 1 1/2 inches long, bright green, turning brown at maturity; bark dark purplish brown, white-striped

PROPAGATION seed, warm stratify for three months then cold stratify for three months; softwood and hardwood cuttings; division

NOTES Naturally thrives in rich circumneutral soils. Although many authors seem to focus on the unusual fruit, its flowers are very attractive; clean foliage and subtle striping of bark are bonuses.

NATURAL RANGE southern Quebec to Minnesota, south to Georgia, west Florida, and Oklahoma

Symphoricarpos albus

SNOWBERRY
CAPRIFOLIACEAE

ZONES 3 to 7

SOIL dry, rocky

LIGHT sun to partial shade

ATTRIBUTES to 4 feet high and wider, forming dense mound by root suckers; leaves simple, opposite, to 2 inches long, bluish green; flowers pink, 1/4 inch long, late spring to early summer; fruit round, berrylike, white, 1/2 inch wide, persisting into winter

PROPAGATION seed, will require warm then cold stratification; cuttings root readily

Staphylea trifolia

Symphoricarpos albus

Symphoricarpos orbiculatus

NOTES *S. orbiculatus,* coralberry, is also native to this region and has similar attributes except for its yellowish white flowers, smaller and reddish purple fruit, and slightly larger stature. Both species are very well adapted to the driest soils or rocky areas.
NATURAL RANGE Quebec to southern Alaska, south to Virginia, Michigan, Minnesota, and California

Taxus canadensis

CANADA YEW
TAXACEAE

ZONES 2 to 6
SOIL rich, moist, well drained
LIGHT partial shade to shade
ATTRIBUTES sprawling, semi-erect stems that eventually root when they contact the soil; reaches about 6 feet in height; leaves needlelike, dark green, glossy; fruit a gelatinous, orange-red mass that surrounds a very poisonous seed
PROPAGATION seed is difficult, will require long period of warm then cold stratification; cuttings relatively easy
NOTES When I saw this species for the first time, the importance of microsite conditions in supporting plants way outside the heart of their range really registered. It was growing in northeastern Kentucky at the shaded mouth of a cave, which continuously released humid, cool air. Much farther north it grows best on north-facing, lower slopes, where it thrives on moist soils that rarely receive any sunlight. Canada yew's sprawling habit will prevent it from ever replacing the commonly planted cultivars of *Taxus* species and hybrids from Asia and England, but on moist, dark sites, it provides a rich color and interesting architecture. Before planting, be aware that it is a very strong deer magnet!
NATURAL RANGE Newfoundland and Labrador to Minnesota and southeast Manitoba, south to Virginia, Kentucky, and Iowa

Vaccinium angustifolium

LOW SWEET BLUEBERRY
ERICACEAE

ZONES 2 to 5
SOIL dry to moist, acidic, infertile, sandy or rocky
LIGHT sun
ATTRIBUTES to 2 feet high and wider; leaves simple, alternate, to 3/4 inch long, bright green, shiny, turn-

ing shades of red and orange in autumn; flowers urn-shaped, white tinged with pink to red, 1/4 inch long, in mid spring; fruit round, bluish black with white waxy surface, very sweet, 1/4 to 1/2 inch in diameter
PROPAGATION seed, cold stratify for one to two months; softwood or rhizome cuttings
NOTES Also known as the lowbush blueberry. This is the blueberry of Maine fame; an exceptional very small shrub, especially some cultivars, in terms of edible fruit and autumn color (a mini burningbush). Like most members of the heath family (Ericaceae),

Taxus canadensis

Vaccinium angustifolium

Vaccinium angustifolium in fruit

it requires well-drained, acidic soils. Two other native low-growing blueberries are the dryland blueberry (*V. pallidum*) and velvetleaf blueberry (*V. myrtilloides*). Dryland blueberry is common in dry woods and produces a sweet, edible fruit. Velvetleaf blueberry occurs in bogs and on dry sites and produces a sour but edible fruit. Both have beautiful fall color.

NATURAL RANGE Labrador and Newfoundland to Manitoba, south to New Jersey, Pennsylvania, Illinois, and Minnesota, and in the mountains to North Carolina

Vaccinium corymbosum
HIGHBUSH BLUEBERRY
ERICACEAE

ZONES 3 to 7

SOIL moist, well drained, acidic, high in organic matter best, but will tolerate wet, sandy, acidic soils, too

LIGHT sun (best fruit production and autumn colors) to partial shade

ATTRIBUTES somewhat arching stems to 10 feet tall and wider; leaves simple, alternate, dark green, 1 to 3 inches long, turning intense shades of red, purple, orange, and yellow in autumn; flowers urn-shaped, white, 1/3 inch long, late spring; fruit round, bluish black berry, with white waxy surface, 1/4 to 1/2 inch in diameter, tart to sweet, mid summer

PROPAGATION seed, will germinate without pretreatment; softwood cuttings treated with high concentration of rooting hormone

NOTES Alas, much of my field work lately is in upstate New York peatlands that have so many highbush blueberry in fruit in August that I will probably get tired of eating them in a few more years. I acidified the circumneutral soils at my home years ago and planted a hedge of highbush blueberries that rivals my neighbor's burningbush (*Euonymus alatus*) each fall—and she does not have the opportunity to enjoy the fruit that I do, if I can beat the many catbirds to my specimens. This species is the common blueberry of commerce, and there are many cultivars that have larger and more fruit, and more refined forms. Two other attractive native *Vaccinium* species, but with inedible fruit, are farkleberry (*V. arboreum*) and deerberry (*V. stamineum*).

Vaccinium corymbosum

Vaccinium vitis-idaea

Vaccinium corymbosum in autumn

Vaccinium vitis-idaea var. minus

Both better tolerate dry soils and shade than highbush blueberry. Farkleberry will reach about the same height, whereas deerberry matures at half this height.

NATURAL RANGE Maine and Nova Scotia to Florida, west to Michigan, northern Illinois, Kentucky, Arkansas, eastern Oklahoma, and eastern Texas

Vaccinium vitis-idaea
MOUNTAIN CRANBERRY
ERICACEAE
ZONES 2 to 6
SOIL moist, well drained, acidic, high in organic matter

LIGHT sun

ATTRIBUTES to 12 inches tall; leaves alternate, simple, leathery, dark green, evergreen, turning shiny mahogany in winter; flowers urn-shaped, 1/4 inch long, white or pinkish in spring; fruit round, about 1/3 inch wide, dark red, very tart, in late summer

PROPAGATION cuttings taken during dormant season, treated with rooting hormone

NOTES Also known as lingonberry, cowberry. Variety *minus* is about one-half the height of the species and cold hardy to Zone 2; var. *majus* and its cultivars have received much attention for their larger fruits. The cranberry of Thanksgiving season is the native *V. macrocarpon*. A similar native cranberry is the smaller-fruited and -leaved *V. oxycoccos* (small cranberry). Both of these cranberries have very small evergreen leaves along long, trailing, slender woody stems and are found in open bogs throughout the northern half of our region.

NATURAL RANGE boreal North America and Eurasia, south to the higher mountains of New England, the shore of Maine, and to Minnesota and British Columbia

Viburnum acerifolium
MAPLELEAF VIBURNUM
CAPRIFOLIACEAE

ZONES 4 to 8

SOIL dry to moist

LIGHT shade to sun

ATTRIBUTES to about 5 feet high and wide, spreading by root suckers; leaves simple, opposite, resemble a maple, about 3 inches long, dark green, turning shades of pink, purple, and red in autumn; flowers white, small, in 1- to 3-inch-wide, flat terminal cluster in late spring; fruit elliptical, 1/3 inch long, bluish black

PROPAGATION seed, will require warm then cold stratification; softwood cuttings

NOTES Its somewhat washed-out pink, purple, and red autumn colors are difficult to describe—I cannot think of any other woody plant species with these same attractive, soft, fall colors.

NATURAL RANGE Quebec and New Brunswick to Minnesota, south to Florida and Louisiana

Viburnum acerifolium fruit

Viburnum acerifolium

Viburnum alnifolium

HOBBLEBUSH
CAPRIFOLIACEAE

ZONES 3 to 5

SOIL moist, well drained

LIGHT partial sun to shade

ATTRIBUTES to about 7 feet high and wider, spreading by branches that root along the ground; leaves simple, opposite, nearly round, to 8 inches in diameter, dark green, turning shades of red and purple in late summer to autumn; flowers white, in flat clusters about 5 inches in diameter, on outside of the cluster sterile and 1 inch in diameter, on inside of cluster much smaller and fertile; fruit ellipsoidal, red, becoming purple-black in autumn, 1/3 inch long

PROPAGATION seed, will require warm then cold stratification; sofwood cuttings

NOTES Also listed as *V. lantanoides*. Hobblebush is a very shade-tolerant, medium-size shrub with an outstanding flower display in early spring.

NATURAL RANGE Nova Scotia to Michigan, south in the mountains to North Carolina and Tennessee

Viburnum alnifolium

Viburnum cassinoides

WITHEROD VIBURNUM
CAPRIFOLIACEAE

ZONES 3 to 8

SOIL moist to wet

LIGHT sun to shade

ATTRIBUTES to 12 feet high and wide; leaves simple, opposite, about 3 inches long, dull, dark green, turning shades of red, purple, and orange in autumn; flowers creamy white, about 1/4 inch in diameter, borne in 2- to 5-inch-wide, flat clusters in late spring; fruit about 1/3 inch long, ovoid, green turning pink then red then bluish black

PROPAGATION seed, will require warm and cold stratification; softwood cuttings

NOTES Some taxonomists regard *V. cassinoides* as a variety of *V. nudum;* they are indeed very similar except for the more lustrous leaves of *V. nudum.*

NATURAL RANGE Newfoundland to Manitoba and Minnesota south to Georgia

Viburnum cassinoides

Viburnum dentatum

ARROWWOOD
CAPRIFOLIACEAE

ZONES 3 to 8

Viburnum dentatum

SOIL dry to moist, well drained

LIGHT sun to partial shade

ATTRIBUTES about 10 feet high and wide, spreading by root suckers; leaves simple, opposite, coarsely toothed, about 3 inches long, generally shiny, dark green, turning yellow or shades of purple and red in autumn; flowers white, small, in flat clusters, 2 to 4 inches in diameter, in late spring; fruit ovoid, 1/4 inch long, bluish black in autumn

PROPAGATION seed, will require warm then cold stratification; softwood cuttings

NOTES Cultivars with better summer and autumn leaf color, and distinct growth habit are available. There is much variation in this species, which includes, by recent taxonomic treatment, var. *recognitum* (= *V. recognitum,* northern arrowwood).

NATURAL RANGE Maine to Illinois, south to Florida and Texas

Viburnum nudum
SMOOTH WITHEROD
CAPRIFOLIACEAE

ZONES 5 to 9

SOIL moist to wet

LIGHT sun to shade

ATTRIBUTES to 12 feet high and wide; leaves simple, opposite, about 3 inches long, shiny, dark green, turning shades of red and purple in autumn; flowers creamy white, about 1/4 inch wide, borne in 2- to 5-inch-wide, flat clusters in late spring; fruit about 1/3 inch long, ovoid, green turning pink then red then bluish black

PROPAGATION seed, will require warm then cold stratification; softwood cuttings

NOTES Not as cold hardy as *V. cassinoides,* but both are excellent choices for wet soils and their numerous ornamental features (flowers, fruit, and fall color). 'Winterthur' has especially lustrous foliage and is a bit more compact than the species.

NATURAL RANGE Connecticut, Long Island to Florida, west to Kentucky and Louisiana

Viburnum trilobum
AMERICAN CRANBERRYBUSH
CAPRIFOLIACEAE

ZONES 2 to 7

SOIL moist, well drained

LIGHT sun to partial shade

Viburnum nudum

Viburnum trilobum fruit

ATTRIBUTES about 12 feet high and wide; leaves simple, opposite, 2 to 5 inches long, resemble a maple leaf, shiny, dark green, turning yellow or red-purple in autumn; flowers white, in flat clusters to about 4 inches in diameter, flowers on outside of cluster 3/4 inch wide and sterile, interior flowers

Viburnum trilobum

very small and fertile; fruit bright red, round, $1/4$ to $1/3$ inch in diameter

PROPAGATION seed, will require warm then cold stratification; softwood cuttings

NOTES Regarded as a variety of the European cranberrybush or Guelder rose, *V. opulus* (i.e., *V. trilobum* = *V. o.* var. *americanum*), by many taxonomists. The most northern of our native viburnums is the mooseberry or squashberry (*V. edule*). The ripe fruit of mooseberry can be made into a delicious jelly.

NATURAL RANGE Newfoundland to British Columbia, south to Pennsylvania, northern Ohio, Iowa, and Washington

Xanthorhiza simplicissima

YELLOWROOT

RANUNCULACEAE

ZONES 3 to 9

SOIL moist to wet; will tolerate dry soils but not spread vigorously

LIGHT sun to partial shade

ATTRIBUTES 2 to 3 feet high, spreading extensively from root suckers; leaves pinnately compound, shiny, dark green, subtle shades of yellow, orange, and purple in autumn; flowers small, brownish purple, in 2- to 4-inch-long cluster; fruit pale brown, small; roots yellow

Xanthorhiza simplicissima

PROPAGATION division of clump

NOTES Yellowroot is an exceptional ground cover for moist, shaded locations.

NATURAL RANGE southern New York to Pennsylvania and Kentucky, south to South Carolina, western Florida, and Alabama

Yucca filamentosa

Yucca filamentosa
ADAM'S NEEDLE
AGAVACEAE

ZONES 4 to 9

SOIL dry, sandy to moist but well drained

LIGHT sun

ATTRIBUTES habit a mound of erect leaves spreading from the base; leaves long, linear, swordlike, to $2^{1/2}$ feet long, evergreen; flowers yellowish white, pendulous, 2 to 3 inches in diameter, borne along a 3- to 6-foot-high, erect stalk in summer; fruit a capsule

PROPAGATION seed, will germinate without pretreatment, but not immediately; root cuttings

NOTES 'Ivory Tower' and 'Starburst' are the primary cultivars available. Other species of *Yucca* are sold for landscaping purposes in this region, although most are less cold hardy than this species.

NATURAL RANGE Maryland to Florida and Louisiana

Zanthoxylum americanum
PRICKLY-ASH
RUTACEAE

ZONES 3 to 7

SOIL dry, poor to moist

LIGHT sun to shade

ATTRIBUTES in dense thickets to 20 feet high due to root sprouting, or occasionally a small tree; leaves pinnately compound, alternate, about 8 inches long, dark green, armed along the leaf stalk; flowers dioecious, small, yellowish green, before leaves expand; fruit a capsule enclosing shiny, black seeds; stems armed with $1/3$ to $1/2$ inch long prickles

PROPAGATION seed, cold stratify for four months; mechanical scarification may improve germination

NOTES Also known as the toothache tree. I have seen prickly-ash on very dry, wet, shaded and sunny sites. Although it does not have any outstanding attribute, I admire its ability to grow well on such a wide range of site conditions.

NATURAL RANGE southern Quebec to eastern North Dakota, south to South Carolina, Georgia, and Oklahoma but only irregularly east of Ohio and northwest New York

Zenobia pulverulenta
DUSTY ZENOBIA
ERICACEAE

ZONES 5 to 9

SOIL moist to wet, acidic

LIGHT sun to partial shade

ATTRIBUTES somewhat arching stems to 6 feet high and wide; leaves alternate, simple, 1 to 3 inches long, green to bluish, turning yellowish in autumn; flowers urn-shaped, $3/8$ inch wide, white, fragrant, in clusters along the stem in late spring; fruit a capsule

PROPAGATION seed, will germinate without pretreatment

NOTES There is much variation in foliage color, including waxy, nearly blue forms. Perhaps this plant will someday be known and loved by so many people that someone will think of a more appealing common name.

NATURAL RANGE southeast Virginia to South Carolina

Zanthoxylum americanum

Zenobia pulverulenta

TREES

Abies balsamea

BALSAM FIR
PINACEAE

ZONES 3 to 5

SOIL moist to wet

LIGHT sun to shade

ATTRIBUTES very narrow, pyramidal tree (spirelike habit) to about 50 feet high and 20 feet wide; leaves needlelike but blunt at tip, about 1 inch long, borne flat on twigs in shade but much more upright in sun; dark green above, two white waxy bands below, very fragrant; flowers in separate cones; fruit an upright cone 2 to 4 inches long, dark violet until turning brown at maturity, borne on uppermost branches of tree

PROPAGATION seed, cold stratify up to one month

NOTES *A. fraseri* (Fraser fir) is a very similar species but is naturally restricted to the highest elevations of the southern Appalachians; cones of *A. fraseri* differ from balsam fir in having exserted bracts. Both firs, the only firs native to the eastern U.S., thrive on cool, moist, well-drained soils and should not be planted on hot, dry sites that receive full sun, although some sources indicate that *A. fraseri* is slightly more heat- and drought-tolerant than *A. balsamea*.

NATURAL RANGE Newfoundland and Labrador to the Mackenzie Valley, south to New York, Michigan, Minnesota, and in the mountains to West Virginia and northern Virginia

Acer nigrum

BLACK MAPLE
ACERACEAE

ZONES 4 to 8

SOIL dry to moist, well drained

LIGHT sun to shade

ATTRIBUTES large tree (to over 100 feet high) with dense, oval crown; leaves simple, opposite, often with three lobes and drooping appearance, dark green, turning shades of yellow, orange, and sometimes red in autumn; flowers yellowish green, in hanging clusters in early spring; fruit winged, about 1 1/2 inches long, in pairs

PROPAGATION seed, cold stratify for three months

NOTES Black maple is quite abundant in central New York, where it grows very well on rather dry, calcareous soils; seeing so much of it under natural conditions will convince anyone that black maple is truly different from sugar maple. Based on its growing well on such sites and its much greater western geographical range versus sugar maple, one can infer that black maple is relatively drought-tolerant; yet Gleason and Cronquist (1991) indicate that this species is more common along streams and occurs on sites more moist than for sugar maple. Perhaps black maple will tolerate either soil moisture extreme much better than the much more commonly planted sugar maple. Although the fall color is often reported as not as attractive as sugar maple, there is a tremendous range in fall color, at least in some areas. There is much opportunity for horticultural selections of this species.

NATURAL RANGE southern Quebec to southern Minnesota, south to Long Island, New Jersey, Delaware, western Virginia, western North Carolina, Tennessee, and northern Arkansas

Acer pensylvanicum

STRIPED MAPLE
ACERACEAE

ZONES 3 to 7

SOIL cool, moist, well drained

LIGHT sun to shade

ATTRIBUTES typically to about 25 feet tall; leaves simple, opposite, about 6 inches long, bright green, turning yellow in autumn; flowers greenish yellow, in 4- to 6-inch-long clusters in spring; fruit winged;

bark bright green with vertical chalky white stripes, with size becoming gray-brown

PROPAGATION seed, cold stratify for three to four months

NOTES Striped maple is a very beautiful small tree for rich, moist soils and shaded sites. Its green, white-striped bark is striking in any season, and its fall color is very attractive. The cultivar 'Erythrocladum' with bright coral-red young stems is worth looking for.

NATURAL RANGE Nova Scotia and southern Quebec to northern Minnesota, south to New York, Penn-

Acer nigrum

Abies balsamea

Abies fraseri

Acer pensylvanicum

Acer pensylvanicum, fall color

maple have been made primarily for form and fall color; Dirr (1998) lists many cultivars, including hybrids with silver maple (= *A.* ×*freemanii*), which have less problems than straight silver maple. Silver maple (*A. saccharinum*) and boxelder (*A. negundo*) are not thoroughly treated in this guide because—although these species are native to this region, naturally occurring on floodplains—they have too many liabilities in the landscape. However, for wetland restoration projects silver maple and boxelder, as well as red maple, would be very useful.

NATURAL RANGE Newfoundland to southeast Manitoba, south to Florida and eastern Texas, but missing from Iowa, most of Illinois, and northern Missouri

Acer saccharum

SUGAR MAPLE
ACERACEAE

ZONES 4 to 8

SOIL moist, well drained

LIGHT sun to shade

ATTRIBUTES large tree (75+ feet) with oval, dense crown; leaves simple, opposite, 3 to 6 inches long, typically five-lobed, turning one or more of the following colors in autumn: deep orange, red, and occasionally yellow; flowers greenish yellow, in drooping clusters; fruit a brown samara about $1^{1}/2$ inches long

PROPAGATION seed, cold stratify for three months

NOTES Sugar maple is indeed a beautiful tree, especially in autumn, but it really should be reserved for large areas on rich, moist, well-drained soils. Sugar maple is very intolerant of heat and salt stress and therefore generally is not a good street tree where these conditions are prevalent. Many cultivars, primarily selected for fall color and specific form, are available and are described in Dirr (1998). *Acer barbatum,* southern or Florida sugar maple, is native to the southern half of the eastern U.S., including the northern portion of the range covered here. While more heat-tolerant, it does not have the outstanding fall color of the more northern sugar maple.

NATURAL RANGE Nova Scotia and New Brunswick to Minnesota and eastern South Dakota, south to New Jersey, Delaware, western Virginia, northern Georgia, Tennessee, and Missouri

sylvania, Michigan, and in the mountains to North Carolina, Tennessee, and northern Georgia

Acer rubrum

RED MAPLE
ACERACEAE

ZONES 3 to 9

SOIL dry to wet, including occasional standing water

LIGHT sun to partial sun

ATTRIBUTES somewhat open-crowned (relative to sugar maple) tree to 60+ feet; leaves simple, opposite, 2 to 4 inches long, medium to dark green, turning shades of yellow, red, and orange in autumn; flowers in clusters, mostly dioecious, females red, males yellow when anthers open; fruit a red samara to 1 inch long in late spring

PROPAGATION seed, will germinate without pretreatment when ripe in late spring; softwood cuttings

NOTES Red maple is the best native maple for the widest range of growing conditions. Cultivars of red

Acer rubrum samaras

Acer rubrum, fall color

Acer saccharum in autumn

Aesculus flava

YELLOW BUCKEYE

HIPPOCASTANACEAE

ZONES 4 to 8

SOIL moist, well drained

LIGHT sun to partial shade

ATTRIBUTES large tree to 75+ feet high, with broadly oval crown; leaves palmately compound (five leaflets) to 8 inches long, dark green, shades of yellow and orange in autumn; flowers greenish yellow, tubular, about 1 inch long, borne along a 6- to 7-inch-long terminal stalk in early to mid spring; fruit a pear-shaped, smooth husk about 2^1/$_2$ inches in diameter, splitting open to release two seeds that are glossy and rich brown (except for "eye-spot"); bark

Aesculus flava bark

Aesculus flava in flower

Aesculus glabra flowers

initially smooth, but developing large plates with size

PROPAGATION seed, cold stratify for four months

NOTES Also listed as *A. octandra*. Yellow buckeye has some of the richest color in autumn, its leaves turning mostly shades of orange and bronze. It generally has a much nicer appearance toward the end of the growing season than does Ohio buckeye.

NATURAL RANGE southwestern Pennsylvania and southern Ohio to southern Illinois, south to northern Georgia and northern Alabama

Aesculus glabra
OHIO BUCKEYE
HIPPOCASTANACEAE

ZONES 4 to 7

SOIL moist, well drained

LIGHT sun to partial shade

ATTRIBUTES large tree to 75+ feet high, with broadly oval crown; leaves palmately compound (five leaflets), to 6 inches long, dark green, shades of yellow and orange in autumn; flowers greenish yellow, tubular, about 1 inch long, borne along a 4- to 7-inch-long terminal stalk in early to mid spring; fruit a round, prickly husk about 1 1/2 inches in diameter, splitting open to release one (usually) or two seeds that are glossy and rich brown (except for "eyespot"); bark irregular and corky

PROPAGATION seed, cold stratify for four months

NOTES Ohio buckeye is quite showy in flower, but its fruit are a bit messy and its leaves will turn brown

and drop in late summer if the soil is dry; the seed of all *Aesculus* species is poisonous.

NATURAL RANGE western Pennsylvania to southern Ontario, southern Wisconsin, Iowa, and Kansas, south to Tennessee, northern Alabama, Arkansas, and Texas

Aesculus pavia
RED BUCKEYE
HIPPOCASTANACEAE

ZONES 4 to 8

SOIL moist, well drained

LIGHT sun to shade

ATTRIBUTES often shrubby in habit, forming rounded mounds about 20+ feet high and wide; leaves opposite, palmately compound (five leaflets); flowers 1 1/2 inches long, tubular, red, in 4- to 8-inch-long terminal cluster in mid spring; fruit a nearly round, smooth husk, 2 inches in diameter, splitting open to release one or two glossy, brown seeds

PROPAGATION seed, cold stratify for four months

NOTES A hummingbird magnet when in flower in mid spring.

NATURAL RANGE coastal plain from North Carolina to Florida and Texas, and inland south to southern Missouri, southern Illinois, and Kentucky

Aesculus glabra, fall color

Aesculus pavia

Aesculus sylvatica

PAINTED BUCKEYE
HIPPOCASTANACEAE

ZONES 6 to 9

SOIL moist, well drained

LIGHT partial shade to shade

ATTRIBUTES often shrubby in habit, generally to 15 feet high, and spreading by root suckers; leaves opposite, palmately compound (five leaflets), generally turning yellow in autumn; flowers have shades of yellow, green, red, and pink and are in 4- to 8-inch-long clusters in mid spring; fruit a round, smooth husk about 1$1/2$ inches in diameter, splitting to release one to three glossy, rich brown seeds

PROPAGATION seed, cold stratify for four months

Aesculus sylvatica

Aesculus parviflora

Amelanchier arborea

NOTES Another small buckeye, but with a more southeastern U.S. geographical range, is *A. parviflora*, bottlebrush buckeye, which has nearly 1-foot-long terminal clusters of white flowers in early summer. Bottlebrush buckeye is generally a very dense, thicket-forming, tall shrub.

NATURAL RANGE southern Virginia to Georgia, eastern Alabama, and eastern Tennessee

Amelanchier arborea

DOWNY SERVICEBERRY
ROSACEAE

ZONES 4 to 9

SOIL moist, well drained best, but will tolerate dry and wet soils

LIGHT sun to partial shade

ATTRIBUTES one to few stems with rounded crown,

Amelanchier arborea fruit

Amelanchier arborea, fall color

Amelanchier canadensis

to 25+ feet tall; leaves simple, alternate, about 2 inches long, turning shades of red, orange, and yellow in autumn; flowers white, round, about 1 inch in diameter, in drooping clusters 2 to 4 inches long; fruit round, 1/4 to 1/3 inch wide, red to purple at maturity in late spring to early summer; bark gray with darker, longitudinal fissures

PROPAGATION seed, cold stratify for three to four months

NOTES Also known as juneberry, shadbush. Following the taxonomic treatment in Gleason and Cronquist (1991), there are two other similar species of *Amelanchier* in this region, *A. laevis* (smooth serviceberry) and *A. canadensis* (shadbush, eastern serviceberry). *Amelanchier laevis* differs from *A. arborea* in having coppery reddish leaves with hairless undersides about half-grown at flowering, and sweeter, juicier fruit; leaves of *A. arborea* at flowering are much less than half-grown and are green on top and whitish hairy below. *Amelanchier canadensis* differs from these species by its naturally shrubby habit and relatively short flower petals (less than 1/2 inch long, versus 1/2 to 3/4 inch long for *A. arborea* and *A. laevis*). Numerous cultivars from one or more of the above species have been selected, based primarily on flower display, summer leaf color and texture, growth habit, and fall color. Cultivars from the cross between *A. arborea* and *A. laevis* (= *A. ×grandiflora*) are especially nice. There are at least five other *Amelanchier* species native to this region, all mostly shrubby in habit (see *A. stolonifera* in the species descriptions for shrubs).

NATURAL RANGE Maine and New Brunswick and southern Quebec to southwest Ontario and Minnesota, south to Georgia, northwest Florida, Louisiana, and eastern Oklahoma

Aralia spinosa
DEVIL'S-WALKINGSTICK
ARALIACEAE

ZONES 4 to 9

SOIL dry to moist

LIGHT sun to shade

ATTRIBUTES dense, thicket-forming, top-heavy shrub or small tree to 20+ feet high; leaves alternate, twice and thrice pinnately compound, to 3 feet long, leaflets dark bluish green and about 3 inches long; flowers white, very small, but in 12- to 18-inch-wide cluster in mid summer; fruit purple-black, 1/4 inch in diameter, berrylike; stems very stout, heavily armed with sharp prickles

PROPAGATION seed, cold stratify for two to three months; dig root shoots that arise in clump

NOTES Also known as Hercules' club, devil's-walkingstick has a very impressive flower and fruit display, and its foliage is quite tropical-looking; its stout, prickly stems might be interesting in the winter garden. Because it spreads by root suckers, it may require some maintenance to keep in bounds.

NATURAL RANGE Delaware to southern Indiana and Missouri, south to Florida and Texas

Asimina triloba
PAWPAW
ANNONACEAE

ZONES 5 to 8

SOIL moist, well drained

LIGHT sun to shade

ATTRIBUTES pyramidal crown, often in thickets, to 20+ feet high; leaves alternate, simple, 6 to 12 inches long, dark green, turning shades of yellow and bronze in autumn; flowers round, about 1 1/2 inches in diameter, chocolate-red to purple, velvety in appearance, in mid spring; fruit 2 to 5 inches long, bright green, turning light yellow-green with brown blotches when ripe in autumn, with the sweet taste of banana-pineapple and the texture of custard

PROPAGATION seed, cold stratify for two to three months

NOTES The flowers, form, and fall colors are reason enough to plant this tree, and the tropical-tasting fruit is a real bonus. I bring a bag of pawpaw fruits into one of my classes each fall, and nearly everyone finds them very appealing. Do not forget to cut off the peel and remove the few very large, flat seeds.

NATURAL RANGE western New York and southern Ontario to southern Michigan and eastern Nebraska, south to Florida and Texas

Betula alleghaniensis
YELLOW BIRCH
BETULACEAE

ZONES 3 to 7

SOIL moist, well drained

Aralia spinosa

Asimina triloba

Asimina triloba flowers

LIGHT sun to partial sun

ATTRIBUTES large tree with very broad crown, to 75 feet high; leaves simple, alternate, 3 to 5 inches long, dark green, turning yellow in autumn; flowers in catkins; fruit conelike, barrel-shaped, upright, 1 to 1¹/2 inches long; bark initially bright, shiny yellow, becoming golden or bronze on trees to about 18 inches in diameter, then grayish brown with increasing size

PROPAGATION seed, typically will germinate without pretreatment if sown on surface of media

NOTES Yellow birch adds much color and texture to the winter garden, especially when blanketed with snow. It will not tolerate hot, dry conditions.

NATURAL RANGE Newfoundland to southeast Manitoba, south to Delaware, Pennsylvania, Ohio, northern Indiana, Wisconsin, Minnesota, and occasionally Iowa and along the mountains to northern Georgia

Betula alleghaniensis

Betula lenta
SWEET BIRCH
BETULACEAE

ZONES 4 to 7

SOIL moist, well drained best, but will grow on drier soils

LIGHT sun to partial sun

ATTRIBUTES generally to about 50 feet high; leaves alternate, simple, $2^1/2$ to 6 inches long, shiny, dark green, turning golden yellow in autumn; flowers in catkins; fruit upright, barrel-shaped, conelike, about 1 inch long; bark nearly black, developing smaller ridges and resembling black cherry (*Prunus serotina*) but not as dark

PROPAGATION seed, typically will germinate without pretreatment if sown on surface of media

NOTES Both yellow and sweet birch twigs and cut, fresh bark have oil-of-wintergreen fragrance and taste. Neither species, nor the next, is bothered by the bronze birch borer, which kills paper birch. Roundleaf birch (*B. uber*) is an extremely rare species known from only one stand in the Jefferson National Forest in Virginia. Roundleaf birch is supposedly smaller than sweet or yellow birch. The mature specimen I saw recently at the New York Botanical Garden suggested some landscape potential.

NATURAL RANGE southern Maine and southern Quebec to Delaware, Ohio, and Kentucky, and in the mountains to Georgia and Alabama

Betula nigra
RIVER BIRCH
BETULACEAE

ZONES 3 to 9

SOIL moist to wet (will tolerate drought once established)

LIGHT sun to partial sun

ATTRIBUTES wide-spreading crown of arching branches, to 70+ feet high, leaves simple, alternate, $1^1/2$ to $3^1/2$ inches long, shiny, dark green, turning dull yellow in autumn; flowers in catkins; fruit upright, barrel-shaped, conelike, to $1^1/2$ inches long; bark exfoliates into papery sheets, showing underlying colors in shades of pink, brown, gray, and occasionally white

PROPAGATION seed, will germinate without pretreatment; softwood cuttings

NOTES Few trees, native or otherwise, rival river birch for bark display. River birch is also an exceptionally windfirm, disease- and insect-free species that develops a very broad, somewhat pendulous crown with size. If one wants a fast-growing tree for a site in full sun (but not excessively dry) and is concerned about the general weak-wooded nature of trees that grow very fast (like eastern cottonwood and silver maple), I think river birch is the best choice of medium-size trees. Cultivars available include Heritage®, which has glossier leaves and white and white-pink bark underlying exfoliating layers.

NATURAL RANGE New Hampshire to Florida, west to southern Ohio, southern Michigan, southeastern Minnesota, eastern Kansas, and Texas

Betula papyrifera
PAPER BIRCH
BETULACEAE

ZONES 2 to 6

SOIL moist, well drained best, but will tolerate much drier conditions further north in this region

LIGHT sun

ATTRIBUTES to 70 feet high, typically single-stemmed naturally but often sold in clumps by nurseries, etc.; leaves simple, alternate, 2 to 4 inches long, dark green, turning golden yellow in autumn; flowers in catkins; fruit pendent, cylindrical, conelike structure to $1^1/2$ inches long; bark chalky white, slowly exfoliating in large, papery sheets

PROPAGATION seed, sow on surface of media, germination improved with cold stratification for two to three months

NOTES Paper birch is truly a boreal species, thriving at the highest elevations in the Northeast and throughout much of Canada. While no other native species has such a striking chalky white, exfoliating bark, paper birch is susceptible to the bronze birch borer, especially in the hotter portions of this region and further south. Mountain paper birch (*B. cordifolia* = *B. papyrifera* var. *cordifolia*) is a similar species except more limited geographically in the region to the highest mountains. Mountain paper birch has more heart-shaped leaves than paper birch, and its bark is often reddish cinnamon in color, especially younger specimens.

NATURAL RANGE Labrador to Alaska, south to New Jersey, West Virginia, northern Indiana, and northeastern Iowa

Betula lenta

Betula nigra

Betula nigra, fall color

Betula papyrifera

Betula populifolia

GRAY BIRCH

BETULACEAE

ZONES 3 to 7

SOIL dry, sterile, sandy or rocky, to wet; will grow on nearly any site but will become chlorotic on soils with high pH

LIGHT sun

ATTRIBUTES typically a multiple-stemmed clump in nature, to about 30 feet high; leaves simple, alternate, about 3 inches long, glossy, dark green, turning golden yellow in autumn; flowers in catkins; fruit pendent, cylindrical, conelike, about 1 inch long; bark dull white to gray, often with black patches below major branches, not exfoliating

PROPAGATION seed, sow on surface of media, cold stratification for two to three months will improve germination; softwood cuttings

NOTES Gray birch is an exceptional species for the restoration of dry (to wet) acidic, infertile, sandy or rocky sites and has good resistance to the bronze birch borer, although the foliage can be heavily damaged by leaf miner. With all the attention on finding

Betula populifolia

Betula populifolia in autumn

superior cultivars of birch species, it is most surprising that gray birch has been so neglected, especially given its ornamental features and tolerance to such severe growing conditions.

NATURAL RANGE Nova Scotia to southern Quebec, southern New Jersey and Pennsylvania, with outlying stations in northern Virginia, southern Ontario, northern Ohio, and northeastern Indiana

Carpinus caroliniana
AMERICAN HORNBEAM
BETULACEAE

ZONES 3 to 9

SOIL moist, well drained best, but will tolerate drier and wetter conditions

LIGHT sun to shade

ATTRIBUTES leaning or somewhat twisted main stem, often naturally in small clumps, to about 30 feet high; leaves simple, alternate, about 3 inches long, often shiny, dark green, turning shades of red, purple, orange, and yellow in autumn; flowers in catkins; fruit leafy, lobed, attached to very small nutlet; bark slate-gray, smooth, fluted, like a tense muscle in appearance

PROPAGATION seed, warm stratify for two months then cold stratify for two months

NOTES American hornbeam tolerates deep shade and has quite unusual bark and often beautiful fall color.

NATURAL RANGE Nova Scotia to Minnesota, south to Florida and Texas

Carya illinoinensis
PECAN
JUGLANDACEAE

ZONES 5 to 9

SOIL moist, well drained, but will tolerate occasional flooding

LIGHT sun to partial sun

ATTRIBUTES 70 to 100 feet high; leaves pinnately compound, alternate, 12 to 20 inches long, shiny, dark green; flowers in catkins; fruit ellipsoidal, about 1½ inches long, containing single sweet seed; bark becomes scaly with age

Carpinus caroliniana

Carya illinoinensis

PROPAGATION seed, cold stratify for three months
NOTES This species is the commerical source of pecans; many cultivars have been selected for superior fruit characteristics. Although the straight species may not fruit heavily, it is still a fine, large shade tree with very handsome foliage. Pecan also has potential for wetland restoration projects in the central and southern portions of this region because it naturally occurs on stream floodplains. Another native wetland *Carya* species in this region in similar or often more deeply flooded soils is the water hickory (*C. aquatica*).
NATURAL RANGE southwest Ohio to Iowa and eastern Kansas, south to Alabama, Texas, and New Mexico

Carya laciniosa
SHELLBARK HICKORY
JUGLANDACEAE
ZONES 5 to 8
SOIL dry to wet
LIGHT sun to partial sun

Carya laciniosa

ATTRIBUTES to about 75+ feet high; leaves pinnately compound (usually seven leaflets), alternate, 12 to 24 inches long, dark green; flowers in catkins; fruit round, about $2^{1}/_{2}$ inches in diameter, containing single sweet seed; bark slate-gray, peels away from main trunk in broad, long strips
PROPAGATION seed, cold stratify for three months
NOTES Shellbark hickory naturally occurs on floodplains and in other poorly drained areas so would be an exceptional large, long-lived tree with excellent wildlife value for wetland restoration projects; and, like so many species naturally restricted to wetlands, shellbark hickory grows well on well-drained sites.
NATURAL RANGE New York and southern Ontario to Iowa and eastern Kansas, south to North Carolina

Carya ovata
SHAGBARK HICKORY
JUGLANDACEAE
ZONES 4 to 8
SOIL dry to moist
LIGHT sun to partial sun
ATTRIBUTES long, nearly elliptical crown, to 80+ feet high; leaves pinnately compound (usually five leaflets), alternate, deep green, turning golden yellow in autumn; flowers in catkins; fruit round, to $1^{1}/_{2}$ inches in diameter, containing single sweet seed; bark slate-gray, peels away from main trunk in narrow to broad, long strips
PROPAGATION seed, cold stratify for three months
NOTES Shagbark hickory, with its deep taproot, is well adapted to very dry soils. Eight additional *Carya* species are native to this region; most have excellent golden yellow fall color and timber, fuel, and wildlife value but are too large and messy (fruit and nuts especially) for many sites. Four that do especially well on drier sites are pignut (*C. glabra*), pale hickory (*C. pallida*), black hickory (*C. texana*), and mockernut hickory (*C. tomentosa*). Another native hickory, bitternut hickory (*C. cordiformis*), is best suited to moist soils.
NATURAL RANGE southern Maine and southern Quebec to southeastern Minnesota and western Nebraska, south to Georgia and eastern Texas

Carya ovata

Carya glabra

Carya tomentosa

Carya cordiformis

Celtis occidentalis

HACKBERRY

ULMACEAE

ZONES 3 to 9

SOIL dry to wet

LIGHT sun to partial shade

ATTRIBUTES to about 50+ feet high; leaves simple, alternate, 2 to 5 inches long, bright green, occasionally turning pale or golden yellow in autumn; flowers inconspicuous; fruit round, $1/3$ inch wide, dark purple at maturity; bark irregular, consisting of warty projections, unusual but not necessarily attractive

PROPAGATION seed, cold stratify for two to three months

Celtis occidentalis

NOTES Hackberry is a nearly indestructible large tree for a wide range of sites and has unique bark and occasional decent autumn color. A few cultivars with more distinct form and foliage characteristics are available, including 'Prairie Pride'. Hackberry somewhat resembles the native elms in this region but does not develop the majestic, sweeping, vase-shaped form of American elm; however, hackberry is not susceptible to Dutch elm disease and elm yellows, which prevent the planting of native elms. A similar but less common native species, sugarberry (*C. laevigata*), occurs on wet soils in the southern half of this region. Sugarberry leaves are smaller, glossier, and more lance-shaped than hackberry leaves. The third *Celtis* species in our region is the dwarf hackberry (*C. tenuifolia*), which often has a shrub stature and leaves lacking teeth along its margin.

NATURAL RANGE southern Quebec to southern Manitoba, south to Virginia, Arkansas, and Oklahoma, and locally to North Carolina, Georgia, Alabama, and Mississippi

Cercis canadensis
EASTERN REDBUD
FABACEAE

ZONES 4 to 9

SOIL moist, well drained

LIGHT sun to shade

ATTRIBUTES single- or multiple-stemmed, somewhat flat-topped crown, to about 25 feet high; leaves simple, alternate, heart-shaped, about 4 inches in diameter, bluish green, turning pale or golden yellow in autumn; flowers reddish purple in bud, opening to rosy pink, about 1/2 inch long, in clusters along stem, early spring; fruit a leathery, narrow, brown pod to 3 inches long; bark becoming blackish and scaly with age

PROPAGATION seed, acid or mechanically scarify, followed by cold stratification for one to two months

NOTES Eastern redbud is an exceptional, small ornamental tree, especially for shaded conditions. Cultivars include clear pink flowers ('Rubye Atkinson', 'Tennessee Pink'), double pink flowers ('Flame'), white flowers ('Alba', 'Dwarf White', 'Royal White'),

Cercis canadensis

Cercis canadensis in autumn

Cladrastis kentukea flowers

purplish red foliage ('Forest Pansy'), glossy foliage ('Oklahoma', a cultivar of var. *texensis*, Texas redbud) and weeping form ('Covey').

NATURAL RANGE Connecticut and southern New York to southern Michigan, Iowa, and eastern Nebraska, south to Florida and northern Mexico

Chamaecyparis thyoides
ATLANTIC WHITE-CEDAR
CUPRESSACEAE

ZONES 4 to 8

SOIL moist to wet

LIGHT sun to partial sun

ATTRIBUTES narrow crown, to about 50 feet high; leaves scalelike, bluish green, evergreen, turning shades of bronze or brown in winter; flowers inconspicuous; fruit a globose, waxy, wrinkled cone, 1/4 inch wide; bark ash-gray, fibrous

PROPAGATION seed, will require cold stratification for three months; cuttings collected in late fall and early winter

NOTES Atlantic white-cedar naturally occurs on saturated organic (peat) soils not far from the eastern U.S. coast. While it does tolerate very wet, acidic conditions, it also grows well on much drier soils, including the rather basic soils of central New York. Cultivars are becoming increasingly available and have distinct forms (including compact) and foliage colors (including golden yellow). This native plant has been neglected too long because of the much wider availability of so many cultivars of nonnative junipers and other evergreens.

NATURAL RANGE southern Maine and central New Hampshire to Florida and Mississippi

Cladrastis kentukea
YELLOWWOOD
FABACEAE

ZONES 4 to 8

SOIL dry to moist, well drained

LIGHT sun to partial sun

ATTRIBUTES low-branching tree with broad crown, to 50 feet high; leaves pinnately compound, alternate, to 12 inches long, bright green, turning golden yellow in autumn; flowers white, about 1 inch long, fragrant, borne in an 8- to 14-inch-long, pendent cluster in late spring; fruit a leathery pod to 4 inches

Chamaecyparis thyoides

Cladrastis kentukea

long; bark gray, smooth, resembles beech (but slightly darker)

PROPAGATION seed, acid or mechanically scarify then cold stratify for three months

NOTES Yellowwood is quite uncommon over its range and when found is often on limestone cliffs and other calcareous soils. It has no rival when in bloom late in the spring, although it does not bloom profusely every year. Its wood is indeed bright yellow.

NATURAL RANGE irregularly from West Virginia and western North Carolina to southern Ohio, southern Indiana, Alabama, Mississippi, southern Missouri, Arkansas, and Oklahoma

Cornus alternifolia
ALTERNATE-LEAF DOGWOOD
CORNACEAE

ZONES 3 to 7

SOIL moist, well drained

LIGHT sun to partial shade

ATTRIBUTES rather square form of distinct layers of horizontal branches, to about 20 feet tall; leaves simple, slightly alternate, 2 to 5 inches long, turning shades of purple and red and sometimes pink in autumn; flowers yellowish white, very small but packed in a flat-topped cluster about 2 inches in diameter in mid to late spring; fruit bluish black, 1/4 to 1/3 inch wide, borne on pinkish red fruit stalks; bark can be green or red on smaller trees

PROPAGATION seed, warm stratify for two to five months then cold stratify for two to three months

NOTES Also known as the pagoda dogwood, alter-

Cornus alternifolia

Cornus alternifolia, fall color

nate-leaf dogwood lacks the large, white, showy bracts that make such a fine display for flowering dogwood, but its dense clusters of white flowers, often rich fall color, and unusual branch architecture make alternate-leaf dogwood a choice small tree for partially shaded areas. Additionally, this species is much cold hardier than flowering dogwood and is resistant to anthracnose, which is currently devastating flowering dogwood.

NATURAL RANGE Newfoundland and Nova Scotia to Minnesota, south to Florida, Alabama, and Arkansas

Cornus florida
FLOWERING DOGWOOD
CORNACEAE

ZONES 5 to 9

SOIL moist, well drained

LIGHT sun to partial shade

ATTRIBUTES low-branched tree with somewhat horizontal branching, forming a rather mounded crown, to about 25 feet high; leaves simple, opposite, 3 to 6 inches long, dark green, turning shades of red, orange, and purple in autumn; flowers actually very small (about 1/4 inch wide), greenish yellow, in clusters surrounded by four large (about 2 inches long), white bracts before leaves emerge in spring; fruit bright red, ellipsoidal, 1/3 to 1/2 inches long; bark develops small, blocky ridges that resemble an alligator hide

Cornus florida

Cotinus obovatus

Cornus florida fruit

PROPAGATION seed, cold stratify for three to four months

NOTES While flowering dogwood may indeed be the most beautiful native tree of this region, its use should be tempered given its susceptibility to anthracnose, a very serious disease. Cultivars have been selected for disease resistance, as well as variegated foliage, pink and red flowers, double flowers, larger flowers, more flowers, yellow fruit, weeping form, compact form, and greater cold tolerance. Additional selections have been made from crosses between *C. florida* and *C. kousa* (Chinese dogwood) and are sold as the Stellar® series; these are quite

attractive and are resistant to anthracnose. Flowering dogwood should not be planted in poorly or excessively drained soils in full sun.

NATURAL RANGE Maine to southern Ontario, Michigan, Illinois, Missouri, and Oklahoma, south to Florida and northeastern Mexico

Cotinus obovatus
AMERICAN SMOKETREE
ANACARDIACEAE

ZONES 4 to 8

SOIL dry to moist, well drained

LIGHT sun to partial sun

ATTRIBUTES rounded crown often on multiple trunks, to about 25 feet high; leaves simple, alternate, 2 to 5 inches long, broadly elliptical, bluish green, turning shades of orange, yellow, red, and purple in autumn; flowers dioecious, greenish, in open clusters 6 to 10 inches long, in mid to late spring; fruit inconspicuous; bark becoming scaly and dark

PROPAGATION seed, cold stratify for three to five months

NOTES American smoketree is one of the most underutilized, small native trees with outstanding fall color, especially for dry sites. It naturally occurs on soils high in calcium so is tolerant of very high pH.

NATURAL RANGE very local in Tennessee, Alabama, and the Edwards Plateau of Texas

Crataegus crus-galli

COCKSPUR HAWTHORN

ROSACEAE

ZONES 4 to 7

SOIL dry to moist, well drained

LIGHT sun

ATTRIBUTES wide-spreading and dense crown, to 30 feet high; leaves simple, alternate, 1 to 4 inches long, glossy, dark green, turning shades of red, purple, and brown in autumn; flowers white, $1/2$ to $2/3$ inch in diameter, in upright flat clusters 2 to 3 inches wide; fruit deep red, to $1/2$ inch wide, persisting into winter; stems with very sharp, slender, slightly curved thorns, $1^1/2$ to 3 inches long

PROPAGATION seed, acid or mechanically scarify, followed by warm stratification for four months, then cold stratification for five months

NOTES The flower display of cockspur hawthorn contrasts very nicely with its very dark, glossy foliage. While thorns are generally present on hawthorn species, those of cockspur hawthorn are especially large, sharp, and numerous. Hawthorns are excellent choices for dry, hot sites, although they are susceptible to a number of insect and disease problems. Taxonomically, they are a most difficult group; Gleason and Cronquist (1991) recognize twenty-two native or naturalized hawthorns in the Northeast.

NATURAL RANGE Quebec to Florida, west to Minnesota, Kansas, and Texas

Crataegus mollis

DOWNY HAWTHORN

ROSACEAE

ZONES 3 to 6

SOIL dry to moist, well drained

LIGHT sun

ATTRIBUTES wide-spreading crown, to about 25 feet high; leaves simple, alternate, 2 to 4 inches long and nearly as broad, turning shades of yellow, brown, and red in fall; flowers white, 1 inch in diameter, in 3- to 4-inch-wide clusters in spring; fruit red, nearly round, $1/2$ to 1 inch in diameter

PROPAGATION seed, warm stratify for four months then cold stratify for four months

NOTES Downy hawthorn can have very serious problems with rust disease, which covers its fruit and leaves.

Crataegus crus-galli

Crataegus phaenopyrum

NATURAL RANGE New England and southeast Canada to Alabama, west to Minnesota, Kansas, and Oklahoma

Crataegus phaenopyrum

WASHINGTON HAWTHORN

ROSACEAE

ZONES 4 to 8

SOIL dry to moist, well drained

LIGHT sun

ATTRIBUTES wide-spreading, dense crown, to 30 feet high; leaves simple, alternate, 1 to 3 inches long, glossy, dark green, with shades of red, purple, and orange in autumn; flowers white, $1/2$ inch wide, in flat clusters in late spring; fruit orange-red, glossy, $1/4$ inch wide, persisting into winter; stems covered with 1- to 3-inch-long thorns

PROPAGATION seed, warm stratify for four months then cold stratify for four months

NOTES Washington hawthorn is one of the most attractive native hawthorns in flower, foliage, and fruit.

NATURAL RANGE Pennsylvania to northern Florida, west to Illinois and Missouri

Crataegus punctata

THICKET HAWTHORN
ROSACEAE

ZONES 4 to 7

SOIL dry to moist, well drained

LIGHT sun

ATTRIBUTES wide-spreading crown, to 35 feet high; leaves rather elliptical, not lobed, about 3 inches long, turning scarlet in autumn; flowers white, about $3/4$ inch wide, in mid spring; fruit dull red, $3/4$ inch wide

PROPAGATION seed, warm stratify for four months then cold stratify for four months

NOTES Thicket hawthorn is especially sensitive to rust disease. Variety *inermis* (= 'Ohio Pioneer') is an excellent selection for its lack of thorns and its showy flower and fruit display.

NATURAL RANGE Newfoundland, Quebec, and New England, to South Carolina and Georgia, west to Minnesota, Iowa, and Oklahoma

Crataegus viridis

GREEN HAWTHORN
ROSACEAE

ZONES 4 to 7

SOIL dry to moist, well drained

LIGHT sun

ATTRIBUTES dense, wide-spreading crown, to 30 feet high; leaves simple, alternate, $11/2$ to $31/2$ inches long, glossy, dark green, turning shades of red and purple in autumn; flowers white, $3/4$ inch in diameter, in a 2-inch-wide cluster in spring; fruit bright red, $1/4$ to $1/3$ inch wide, persisting into winter; stems covered with thorns to $11/2$ inches long; bark exfoliates as tree size increases, exposing underlying orange-brown bark

Crataegus viridis

PROPAGATION seed, warm stratify for four months then cold stratify for four months

NOTES The cultivar 'Winter King' has larger ($1/2$ inch wide), deeper red fruit.

NATURAL RANGE Delaware to Florida and Texas, and north in the Mississippi Valley to southwest Indiana, Missouri, southeast Kansas, and Oklahoma

Diospyros virginiana

PERSIMMON
EBENACEAE

ZONES 4 to 9

SOIL dry to wet

LIGHT sun to partial shade

ATTRIBUTES modest size and often in thickets on drier sites, reaching 90+ feet high on rich, moist, well-drained sites; leaves simple, alternate, $21/4$ to $51/2$ inches long, dark green, turning pale yellow-green or reddish purple in autumn; flowers dioecious, whitish, bell-shaped, $1/3$ (male) to $3/5$ (female) inch long; fruit nearly round, about $11/4$ inches in diameter, bright green, waxy, and firm, turning pale orange and gooey when ripe in autumn and holding one to eight rather large seeds; bark consists of thick, nearly black, blocky ridges that resemble an alligator hide

Diospyros virginiana

Fagus grandifolia

Diospyros virginiana flowers

PROPAGATION seed, cold stratify for two to three months

NOTES Persimmon fruit, when ripe, reminds me of an overripe apricot soaked in honey. Cultivars have been selected for improved fruit characteristics.

NATURAL RANGE southeast Connecticut and southern New York to Florida, west to Iowa, Kansas, and Texas

Fagus grandifolia
AMERICAN BEECH
FAGACEAE

ZONES 4 to 9
SOIL moist, well drained
LIGHT sun to shade
ATTRIBUTES massive, dense crown, often with numerous, much smaller root suckers beneath; to 70+

feet high; leaves simple, alternate, 2 to 5 inches long, glossy, dark green, turning golden bronze in autumn; flowers inconspicuous; fruit about 3/4 inch long, prickly, holding one to three triangular, edible seeds; bark light gray and smooth regardless of size

PROPAGATION seed, cold stratify for three months
NOTES One of the most stately native trees but has been affected quite seriously by beech bark disease in much of the Northeast, and resistant cultivars are not yet available.
NATURAL RANGE Nova Scotia to northern Florida, west to Wisconsin, eastern Illinois, southeast Missouri, eastern Oklahoma, and eastern Texas

Fraxinus americana
WHITE ASH
OLEACEAE

ZONES 4 to 9
SOIL moist, well drained
LIGHT sun to partial sun
ATTRIBUTES pyramidal crown when small, becoming rounded with size, to 80 feet high; leaves pinnately compound (five to nine leaflets), opposite, 8 to 15 inches long, dark green, turning shades of purple, red, orange, and yellow; flowers dioecious, inconspicuous; fruit brown, 1 to 2 inches long, shaped like an oar; bark consists of narrow, interlacing ridges

PROPAGATION seed, warm stratify for one month then cold stratify for two months
NOTES Of the native ashes, site selection is most

Fraxinus americana

critical for white ash as it will not do well on dry or
wet soils, or sites subjected to other stresses. But on
suitable sites (i.e., rich, moist, well-drained soils),
white ash becomes an exceptional shade tree, often
with outstanding autumn color. Numerous cultivars
have been selected for absence of fruit (i.e., male
trees) and superior form and fall color.

NATURAL RANGE Nova Scotia to Minnesota, south
to Florida and Texas

Fraxinus nigra
BLACK ASH
OLEACEAE

ZONES 2 to 5

SOIL moist to wet, including occasional standing
water

LIGHT sun to partial sun

ATTRIBUTES to 50 feet high; leaves pinnately compound (seven to eleven leaflets), opposite, 12 to 18
inches long, bright to dark green, occasionally turning golden in autumn; flowers dioecious, inconspicuous; fruit elliptical, brown, about $1^1/2$ inch long;
bark corky and scaly

PROPAGATION seed, warm stratify for one month
then cold stratify for two months

NOTES Black ash and green ash (*F. pennsylvanica*)
are naturally found primarily in wetlands, so have
much potential for wetland restoration projects.
Water ash (*F. caroliniana*) and pumpkin ash (*F. profunda*) also are native wetland species in this region.

Fraxinus nigra

Of these four, black ash is by far the most cold-
tolerant.

NATURAL RANGE Newfoundland and Quebec to
Manitoba, south to Delaware, West Virginia, Indiana, and Iowa

Fraxinus pennsylvanica
GREEN ASH
OLEACEAE

ZONES 3 to 9

SOIL dry to wet

LIGHT sun to partial sun

ATTRIBUTES rounded crown, to 60 feet high; leaves
pinnately compound (five to nine leaflets), to 12

Fraxinus pennsylvanica

inches long, glossy, bright green, turning yellow in autumn; flowers dioecious, inconspicuous; fruit 1 to 2 inches long, brown, rather cyclindrical; bark consists of narrow, interlacing ridges

PROPAGATION seed, warm stratify for two months then cold stratify for four months

NOTES Green ash and its many cultivars are widely planted as street trees because this species tolerates such a wide range of site conditions and has excellent foliage (including fall color) and form. Some cultivars are seedless, or have superior form and foliage (including fall color).

NATURAL RANGE Nova Scotia and Quebec, to Alberta, south to Florida and Texas

Fraxinus quadrangulata
BLUE ASH
OLEACEAE

ZONES 4 to 7

SOIL dry to moist, well drained

LIGHT sun to partial sun

ATTRIBUTES to about 60 feet high; leaves pinnately compound (seven to eleven leaflets), opposite, 7 to 14 inches long, shiny, dark green, turning pale yellow in autumn; flowers dioecious, inconspicuous; fruit elliptical, about 1 inch long; young stems four-sided; bark scaly

PROPAGATION seed, warm stratify for two months then cold stratify for four months

NOTES The cultivar 'True Blue' may be faster growing than the species.

NATURAL RANGE southern Ontario to southern Michigan, southern Wisconsin, and eastern Kansas, south to West Virginia, Georgia, Alabama, and Oklahoma

Gleditsia triacanthos
HONEYLOCUST
FABACEAE

ZONES 4 to 9

SOIL dry to wet

LIGHT sun

ATTRIBUTES wide-spreading crown, 50 to 70+ feet high; leaves pinnately and bipinnately compound, alternate, 6 to 8 inches long, shiny, bright green, turning shades of yellow in autumn; flowers greenish yellow, borne in a 2- to 4-inch-long, cylindrical cluster; fruit (on female trees only) a leathery, finally brownish black pod, strap-shaped, about 12 inches long and 1 inch wide, filled with numerous beanlike but very hard seeds; bark dark, eventually developing broad plates; stems and main bole of naturally occurring trees covered with numerous very sharp and long, branched thorns

PROPAGATION seed, acid scarify for one to two hours (will result in individuals that will develop thorns; cultivars are budded onto these seedlings)

NOTES Honeylocust has an exceptionally light-textured crown and tolerates a great range of difficult site conditions. It has been overplanted because of these characteristics, and because of the loss of American elm (*Ulmus americana*) to the landscape. All honeylocust sold are cultivars of var. *inermis,* or thornless honeylocust, as the straight species has numerous, long, vicious thorns. Cultivars have been further selected for interesting foliage characteristics (golden or ruby-red new growth) or form, and are typically male selections so there is no fruit litter (which can be substantial on female trees). Water locust (*G. aquatica*) is the only other species of *Gleditsia* native to this region. Water locust occurs in swamps, especially along larger rivers of the Midwest. It differs from honeylocust mainly in having a much shorter pod (to only 2 inches long) and in its greater tolerance to deeper and more prolonged flooding.

NATURAL RANGE Pennsylvania to Tennessee and western Florida, west to southern Minnesota, southeastern South Dakota and Texas, and widely escaping cultivation elsewhere

Gymnocladus dioicus
KENTUCKY COFFEETREE
FABACEAE

ZONES 3 to 8

SOIL dry to moist, well drained

LIGHT sun

ATTRIBUTES narrow, contorted crown of stout branches, to about 75 feet high; leaves bipinnately compound, to 3 feet long, dark or bluish green, turning shades of yellow in autumn; flowers dioecious, about 1/3 inch long, in pyramidal clusters 8 to 12 inches long (male cluster shorter), late spring; fruit a leathery, thick, dark brown pod, about 6 inches long

Fraxinus quadrangulata fruit

Gleditsia triacanthos, immature fruit

Gleditsia triacanthos in autumn

and to 2 inches wide, holding a few large, very hard, blackish seeds; bark gray, scaly

PROPAGATION seed, acid scarify for four to six hours

NOTES Kentucky coffeetree is a naturally uncommon tree that may be a bit coarse (especially large leaves and stout stems) for some tastes. If the main stem is damaged, it will develop prolific root sprouts, eventually forming a thicket. A few cultivars promise unique form.

NATURAL RANGE New York to southern Minnesota and southeastern South Dakota, south to western Virginia, Tennessee, Arkansas, and Oklahoma

Halesia carolina
CAROLINA SILVERBELL
STYRACACEAE

ZONES 4 to 8

SOIL moist, well drained

LIGHT sun to partial shade

ATTRIBUTES to about 50 feet high; leaves simple, alternate, 2 to 5 inches long, dark green, turning yellow or yellow-green in autumn; flowers white, bell-shaped, about 3/4 inch long, in clusters all along stem, in spring; fruit woody, four-winged, brown, about 1 inch long

PROPAGATION seed, warm stratify for two to four months then cold stratify for two to three months

NOTES Also listed as *H. tetraptera*. Cultivars have been selected for larger or pinkish flowers, variegated foliage, and unusual form. There is quite a bit of flower and overall size variation in this species if one accepts the decision among most taxonomists to put *H. monticola* (mountain silverbell) into *H. carolina*. The former species has larger flowers, fruit, and overall height—I have seen some in the southern Appalachians that reach 4 feet in diameter! Regardless, *Halesia* species are really choice shade-tolerant trees.

NATURAL RANGE western Virginia to southern Ohio and southern Illinois, south to Florida and eastern Texas

Ilex montana
MOUNTAIN WINTERBERRY
AQUIFOLIACEAE

ZONES 5 to 7

SOIL moist, well drained

Gymnocladus dioicus

Halesia carolina

Ilex montana

LIGHT sun to shade

ATTRIBUTES typically a large shrub but can reach 30+ feet high; leaves simple, alternate, about 4 inches long; flowers dioecious, very small; fruit rich red, round, $1/3$ to $1/2$ inch in diameter

PROPAGATION seed is difficult, will require multiple cycles of warm and cold stratification for germination; softwood cuttings treated with rooting hormone

NOTES Mountain winterberry will never lessen the popularity of the American holly (*I. opaca*), but female specimens do have a nice fruit display from autumn into early winter, and it is a very shade-tolerant small tree or large shrub. With all the attention to selecting cultivars for *I. verticillata* (winterberry), perhaps there is some potential to find individuals of mountain winterberry with better fruit production, retention, and color.

NATURAL RANGE New York to Tennessee, Georgia, and eastern Alabama

Ilex opaca
AMERICAN HOLLY
AQUIFOLIACEAE

ZONES 5 to 9

SOIL moist, well drained

LIGHT sun to partial shade

ATTRIBUTES dense, pyramidal crown with foliage from top to bottom, to 50 feet high; leaves simple, alternate, about 3 inches long, leathery, with spine-tipped margin, dark green (although older leaves become yellow-green before falling), evergreen; flowers dioecious, small, in clusters; fruit round,

red, $1/4$ to $1/2$ inch wide, persisting into winter; bark smooth, gray, beechlike

PROPAGATION seed is difficult, will require multiple cycles of warm and cold for germination; stem cuttings just after summer growth hardens

NOTES Where cold hardy, this species is among the finest native woody plants in the region for landscaping purposes, because of its thick, leathery, dark, evergreen leaves; clusters of bright red fruit; and dense, pyramidal form. More than one thousand available cultivars promise better form, foliage, or fruit characteristics (including yellow or orange).

NATURAL RANGE near the coast from Maine to Maryland, widely distributed in the southern states from Virginia to Kentucky and southern Missouri, south to Florida and Texas

Juniperus virginiana
EASTERN REDCEDAR
CUPRESSACEAE

ZONES 3 to 9

SOIL dry to moist, well drained

LIGHT sun

ATTRIBUTES dense, pyramidal crown, to about 45

Ilex opaca

Juniperus virginiana

Larix laricina in bog, backed by *Picea mariana*, autumn

feet high; leaves evergreen, on young specimens needlelike and bluish green, on older specimens scalelike and dark green; flowers dioecious, inconspicuous; fruit somewhat round, bluish black, white waxy on surface, 1/4 inch wide, when crushed has smell of gin; bark fibrous, reddish brown

PROPAGATION seed is difficult, remove waxy seed coat by mechanical scarification (e.g., in a blender) then cold stratify to improve germination; softwood cuttings

NOTES Eastern redcedar is a real workhorse on barren, dry soils (regardless of pH) in full sun throughout its range and is often overlooked for the landscape because of the many cultivars of Chinese, savin, Rocky Mountain, and singleseed junipers (*J. chinensis, J. sabina, J. scopulorum,* and *J. squamata,* respectively)—all not native to this region. Many cultivars have been selected for form (including dwarf, compact, columnar, and spreading) and foliage color (including bluish, bright green, golden, and silvery gray). This species is the alternate host for cedar apple rust, which is more of a problem for apple than for juniper species.

NATURAL RANGE southern Maine and southern Quebec to North Dakota, south to Georgia, northwest Florida and Texas

Larix laricina
TAMARACK
PINACEAE

ZONES 2 to 4

SOIL moist to wet

LIGHT sun

ATTRIBUTES wide-spreading, open crown, to about 50+ feet high; leaves needlelike, alternate along current season's growth or whorled on spur shoots, about 1 inch long, bluish green, turning golden yellow in mid to late autumn; flowers inconspicuous; fruit a brown, egg-shaped cone to 2/3 inch long, borne upright along twig; bark dark brown, scaly

PROPAGATION seed, cold stratify for one to two months to improve germination

NOTES Also known as the eastern larch. While its European (*L. decidua*) and Japanese (*L. kaempferi*) relatives are much more commonly planted, tamarack is a beautiful, deciduous conifer that thrives on cold, wet sites in full sun. I encounter tamarack regularly in both acidic and alkaline peatlands of upstate New York. Given its tremendous geographical range, it is surprising that interesting cultivars have not been selected and become popular.

NATURAL RANGE Newfoundland and Labrador to Alaska, south to northern New Jersey, West Virginia, Ohio, northern Illinois, and Minnesota

Liquidambar styraciflua
SWEETGUM
HAMAMELIDACEAE

ZONES 5 to 9

SOIL moist to wet, including occasional standing water (will tolerate drought once established)

Larix laricina

Liquidambar styraciflua

LIGHT sun

ATTRIBUTES initially pyramidal crown, wide-spreading with age, to 75+ feet high; leaves simple, alternate, five-lobed, about 5 inches in diameter, shiny, dark green, turning shades of purple, red, and orange in autumn; flowers inconspicuous; fruit leathery, to 1 1/2 inches in diameter, covered by pointed projections; stems may develop corky wings

PROPAGATION seed, cold stratify for one to three months

NOTES Sweetgum is an exceptional wetland restoration species where it is hardy. Anyone choosing to use it as a large lawn or park tree needs to consider that the fruit can be a litter problem and should not be stepped on by barefeet. Cultivars have been selected for foliage (variegated summer or specific fall colors, rounded leaf lobes), form (columnar, globose), fewer fruit, and improved cold hardiness.

NATURAL RANGE Connecticut to southern Ontario, southern Illinois and Oklahoma, south to Florida and Guatemala

Liriodendron tulipifera
YELLOW-POPLAR
MAGNOLIACEAE

ZONES 4 to 9

SOIL moist, well drained

LIGHT sun

ATTRIBUTES initially pyramidal crown that becomes very broad and open with age, to 100+ feet high; leaves simple, alternate, shaped like a tulip, about 5 inches wide and long, bright green, turning yellow or golden in autumn; flowers also tulip-shaped, about 2 1/2 inches long, in late spring; fruit brown, 2 to 3 inches long, conelike structure that holds numerous winged seeds that are slowly dispersed throughout the winter

PROPAGATION seed, cold stratify for two to three months

NOTES Also known as the tuliptree. I cannot think of a more impressive tree in the eastern U.S. than the magnificent old-growth yellow-poplar in the southern Appalachians, where trees to 9 feet in diameter (not circumference!), 175 feet tall, and four hundred years old occur. This species needs a very large space, even if one does not expect to see it really mature centuries later. A few cultivars have

been selected for smaller stature, upright and narrow form, and variegated or nearly unlobed foliage.

NATURAL RANGE Vermont to southern Michigan, southern Illinois, and southeast Missouri, south to Florida and Louisiana

Magnolia acuminata
CUCUMBERTREE
MAGNOLIACEAE

ZONES 4 to 8

SOIL moist, well drained

LIGHT sun

ATTRIBUTES crown initially pyramidal, then becoming broad, to 80 feet high; leaves alternate, simple, 4 to 10 inches long, dark green, turning brown in autumn; flowers consist of upright, greenish yellow petals to 3 inches long, resembling an open tulip with narrow petals; fruit conelike, 2 to 3 inches long, turning pinkish red in autumn and releasing bright reddish orange seeds

PROPAGATION seed, cold stratify for three to six months

NOTES Cucumbertree is more like yellow-poplar in stature than the next three *Magnolia* species. While it does not reach the extreme size of yellow-poplar, it does grow quite large and fairly quickly. If grown in an open setting and not limbed up, the flower display will be greatly enhanced. Cucumbertree is an excellent shade tree, although its leaves are a bit coarse. Cultivars have been selected in an attempt at reaching a pure yellow flower, but they are a result of crosses between the native cucumbertree and the Yulan magnolia (*M. denudata*) of central China.

NATURAL RANGE southern and western New York and southern Ontario to southern Missouri and eastern Oklahoma, south to Georgia, western Florida, and Louisiana

Magnolia fraseri
FRASER MAGNOLIA
MAGNOLIACEAE

ZONES 5 to 8

SOIL moist, well drained

LIGHT sun to shade

ATTRIBUTES one to few stems that branch at or near ground, to 75 feet high; leaves simple, alternate, about 12 inches long, dark green above and whitish

Liriodendron tulipifera

Liriodendron tulipifera, fall color

Magnolia acuminata

Magnolia acuminata fruit

Magnolia fraseri

Magnolia fraseri fruit

waxy below; flowers white, round, about 9 inches in diameter; fruit narrow, conelike; bark gray, relatively smooth

PROPAGATION seed, cold stratify for three to six months

NOTES Fraser magnolia differs from umbrella magnolia (*M. tripetala*) primarily by its earlike lobes at the base of the leaf and its larger size. I have seen many Fraser magnolias over 1 foot in diameter at mid to upper elevations in the southern Appalachians.

NATURAL RANGE mountains of western Virginia to eastern Kentucky, south to northern Georgia and Alabama

Magnolia macrophylla
BIGLEAF MAGNOLIA
MAGNOLIACEAE

ZONES 5 to 8

SOIL moist, well drained

LIGHT sun to shade

ATTRIBUTES one to few main stems at or near ground level, to 50+ feet high; leaves simple, alternate, to 32 inches long and 12 inches wide; flowers creamy white, round, about 10 inches in diameter, in mid to late spring; fruit conelike (some round), about 3 inches long, rose-pink, opening to release bright reddish orange seeds; bark gray, relatively smooth

PROPAGATION seed, cold stratify for three to six months

NOTES A few cultivars have been selected with even larger flowers and leaves. Although *M. fraseri, M.*

Magnolia macrophylla

macrophylla, and *M. tripetala* are all very striking for their large flowers, fruit, and leaves, *M. macrophylla* is the most impressive with leaves over 2^1/$_2$ feet long and flowers to nearly a foot in diameter. I was fortunate to do some graduate work in the Cumberland Plateau of eastern Kentucky, where I spent two full field seasons regularly seeing *M. macrophylla* and *M. tripetala* on the way to research sites. I have these and other associated species to thank for regularly distracting me from the work I should have been doing more immediately.

NATURAL RANGE chiefly in Appalachian mountain region from Virginia, Kentucky, and southern Ohio to northern Georgia, west to Arkansas and Louisiana

Magnolia tripetala
UMBRELLA MAGNOLIA
MAGNOLIACEAE

ZONES 5 to 8

SOIL moist, well drained

LIGHT sun to shade

ATTRIBUTES one to few main stems at or near ground level, to about 30 feet high; leaves simple, alternate, 1 to 2 feet long, clustered near end of branches; flowers creamy white, round, 6 to 10 inches in diameter, in mid to late spring; fruit conelike, 4 inches long, rose-pink, opening to release bright reddish orange seeds; bark gray, smooth

PROPAGATION seed, cold stratify for three to six months

NOTES A few cultivars have been selected for larger flowers and foliage.

NATURAL RANGE Georgia to Arkansas, north to southern Pennsylvania, West Virginia, Ohio, Kentucky, and eastern Missouri

Magnolia virginiana
SWEETBAY MAGNOLIA
MAGNOLIACEAE

ZONES 5 to 9

SOIL moist to wet

LIGHT sun to shade

ATTRIBUTES single or multiple stems arising at the ground, to 25+ feet high (grows taller further south); leaves simple, alternate, about 4 inches long, dark green above, waxy and white below, evergreen in

Magnolia tripetala in fruit

Magnolia tripetala

Magnolia virginiana

warmer portions of its range; flowers creamy white, round, about 2¹/₂ inches in diameter, lemon-scented, in early summer; fruit conelike, 2 inches long, dark red at maturity, opening to release bright red seeds; bark smooth, brownish gray
PROPAGATION seed, cold stratify for three months
NOTES Sweetbay magnolia is one of my favorite trees to encounter when visiting swamps in the New Jersey Pine Barrens, where it is found often with

Atlantic white-cedar, blackgum, summersweet clethra, swamp azalea, and many other very beautiful native plants. Unfortunately, this species is not particularly cold hardy in the northern half of this region (although it will grow at least up to central New York at lower elevations), but it is an excellent choice for very wet soils where cold temperatures are not limiting. Numerous cultivars are available with distinct foliage, flower, and form characteristics.

Magnolia virginiana fruit

Nyssa sylvatica fruit

Ostrya virginiana

NATURAL RANGE Florida to Texas, north to Pennsylvania, New Jersey, Long Island, and eastern Massachusetts

Malus coronaria

WILD SWEET CRABAPPLE
ROSACEAE

ZONES 4 to 7

SOIL moist, well drained

LIGHT sun

ATTRIBUTES small to medium-size tree to 30 feet tall, with wide-spreading crown on short trunk; leaves alternate, simple, dark green; flowers white tinged with rose, to 2 inches in diameter; fruit a yellowish green, astringent apple to 1 1/2 inches in diameter

PROPAGATION seed, cold stratify for two to three months

NOTES Because of its susceptibility to disease, especially rust, this and other native crabapples will likely not replace the many hundreds of crabapple cultivars in the landscape. However, this and other native crabapples are beautiful when they bloom, and produce crabapples that can be made into jelly or left alone for wildlife to eventually consume. The other native crabapples in this region are the southern crabapple (*M. angustifolia*) and prairie crabapple (*M. ioensis*). Some taxonomists elevate the variety *glaucescens* of *M. coronaria* to a distinct species, *M. glaucescens*.

NATURAL RANGE New York to Michigan, Illinois,

Nyssa sylvatica in autumn

and Missouri, south to northern Georgia, northern Alabama, and northeastern Arkansas

Nyssa sylvatica

BLACKGUM
CORNACEAE

ZONES 4 to 9

SOIL dry to wet

LIGHT sun to shade

ATTRIBUTES narrow crown with distinct network of fine, horizontal branches; to 50+ feet high; leaves alternate, simple, 3 to 6 inches long, shiny, dark green, turning any or all shades of red, purple, orange, and yellow in autumn, when it is spectacular; flowers inconspicuous; fruit oblong, bluish black, to 1/2 inch long; bark quite variable but often blocky, resembling an alligator hide

PROPAGATION seed, cold stratify for two to three months

NOTES Also known as black tupelo. In natural stands, blackgum can form thickets from root sprouts. Some cultivars have been selected for specific form or fall color. Variety *biflora*, swamp tupelo, which naturally occurs on the coastal plain from Delaware to Florida and Louisiana, grows in deep, standing water.

NATURAL RANGE southern Maine to Florida, west to southeastern Wisconsin, eastern and southern Illinois, Missouri, and Texas

Ostrya virginiana

EASTERN HOPHORNBEAM
BETULACEAE

ZONES 3 to 9

SOIL dry to moist, well drained

LIGHT sun to partial shade

ATTRIBUTES rounded crown, to 40 feet high; leaves simple, alternate, about 4 inches long, dark green; flowers in catkins; fruit a cluster of sacs inflated around small nutlets, to 2 1/2 inches long, resembling the fruit of hops; bark consists of very thin ridges

PROPAGATION seed, warm stratify for three months then cold stratify for three or more months

NOTES Eastern hophornbeam has no really outstanding attributes except it does tolerate very dry soils, a fair amount of shade, and is relatively small at maturity.

NATURAL RANGE Nova Scotia to Manitoba, south to Florida and Texas

Oxydendrum arboreum

SOURWOOD
ERICACEAE

ZONES 5 to 9

SOIL moist, well drained (although will tolerate drought once established), high in organic matter best

LIGHT sun to partial shade

ATTRIBUTES narrow, flat-topped crown, to 30+ feet high; leaves alternate, simple, about 6 inches long, bright to dark green, turning shades of red, purple, and yellow in autumn; flowers bell-shaped, 1/4 inch long, borne along a 4- to 10-inch-long branched stalk; fruit a capsule; bark blocky, resembling an alligator hide

PROPAGATION seed, sow on surface of media and keep moist; difficult to believe this species is so hard to propagate when one sees it thriving throughout the southern Appalachians along many road cuts

NOTES After growing up in Kentucky and spending so much time in the forests of eastern Kentucky, then the southern Appalachians of North Carolina, I think I miss this tree the most each summer and autumn in upstate New York. There is one growing well near our campus in Syracuse but in a protected location. Only a few cultivars of sourwood have been selected so far.

NATURAL RANGE Pennsylvania to southern Indiana, south to Florida and Louisiana

Oxydendrum arboreum

Picea glauca
WHITE SPRUCE
PINACEAE

ZONES 2 to 6

SOIL dry (if not too far south) to wet, but best in moist, well drained

LIGHT sun to partial shade

ATTRIBUTES densely, broad pyramidal crown, to 60+ feet high; leaves needlelike, bluish green, stiff, to 3/4 inch long; flowers inconspicuous; fruit a brown, narrow-cylindrical cone about 2 inches long

PROPAGATION seed, will germinate without pre-treatment; cuttings taken in mid summer

NOTES Like black spruce, tamarack, jack pine, and balsam fir, white spruce is truly a boreal species. There are some interesting, often better-known cultivars of white spruce, including 'Conica', the dwarf Alberta spruce. Other selections have various foliage colors and textures or other distinct forms.

NATURAL RANGE Newfoundland and Labrador to Alaska, south to northern New York, Michigan, Minnesota, South Dakota, and British Columbia

Picea mariana
BLACK SPRUCE
PINACEAE

ZONES 3 to 5

SOIL moist to wet, but will tolerate dry soils in northern portion of region

LIGHT sun to partial sun

ATTRIBUTES broad, pyramidal crown, to about 40 feet tall; leaves needlelike, bluish green, soft when grown in shade, to 1/2 inch long; flowers inconspicuous; cones blackish, nearly round, about 1 inch in diameter, persist on tree; bark blackish, scaly

PROPAGATION seed, will germinate without pre-treatment

NOTES A few cultivars of black spruce have been selected for unusual form or foliage. It is an amazing tree to see in acidic, boreal peatlands, where individuals only a few inches in diameter are often over a hundred years old. It is also interesting as a dense, prostrate shrub in northeastern alpine habitats, like balsam fir.

NATURAL RANGE Newfoundland and Labrador to Alaska, south to northern New Jersey, Pennsylvania, Michigan, Wisconsin, and British Columbia

Pinus banksiana
JACK PINE
PINACEAE

ZONES 2 to 6

SOIL dry, barren, sandy or rocky, and acidic to moist and well drained

LIGHT sun

ATTRIBUTES initially pyramidal but developing narrow, flat-topped crown, to 50 feet high; leaves needlelike, in spreading clusters of two, about 1 1/2 inches long, dark green; flowers inconspicuous; cones asymmetrical, unarmed, initially light brown but becoming silver-gray with age, about 2 inches long, persist on tree

PROPAGATION seed, cold stratify for one to two months to improve germination

NOTES Jack pine is likely the least attractive of all pines native to this region, but it is one of the most cold hardy trees in North America and is exceptionally tolerant of barren, dry, acidic conditions in full sun. It also has interesting cones, which persist for decades on the tree, often requiring heat from wildfire (or other sources) to open them.

NATURAL RANGE Quebec to Maine, Vermont, and northern New York, west to northwestern Indiana, Minnesota, and the Mackenzie Valley

Pinus echinata
SHORTLEAF PINE
PINACEAE

ZONES 6 to 9

SOIL dry to moist, well drained

LIGHT sun

ATTRIBUTES crown initially pyramidal, becoming broad with age, to 80+ feet high; leaves needlelike, in clusters of two (occasionally three), 2 to 4 1/2 inches long, slender; flowers inconspicuous; cones egg-shaped, about 2 inches long, armed with small and sharp prickles; bark developing large, reddish brown, blocky plates with age

PROPAGATION seed, will germinate without pre-treatment

NOTES Pine species in general are excellent for restoring degraded lands of well-drained soils, and shortleaf pine can serve this purpose well in the southern half of this region.

NATURAL RANGE southern New York to northern

Picea mariana

Pinus banksiana

Picea glauca

Pinus echinata bark

Pinus echinata

Florida, west to southern Ohio, southern Missouri, eastern Oklahoma, and eastern Texas

Pinus resinosa

RED PINE

PINACEAE

ZONES 2 to 5

SOIL dry to moist, well drained

LIGHT sun

ATTRIBUTES dense, tufted crown with age, to 80+ feet high; leaves needlelike, in clusters of two, 5 to 6 inches long; flowers inconspicuous; cones egg-shaped, about 2 inches long; bark develops large, thick plates with age

PROPAGATION seed, will germinate without pretreatment

NOTES Because of red pine's tolerance to exposed sites with dry, raw soils, it makes an excellent roadside screen and windbreak.

NATURAL RANGE Newfoundland and Nova Scotia to southeast Manitoba, south to Connecticut, Pennsylvania, northern Illinois, and Minnesota, and in the mountains to West Virginia

Pinus rigida

PITCH PINE

PINACEAE

ZONES 4 to 7

SOIL dry, infertile, acidic, sandy or rocky, to moist and well drained (also naturally occurs on acidic, saturated peat soils)

LIGHT sun

ATTRIBUTES contorted crown, to 60 feet high; leaves needlelike, in clusters of three, 3 to 5 inches long; flowers inconspicuous; cones egg-shaped but flat-topped when open, 2 to 3 inches long, heavily armed, initially brown but turning silver-gray with age, persist on tree

PROPAGATION seed, will germinate without pretreatment

NOTES Pitch pine, while it will tolerate nearly any growing condition as long as the site is very sunny, is especially adapted to dry, acidic sites. Although it is widely regarded as an upland species, I have seen it many times in acidic swamps, growing on saturated peat soils. I also have seen numerous individuals of pitch pine with witches brooms and other features

Pinus resinosa

Pinus rigida bark

Pinus rigida

that suggest it should be possible to select some interesting cultivars. Two other similar pines are native to this region, Table Mountain pine (*P. pungens*) and pond pine (*P. serotina*). Table Mountain pine also will tolerate very dry soils; it is naturally restricted to the Appalachians and has striking, heavily armed cones that tend to stay closed until subjected to fire. Pond pine will tolerate wet soils, unlike most pine species; its cones also tend to remain closed until after fire.

NATURAL RANGE southern Maine to southern Quebec and southern Ontario, south to northern Georgia, and with outlying stations in central and western Kentucky

Pinus strobus

EASTERN WHITE PINE
PINACEAE

ZONES 3 to 7

SOIL moist, well drained best, but it does occur naturally on very dry and wet sites

LIGHT sun to partial sun

Pinus strobus

Pinus virginiana

ATTRIBUTES crown initially pyramidal, becoming flat-topped with plumelike outline with age, to 100+ feet high; leaves needlelike, in clusters of five, bluish green, slender; flowers inconspicuous; cones pinkish brown, 4 to 7 inches long, unarmed; bark develops thick, broad, rectangular ridges with age

PROPAGATION seed, cold stratify for two months

NOTES Of the pine species included here, the most beautiful and majestic of all, and one of the finest of all the nearly one hundred pine species in the world; eastern white pine colonized much of the old-field habitat in New England. It is also abundant in swamps throughout the Northeast, and can tolerate prolonged periods of wet and very dry soils. Eastern white pine tolerates heavy shearing. Dozens of cultivars have been selected primarily for unusual forms (compact, rounded, columnar, pendulous).

NATURAL RANGE Newfoundland to Minnesota and southeast Manitoba, south to Delaware, northern Georgia, Kentucky, and Iowa

Pinus virginiana
VIRGINIA PINE
PINACEAE

ZONES 4 to 8

SOIL dry, sandy, infertile, acidic

LIGHT sun

ATTRIBUTES broadly pyramidal and flat-topped crown, to 40 feet high; leaves needlelike, in clusters of two, 1 1/2 to 3 inches long; flowers inconspicuous; cones oblong, to 3 inches long, heavily armed, initially dark brown but turning silver-gray with age, persist on tree; bark develops scaly, thin plates

PROPAGATION seed, will germinate without pretreatment

NOTES Similar to jack and pitch pines in terms of tolerance to very poor sites, but not as cold hardy as jack pine.

NATURAL RANGE southern New York to southern Indiana, south to Georgia, Alabama, and northeastern Mississippi

Platanus occidentalis
AMERICAN SYCAMORE
PLATANACEAE

ZONES 4 to 9

SOIL moist to wet (will tolerate drought once established, and weeks of deep flooding)

LIGHT sun

ATTRIBUTES crown initially pyramidal but quickly becoming open, irregular, and very broad; a tall, massive tree to 100+ feet high; leaves alternate, simple, three- or five-lobed, 4 to 9 inches wide, dark green; flowers inconspicuous; fruit (actually a multiple of one-seeded fruits) dry, round, a little over 1 inch in diameter; bark exfoliates, revealing browns, grays, greens, whites, and cream

PROPAGATION seed, will germinate without pretreatment

NOTES Cool, moist springs can be devastating to American sycamore, as these conditions greatly promote the development of anthracnose. By late June 2003, few American sycamores in upstate New York had many (or even any) leaves because of the serious

Platanus occidentalis leaf

Platanus occidentalis bark

Platanus occidentalis

Populus deltoides

anthracnose outbreak earlier in the spring. Yet, by late summer, nearly all appeared fine. Despite this very serious problem, I think this species can be planted sparingly in very large areas, like parks, or in greater numbers in wetland restoration projects. American sycamore grows too large too fast to plant along streets and other sites with limited space. American sycamore is one of the parents of the London planetree, *P. ×acerifolia* (= *P. ×hispanica; P. occidentalis × P. orientalis*), which is generally not seriously affected by anthracnose.

NATURAL RANGE southwest Maine to southern Michigan and southeastern Minnesota, south to Florida and Texas

Populus deltoides in fruit

Populus deltoides

EASTERN COTTONWOOD
SALICACEAE

ZONES 3 to 9

SOIL dry to wet, including occasionally and deeply flooded

LIGHT sun

ATTRIBUTES large tree with very open, broad crown, to 100 feet high; leaves alternate, simple, 3 to 5 inches long, nearly triangular in shape, shiny, dark green, turning brown, yellow, or golden in autumn; flowers dioecious, in catkins about 6 inches long, in early spring; fruit a capsule borne along pendent stalk; bark deeply ridged and furrowed

PROPAGATION seed, short-lived, require no pre-treatment to germinate but only viable for a few weeks in late spring; cuttings any size and time

NOTES As with American sycamore, I have reservations listing eastern cottonwood here because I am all too aware of the many liabilities of this species (very fast-growing and short-lived, many disease problems, really messy, crushes cars and houses after strong storms). However, eastern cottonwood is an exceptional wetland restoration species because of its fast growth and tolerance to very wet and dry conditions. And it is very easy to propagate from even large (1+ inch in diameter) stem cuttings; a tree of decent size will result in just a few years. Eastern cottonwood is hybridized with the black cottonwood (*P. nigra*) of Europe to produce even faster-growing selections. Swamp cottonwood (*P. heterophylla*) is another native *Populus* species very well adapted to wet soils.

NATURAL RANGE Quebec and New England to Florida and Texas, and west to the base of the Rocky Mountains

Populus grandidentata

BIGTOOTH ASPEN
SALICACEAE

ZONES 3 to 5

SOIL dry to moist, well drained

LIGHT sun

ATTRIBUTES crown initially pyramidal, becoming irregularly open with few branches along lower half of bole, about 60 feet high, typically in thickets due to root sprouts; leaves simple, alternate, somewhat oval-shaped, 3 to 4 inches long, dark green, turning shades of orange, red, and yellow in autumn; flowers dioecious, in catkins, early spring; fruit a capsule borne along a stalk; bark initially smooth, olive-gray, becoming deeply furrowed and darker with age

PROPAGATION seed, short-lived, require no pre-treatment to germinate but only viable for a few weeks in late spring; transplanting of very small root suckers

NOTES While I cannot recall ever seeing a planted specimen of this tree, I always enjoy seeing this species, especially in spring, when its grayish green leaves expand, and again in the autumn, when its fall colors develop. Bigtooth aspen will tolerate dry sandy or rocky soils.

NATURAL RANGE Nova Scotia to Minnesota, south to North Carolina, Tennessee, and northern Missouri

Populus grandidentata, fall color

Populus tremuloides

QUAKING OR TREMBLING ASPEN

SALICACEAE

ZONES 1 to 6

SOIL dry to moist

LIGHT sun

ATTRIBUTES crown initially pyramidal, becoming irregularly open with few branches along lower half of bole, about 50 feet high; leaves simple, alternate, nearly round, about 2 inches in diameter, dark green, turning yellow or golden in autumn; flowers dioecious, in catkins; fruit a capsule borne along pendent stalk; bark initially smooth, gray or occasionally chalky white, developing dark ridges and furrows

PROPAGATION seed, will germinate without pretreatment but only viable for a few weeks in late spring; transplanting of very small root suckers

NOTES No tree rivals a dense stand of quaking aspen during autumn in the boreal forest of North America. Although it is short-lived, as all *Populus* species are, its bark, fall color, and tolerance to extreme cold and a variety of sites are reasons to seriously consider planting quaking aspen in the northern half of this region.

NATURAL RANGE Labrador to Alaska, south to New Jersey, Virginia, Tennessee, Missouri, and Mexico

Prunus americana

AMERICAN PLUM

ROSACEAE

ZONES 3 to 8

SOIL moist to dry

LIGHT sun

ATTRIBUTES thicket-forming small tree or large shrub about 20 feet tall; leaves simple, alternate, elliptical in shape; flowers white, about 1 inch in diameter, opening before leaves expand; fruit round, about 1 inch long, yellow or red

PROPAGATION seed, cold stratify for three months

NOTES American plum will grow on a wide range of soil conditions, often thriving along roadsides where it forms dense thickets via root sprouts. Other native, generally treelike plums in this region are chickasaw plum (*P. angustifolia*), hortulan plum (*P. hortulana*), bigtree plum (*P. mexicana*), wildgoose plum (*P. munsoniana*), and Canada plum (*P. nigra*).

Populus tremuloides in autumn

Prunus americana

All have attractive flowers and fruit that can be made into jellies and jams, or left to wildlife.

NATURAL RANGE New Hampshire to Manitoba and Montana, south to northern Florida and Oklahoma

Prunus pensylvanica

PIN CHERRY
ROSACEAE

ZONES 2 to 5

SOIL dry to moist, well drained

LIGHT sun

ATTRIBUTES crown narrow, individuals often in dense thickets due to root sprouts, about 40 feet high; leaves simple, alternate, about 3^1/$_2$ inches long, shiny, deep green, turning intense shades of red, orange, and yellow in autumn; flowers white, ^{1}/$_2$ inch wide, in flat clusters in mid spring; fruit round, ^{1}/$_4$ inch wide, bright shiny red, in summer, sour; bark smooth, initially shiny, often cinnamon-red, turning much darker with age

PROPAGATION seed, cold stratify for three months

NOTES Also known as fire cherry. Although pin cherry will never replace the Asian *Prunus* species and cultivars for widespread landscape use, this

Prunus pensylvanica fruit

Prunus pensylvanica bark

Prunus pensylvanica

small, native cherry does have really outstanding ornamental flowers, fruit, fall color, and bark. It also tolerates very dry, barren soils in full sun, where it can form dense thickets of narrow-crown individuals. When it gets too large, one can cut it to the ground and allow it to sprout. Black cherry, *P. serotina*, is a common native throughout this region, but because of its large size, its flower display is often missed, and its fruit, fall color, and bark are not as ornamental. However, black cherry is one of the most valuable timber species in North America for fine furniture, cabinets, woodenware, and many other uses.

NATURAL RANGE Newfoundland and Labrador to Mackenzie and British Columbia, south to Pennsylvania and Minnesota, irregularly in the mountains to North Carolina and Tennessee, and elsewhere to Illinois, Iowa, and Colorado

Ptelea trifoliata
HOPTREE
RUTACEAE

ZONES 3 to 9
SOIL moist, well drained
LIGHT sun to partial shade
ATTRIBUTES short, flat-topped tree or large shrub, to 20 feet high; leaves compound (trifoliate), alternate, 3 to 5 inches long, glossy, dark green, turning yellow-green in autumn; flowers greenish white, to $1/2$ inch in diameter, borne in terminal clusters 2 to 3 inches wide in late spring and early summer; fruit nearly round, flat, brown, to 1 inch in diameter; bark smooth, glossy, dark purple-brown
PROPAGATION seed, cold stratify for three to four months
NOTES Also known as the wafer-ash, hoptree is very well suited to shaded, small places. While it does not have any outstanding ornamental attributes, it looks nice every day of the year.

Ptelea trifoliata

NATURAL RANGE Mexico and southwestern U.S., north and east to Kansas, southern Wisconsin, southern Michigan, Ohio, North Carolina, and Florida, irregularly to southern Quebec, Vermont, western New York, New Jersey, and Virginia

Quercus alba leaf, fall color

Quercus falcata fruit

Quercus alba

WHITE OAK
FAGACEAE

ZONES 3 to 9

SOIL moist, well drained best, but will tolerate less ideal conditions

LIGHT sun

ATTRIBUTES broad, dense crown, to about 80 feet high; leaves simple, alternate, 4 to 8 inches long, lobed, bluish green, turning shades of red or brown in autumn; flowers in catkins; fruit an acorn, to 1 inch long, rather oblong, with shallow, warty cap; bark ashy gray, platy in upper half of tree, rectangular ridges on bottom half

PROPAGATION seed, will germinate without pretreatment

NOTES Of the twenty-nine oak species native to this region, the oak species treated here belong to one of two main groups: white oaks (*Q. alba, Q. bicolor, Q. lyrata, Q. macrocarpa, Q. michauxii, Q. muehlenbergii, Q. prinoides, Q. prinus,* and *Q. stellata*) and red oaks (*Q. cinerea, Q. coccinea, Q. ellipsoidalis, Q. falcata, Q. hemisphaerica, Q. ilicifolia, Q. imbricaria, Q. laevis, Q. laurifolia, Q. nigra, Q. pagoda, Q. palustris, Q. phellos, Q. rubra, Q. shumardii, Q. velutina,* and *Q. virginiana*). White oaks tend to grow more slowly but live about twice as long as the red oaks; they also have lobed leaves without bristles and seeds that germinate without pretreatment, among other important differences. Oaks generally are not consistently outstanding in terms of fall color (other than rich browns), but *Q. alba, Q. coccinea, Q. palustris,* and *Q. rubra* display excellent autumn color, at least in some years. *Quercus alba*—*the* white oak—is an exceptional shade tree once it is at least fifty or so years old; it can live for about four hundred years and is a very valuable timber tree.

NATURAL RANGE Maine to Michigan and Minnesota, south to northern Florida and eastern Texas

Quercus bicolor

SWAMP WHITE OAK
FAGACEAE

ZONES 4 to 8

SOIL dry to wet, including occasional standing water

LIGHT sun to partial sun

Quercus bicolor

ATTRIBUTES dense, wide-spreading crown, to 75+ feet high; leaves simple, alternate, irregularly lobed, about 6 inches long, shiny, dark green above and light below; flowers in catkins; fruit an acorn, about 1 inch wide, on a 1- to 4-inch-long stalk; branches show moderate bark exfoliation; bark on larger trees ridged and furrowed

PROPAGATION seed, will germinate without pre-treatment

NOTES Swamp white oak, like many trees adapted to poorly drained soils, is also quite drought-tolerant and therefore is a better choice than white oak for soils that tend to be wet or dry. Its leaves are very dark and glossy, forming an attractive crown. Swamp chestnut oak (*Q. michauxii*) is another oak well adapted to wet soils. It is similar in appearance to swamp white oak but has a more southern range.

NATURAL RANGE Quebec and Maine to southern Michigan and central Minnesota, south to North Carolina, Tennessee, and northern Arkansas

Quercus coccinea
SCARLET OAK
FAGACEAE
ZONES 4 to 9
SOIL dry to moist, well drained
LIGHT sun

Quercus coccinea leaf, fall color

ATTRIBUTES irregular, open crown, to 75 feet high; leaves simple, alternate, about 7 inches long, bristle-tipped along lobes, distinct C-shaped sinuses, shiny, dark green, turning scarlet to brownish red in autumn; flowers in catkins; fruit a 1-inch-wide acorn covered two-thirds of its length by a thick cap; bark rough, shallowly furrowed

PROPAGATION seed, will require three months of cold stratification

NOTES Scarlet oak resembles pin oak, except its crown does not maintain a strong pyramidal habit for very long, and its acorns are much larger. Under natural conditions, scarlet oak is restricted to dry, upper slopes, while pin oak is found on very poorly drained soils. Two other native oaks similar to scarlet oak in appearance and their ability to tolerate very dry soils are black oak (*Q. velutina*) and northern pin oak (*Q. ellipsoidalis*). Both thrive on excessively drained, infertile soils because of a deep taproot, which makes transplanting larger specimens very difficult.

NATURAL RANGE southwest Maine to Georgia, west to southern Michigan, Missouri, and Mississippi

Quercus imbricaria
SHINGLE OAK
FAGACEAE
ZONES 4 to 8
SOIL dry to moist, well drained
LIGHT sun
ATTRIBUTES broadly rounded, dense crown, to 75 feet high; leaves simple, alternate, unlobed, about

Quercus imbricaria

4 inches long and 2 inches wide, tipped with single slender bristle, glossy, dark green; acorn about 3/4 inch long

PROPAGATION seed, will require one to two months of cold stratification

NOTES Shingle oak has an unlobed, elliptical leaf that ends with a single, fine bristle-tip, much like willow oak, but its leaves are larger and it is more cold hardy than willow oak. It is really a fine tree that more people need to discover.

NATURAL RANGE eastern Pennsylvania to southern Michigan, Ohio, and Kansas, south to North Carolina, Georgia, and Arkansas

Quercus laurifolia
LAUREL OAK
FAGACEAE

ZONES 6 to 9

SOIL moist to wet

LIGHT sun

ATTRIBUTES large tree with pyramidal-rounded crown, to 80 feet tall; leaves alternate, simple, persistent to evergreen into late winter further south, dark green, with entire margin and bristle-tipped, occasionally shallowly lobed

PROPAGATION seed, cold stratify for one to two months to improve germination

NOTES Laurel oak barely reaches into our region along with a group of similar southern oak species. Some taxonomists refer to this species as swamp laurel oak or diamondleaf oak, and reserve laurel oak for *Q. hemisphaerica,* also known as Darlington oak, which has a similar range. Regardless of how these species are treated, they are beautiful, majestic shade trees in the southern U.S. into the lower Midwest. Other southern red oaks that reach into our region include bluejack oak (*Q. cinerea*), turkey oak (*Q. laevis*), and live oak (*Q. virginiana*). Bluejack and turkey oaks tolerate extremely dry soils and should be more carefully examined for improved cold hardiness especially. Live oak is considered by many to be the most beautiful tree of eastern North America, especially in the Deep South, where its wide-spreading, interior branches are draped in the flowering plant Spanish moss (*Tillandsia usneoides*). Live oak also tolerates very dry soils but is cold hardy only to Zone 7 or 8. While many of the southern oaks tend

to have persistent leaves, live oak leaves are evergreen.

NATURAL RANGE southeastern Virginia to Florida, southern Arkansas, and eastern Texas

Quercus lyrata
OVERCUP OAK
FAGACEAE

ZONES 5 to 9

SOIL dry to wet, including occasional standing water

LIGHT sun

ATTRIBUTES somewhat rounded crown at maturity, to about 50 feet high; leaves simple, alternate, resemble white oak but dark green and not as strongly lobed; flowers in catkins; fruit an acorn about 1 inch in diameter and nearly covered by cap

PROPAGATION seed, will germinate without pretreatment

NOTES Overcup, swamp white, swamp chestnut, bur, willow, cherry bark, water, and pin oaks naturally occur in wetlands and would be a fine mix of species for restoring these habitats throughout much of this region. All produce good crops of acorns that are eaten by many species of birds and mammals.

NATURAL RANGE southern New Jersey to Florida and Texas, north in the interior to southern Indiana, southern and western Illinois, and Missouri

Quercus macrocarpa
BUR OAK
FAGACEAE

ZONES 3 to 8

SOIL dry to wet

LIGHT sun to partial sun

ATTRIBUTES wide-spreading, open crown on short, stout trunk; leaves simple, alternate, to 10 inches long, irregularly lobed (more deeply on lower half of leaf), glossy, dark green; flowers in catkins; fruit an acorn to 2 inches in diameter, nearly covered by a cap that is loosely fringed around the rim; bark ridged and deeply furrowed

PROPAGATION seed, will germinate without pretreatment

NOTES I think that bur oak is the largest, most majestic of all oaks in this region. It naturally occurs on

Quercus lyrata

floodplains, and is often the only tree in dry, midwestern prairies that frequently burn.

NATURAL RANGE New Brunswick and Quebec to Ontario and southern Manitoba, south to Virginia, Louisiana, and Texas

Quercus muehlenbergii

CHINKAPIN OAK
FAGACEAE

ZONES 5 to 7

SOIL dry to moist

LIGHT sun to partial sun

ATTRIBUTES open, rounded crown, to 50+ feet tall; leaves simple, alternate, about 6 inches long, shallowly lobed, glossy, dark green; flowers in catkins; fruit an acorn, about 3/4 inch long, about half covered by a thin cap

PROPAGATION seed, will germinate without pretreatment

NOTES Chinkapin oak naturally occurs on calcium-rich soils and can tolerate prolonged, dry conditions.

NATURAL RANGE Vermont to southeast Minnesota and western Nebraska, south to northern Florida, Alabama, and Texas

Quercus muehlenbergii

Quercus macrocarpa

Quercus palustris, fall color

Quercus palustris fruit

Quercus palustris
PIN OAK
FAGACEAE

ZONES 4 to 8

SOIL moist to wet (will tolerate occasional, shallow standing water, and drier soils once established)

LIGHT sun

ATTRIBUTES crown strongly pyramidal when young, becoming very open and wide-spreading with age, to 70 feet high; leaves simple, alternate, about 5 inches long, deeply lobed, lobes tipped with a fine bristle, glossy, dark green, turning red, reddish brown, or bronze in autumn; flowers in catkins; fruit a barrel-shaped acorn about 1/2 inch long, cap thin

and shallow; bark irregular, lacking network of ridges and furrows

PROPAGATION seed, cold stratify for one to two months

NOTES Pin oak is relatively fast-growing and easy to transplant—two reasons it is the most commonly planted oak in this region. On soils high in calcium, pin oak leaves become chlorotic or turn lime-green.

NATURAL RANGE Massachusetts and Vermont to Michigan, Iowa, and Kansas, south to North Carolina, Tennessee, and Oklahoma

Quercus phellos
WILLOW OAK
FAGACEAE

ZONES 5 to 9

SOIL moist to wet (will tolerate occasional standing water, and drier soils once established)

LIGHT sun

ATTRIBUTES crown initially pyramidal, becoming rather oblong with age; leaves simple, alternate, lance-shaped, about 4 inches long, unlobed, with single bristle at tip, glossy, dark green; flowers in catkins; fruit an acorn, about 1/2 inch long, cap thin and very shallow

PROPAGATION seed, cold stratify for one to two months

NOTES Willow oak, with its narrow leaves and slender stems, has the finest texture of all oaks in this region. Water oak, *Q. nigra,* has many similar ecological and physical characteristics, except for its broader (often spatulate) leaf. Both species naturally occur throughout the southern U.S. in wetlands that are flooded each spring. They also make fine, large shade trees where they are cold hardy.

NATURAL RANGE southern New York to Florida and Texas, chiefly on the coastal plain, north in the interior to southern Illinois

Quercus prinus
CHESTNUT OAK
FAGACEAE

ZONES 4 to 8

SOIL dry to moist, well drained

LIGHT sun

ATTRIBUTES rounded, dense crown, to 70 feet high; leaves simple, alternate, about 6 inches long, glossy,

Quercus phellos

Quercus prinus in autumn

dark green, turning shades of yellow, orange, and brown in autumn; flowers in catkins; fruit an oblong acorn, about 1 inch long, covered about one-third by thin cap; bark gray, deeply furrowed, with thick and relatively broad ridges

PROPAGATION seed, will germinate without pre-treatment

NOTES Also known as *Q. montana*. Of the oaks included here, this species is perhaps the most drought-tolerant, along with bur oak and chestnut

oak's common, natural associate, scarlet oak. Both chestnut and scarlet oaks will tolerate dry, rocky, hot sites.

NATURAL RANGE Maine to northern Georgia, extending to the coast as far south as Virginia, and west to southern Illinois and northern Mississippi

Quercus rubra
NORTHERN RED OAK
FAGACEAE

ZONES 3 to 7

SOIL moist, well drained

LIGHT sun

ATTRIBUTES crown rounded, dense, to 75 feet high; leaves simple, alternate, about 7 inches long, lobes tipped with slender bristles, shiny, dark green, turning shades of red, orange, and bronze in autumn—not often as interesting as this description; flowers catkins; fruit a barrel-shaped acorn about 1 inch long, with shallow, thick cap

PROPAGATION seed, cold stratify for one to two months

NOTES With other oaks more suited to drier and wetter sites, northern red oak should be reserved for better sites. This and other red oak species grow about twice as fast as the white oaks, so if one wants to enjoy the shade of an oak in one's lifetime, northern red oak is an excellent choice. Southern red oak (*Q. falcata*) is somewhat similar to northern red oak but, as the common name suggests, has a more southern geographical distribution. It is also more tolerant of very dry and hot, and wet soils than northern red oak. Cherrybark oak (*Q. pagoda* = *Q. falcata* var. *pagodifolia*) has a range similar to southern red oak but is generally restricted to wet floodplain soils. Because floodplain tree species generally have relatively shallow root systems and tolerate extremes of urban conditions, there may be significant opportunities to select for cherrybark oaks that are better adapted to these conditions than is the much better-known northern red oak. Improved cold hardiness would be one of the most important characteristics to find. The black cherry-like bark and dark green, glossy leaves are good foundations on which to build.

NATURAL RANGE Nova Scotia to Pennsylvania, west to Minnesota and Iowa

Quercus rubra

Quercus shumardii

SHUMARD OAK

FAGACEAE

ZONES 5 to 9

SOIL dry to moist

LIGHT sun to partial sun

ATTRIBUTES wide-spreading crown, to 75+ feet high; leaves simple, alternate, about 6 inches long, lobes tipped with slender bristles, shiny, dark green, turning shades of yellow, red, and brown in autumn; flowers catkins; fruit a barrel-shaped acorn about 1 inch long, with shallow, thick cap; bark dark, developing shallow furrows

PROPAGATION seed, cold stratify for one to two months

NOTES Some of the largest red oaks I have seen throughout the Midwest are actually Shumard oak, which has bark and form that look much like northern red oak, and leaves (grown in full sun) that look much like pin and scarlet oaks. Its buds (straw-colored) and acorns (dull cap) are quite unique among all oaks. Shumard oak is also regarded as fairly drought-tolerant and thrives on basic soils.

NATURAL RANGE Pennsylvania and Virginia to Indiana, southern Michigan, Missouri, and Kansas, south to Florida and Texas

Robinia pseudoacacia

BLACK LOCUST

FABACEAE

ZONES 4 to 8

SOIL dry to moist, well drained

LIGHT sun

ATTRIBUTES narrow, twisted, open crown, to 75 feet high; often in thickets due to extensive root sprouting; leaves pinnately compound, alternate, 6 to 14 inches long, bluish green, turning pale yellow-green in autumn; flowers resemble those of peas and beans, asymmetrical, white, about 1 inch wide, borne along a 4- to 8-inch-long pendent stalk, in mid spring; fruit a leathery, brown pod, 2 to 4 inches long, opening to release about eight black, hard

Quercus shumardii

Robinia pseudoacacia flowers

Robinia pseudoacacia fruit

too familiar to the public to be appreciated. Yet, few tree species have such a wonderful flower display, and the ability to restore the most degraded land in eastern North America. Black locust is a significant nitrogen-fixer, and its wood is nearly hard as a rock. It does have problems with two insects (locust borer and leaf miner), is relatively short-lived, and root suckers like the most vigorous aspens, but it is still worthy of consideration, especially on dry, infertile, hot sites of any soil type. It can become an invasive species, however, on sites in the Northeast that support barrens-type plant species like pitch pine and scrub oak and their many associates.
NATURAL RANGE Pennsylvania and southern Indiana to Oklahoma, south to Georgia and Alabama

Salix amygdaloides
PEACHLEAF WILLOW
SALICACEAE
ZONES 3 to 7
SOIL moist to wet, including occasional standing water
LIGHT sun
ATTRIBUTES leaning, often multiple trunks, large shrub to tree, to 50 feet high; leaves simple, alternate, lance-shaped, about 4 inches long, yellowish green above, white and waxy below; flowers in catkins; fruit a capsule
PROPAGATION seed, will germinate when mature in late spring and early summer; cuttings of any kind
NOTES Peachleaf willow, similar to nearly all willow species, is especially well suited to wet, even occasionally flooded, soils.
NATURAL RANGE Vermont, New Hampshire, northeastern New York and adjacent Quebec, west to southeastern British Columbia, and south to Pennsylvania, Kentucky, Arkansas, and Arizona

Salix discolor
PUSSY WILLOW
SALICACEAE
ZONES 2 to 7
SOIL moist to wet, including occasional standing water
LIGHT sun
ATTRIBUTES few-stemmed shrub or small tree, to 20 feet high; leaves simple, alternate, elliptical,

seeds that resemble little beans; bark deeply furrowed with thick, fibrous ridges
PROPAGATION seed, mechanically or acid scarify, or place in hot water
NOTES Black locust, like other common roadside natives (sumacs, goldenrods, asters), is apparently

Salix discolor catkins

Salix nigra

about 3 inches long, dark green above, often whitish and waxy below; flowers in catkins; fruit a capsule
PROPAGATION seed, will germinate when mature in late spring and early summer; cuttings of any kind
NOTES Pussy willow is an excellent large, wide-spreading shrub or small tree for wetland restoration projects. Its emerging, silky catkins in late winter are popular for dried arrangements.
NATURAL RANGE Newfoundland to Alberta, south to Delaware, Kentucky, Missouri, South Dakota, and Montana

Salix nigra

BLACK WILLOW
SALICACEAE
ZONES 3 to 8
SOIL moist to wet, including occasional standing water
LIGHT sun
ATTRIBUTES one- to few-stemmed tree to 60 feet high; leaves simple, alternate, narrowly lance-shaped, about 4 inches long, dark green above and pale below; flowers in catkins; fruit a capsule; bark dark, deeply furrowed, with thick, somewhat scaly ridges
PROPAGATION seed, will germinate when mature in early summer; cuttings of any kind
NOTES I hesitate to include any willow here for the same reasons I am not overly enthusiastic about *Populus deltoides:* these species grow very fast, get very large, and fall down less than fifty years after

planted. However, for wetland restoration purposes, these trees are exceptional because of these same characteristics and their tolerance to wet, flooded soils. And black willow in particular has a nice, light texture and is a fine tree to sit under near water on hot, summer days, as long as conditions are not too windy.
NATURAL RANGE southern New Brunswick to central Minnesota, south to Florida and Texas, and west across southern U.S. to California, south into Mexico

Sassafras albidum

SASSAFRAS
LAURACEAE
ZONES 4 to 9
SOIL dry to wet
LIGHT sun to partial sun
ATTRIBUTES narrow, long crown, to 60 feet high, often in dense thickets due to root sprouting; leaves simple, alternate, lobed or not, bluish green, turning shades of red, purple, orange, and yellow in autumn; flowers dioecious, yellow, about 3/8 inch wide, in terminal clusters about 1 1/2 inches long in early spring; fruit round, 1/2 inch wide, dark blue, on scarlet stalks; stems bright green, aromatic when crushed; bark deeply furrowed, with thick ridges that are aromatic when cut
PROPAGATION seed, cold stratify for four months
NOTES I think sassafras is simply the most beautiful tree in autumn—the range of its fall colors exceeds even sugar maple, and its twisted, dark stems, which

Sassafras albidum, fall color

often develop into dense thickets, provide a wonderful contrast to its bright foliage colors. Although many sources suggest sassafras is small in stature, I have seen two (northern Kentucky and northwest Indiana) that are over 3 feet in diameter and 60 feet tall. If sassafras ever becomes readily available, I believe it will become one of the most popular of all native shade trees.

NATURAL RANGE southeastern Maine to Michigan and Missouri, south to Florida and eastern Texas

Sorbus americana
AMERICAN MOUNTAIN-ASH
ROSACEAE

ZONES 2 to 5

SOIL moist (will tolerate dry conditions in northern portions or higher elevations of region)

LIGHT sun to partial shade

ATTRIBUTES crown round, flat-topped, often multiple-stemmed, generally to 30 feet high; leaves pinnately compound, alternate, 6 to 12 inches long, dark green, turning shades of red, purple, orange, and yellow in autumn; flowers white, 1/3 inch in diameter, in a 3- to 5-inch-wide, flat cluster; fruit bright orange-red to scarlet

PROPAGATION seed, cold stratify for two to four months

NOTES American mountain-ash is an outstanding small tree for cold, moist climates. Showy mountain-ash (*S. decora*) is a similar native species but

Sorbus americana

Sorbus americana fruit

with a larger flowers and fruit (similar to the European mountain-ash, *S. aucuparia*). It is found more on both moist and dry, rocky sites, whereas American mountain-ash is usually found on moist to wet soils.

NATURAL RANGE Newfoundland to Minnesota, south to Pennsylvania and northern Illinois, and in the mountains to northern Georgia

Stewartia ovata
MOUNTAIN STEWARTIA
THEACEAE

ZONES 5 to 8

SOIL moist, acidic, high in organic matter

LIGHT partial sun

ATTRIBUTES wide-spreading, open crown, to 15 feet high; leaves simple, alternate, 2 to 5 inches long, dark green, turning shades of orange and red in autumn; flowers very showy, white, round, about 3 inches wide, early to mid summer; fruit an angled capsule, about 1 inch long

PROPAGATION seed, warm stratify for three to five months then cold stratify for three months

NOTES What a treat it is to see this small, understory tree in flower, especially after hiking in the hot, humid conditions common where and when this tree is blooming. Much like mountain-laurel and native azaleas and rhododendrons, this species needs a fairly specific suite of site factors to thrive, but it is well worth the effort.

NATURAL RANGE eastern Kentucky to northern Virginia and northern Alabama

Styrax americanus
AMERICAN SNOWBELL
STYRACACEAE

ZONES 5 to 9

SOIL moist to wet

LIGHT partial shade to shade

ATTRIBUTES slender, multiple-stemmed small tree with rounded crown, to 10 feet high; leaves simple, alternate, 1 1/2 to 3 1/2 inches long, bright green; flowers white, bell-shaped, consisting of five narrow and reflexed petals, to 3/4 inch long, one to four in a cluster; fruit 1/3 inch long, roundish, hairy

PROPAGATION seed, cold stratify for three months; softwood cuttings

Stewartia ovata

Styrax americanus

Styrax grandifolius

NOTES American snowbell should be planted on cool, moist, acidic soils. The big-leaf snowbell, *S. grandifolius*, is native to more southern portions of this region, typically on drier sites than those on which one would find the American snowbell.

NATURAL RANGE chiefly on the coastal plain, southeast Virginia to Florida and Louisiana, north in the Mississippi Valley to southern Indiana and at scattered stations in southern Pennsylvania, Kentucky, southern Ohio, and northern Indiana

Taxodium distichum
BALDCYPRESS
CUPRESSACEAE

ZONES 4 to 11

SOIL moist to wet, including deep, prolonged flooding

LIGHT sun to partial sun

ATTRIBUTES crown initially pyramidal, becoming flat-topped with great age, to 75+ feet high; leaves needlelike, about 1/2 inch long, flattened on branchlet, bright green, turning bronze and becoming deciduous in autumn; flowers inconspicuous; fruit a round, unarmed cone, about 1 inch in diameter, which breaks apart at maturity; bark reddish brown, consisting of very narrow and fibrous ridges

PROPAGATION seed, cold stratify for three months

NOTES Baldcypress is one of the few trees of the eastern U.S. that can grow in deep, permanent, standing water. With age it develops a flat crown and becomes a magnificient specimen. It can live for over two thousand years. In and near standing water, baldcypress develops conical projections, or knees. It is an exceptional species for restoring wetlands, especially those with permanently standing water.

NATURAL RANGE chiefly on the coastal plain, Delaware to Florida and Texas, north in the Mississippi Valley to southern Indiana

Thuja occidentalis
NORTHERN WHITE-CEDAR
CUPRESSACEAE

ZONES 3 to 7

SOIL dry to wet

LIGHT sun to partial shade

ATTRIBUTES oblong, dense crown, to 60 feet high;

Taxodium distichum

Thuja occidentalis

leaves scalelike, bright green above, pale below; flowers inconspicuous; fruit a brown, upright cone to 1/2 inch long

PROPAGATION seed, cold stratify for one to two months; cuttings taken in late fall and through winter

NOTES Also known as arborvitae. I once really disliked this plant, having grown up with it in the midwestern landscape, where it is often, well, really ugly. After seeing it throughout the Northeast, in many natural stands on both dry and wet sites, it has become one of my favorite native trees, although it does not really do anything special (except reach a maximum age of over fifteen hundred years). And I have many times now in swamps witnessed the positive consequences of its otherwise bad habit of toppling, because many of the branches of windthrown northern white-cedar in swamps become new trees by branch layering. Northern white-cedar is especially adapted to soils, dry or wet, that are high in calcium. Many cultivars have been selected for foliage characteristics (dark green, golden, resistance to winter discoloration) and form (columnar, globose, dwarf).

NATURAL RANGE Quebec and Nova Scotia to Hudson Bay, south to New Jersey, Ohio, northern Indiana and Illinois, Wisconsin, Minnesota, and in the mountains to North Carolina and Tennessee

Tilia americana

AMERICAN BASSWOOD
TILIACEAE

ZONES 3 to 8

SOIL moist, well drained (will tolerate drier soils)

LIGHT sun to partial shade

ATTRIBUTES one to multistemmed trunk with dense, rounded crown, to 80+ feet high; leaves simple, alternate, somewhat heart-shaped, 4 to 8 inches long, shiny, dark green; flowers yellow, 1/2 inch wide, in pendent cluster, late spring to early summer; fruit a round, small leathery structure that hangs from long stalk attached to oblong bract

PROPAGATION seed is difficult, remove outer seed coat by mechanical or acid scarification, then cold stratify for three to five months

NOTES Also known as American linden. While American basswood has no single outstanding

Tilia americana

feature, it does make a nice, large shade tree, although its texture is a bit coarse for many tastes. Some cultivars have been selected for more distinct form and deeper foliage color.

NATURAL RANGE New Brunswick to Manitoba, south to Florida and Texas; disjunct in Mexico

Tsuga canadensis

EASTERN HEMLOCK
PINACEAE

ZONES 3 to 7

SOIL moist, well drained

LIGHT sun (if not windy and dry) to shade

ATTRIBUTES crown at any age pyramidal and graceful, branches becoming more pendulous with age, to 75+ feet high; leaves needlelike, to 2/3 inches long, mostly flattened along twig, dark green above, two white stripes below; flowers inconspicuous; fruit a pendent, brown, nearly egg-shaped cone to 1 inch long; bark deeply furrowed, with thick ridges

PROPAGATION seed, cold stratify for two to four months

NOTES Also known as the Canada hemlock. There is no more graceful looking tree at any age in eastern North America, and few better species for screens

Tsuga canadensis

Tsuga canadensis fruit

Tsuga caroliniana

and hedges. But site selection for eastern hemlock needs careful consideration as it is not as tolerant of poor conditions as are many other conifers. Dozens of cultivars have been selected primarily for dwarf or pendulous forms; 'Sargentii' is one of the most striking pendulous conifers one might ever encounter. Carolina hemlock (*T. caroliniana*) is the only other hemlock native to eastern North America and is a southern Appalachian endemic. Carolina hemlock is hardy to Zone 4, and has a distinct foliage texture compared to eastern hemlock: the foliage of Carolina hemlock radiates out from the twig instead of lying flat. While not quite as graceful as eastern hemlock, it is still a beautiful tree.

NATURAL RANGE Nova Scotia to Michigan, Wisconsin, and occasionally Minnesota, south to New Jersey, Delaware, Ohio, and Indiana, and in the mountains to Georgia and Alabama

Viburnum lentago
NANNYBERRY
CAPRIFOLIACEAE

ZONES 3 to 7

SOIL dry to moist

LIGHT sun to partial shade

ATTRIBUTES thicket-forming, dense shrub or single-stemmed tree with somewhat arching crown, to 25 feet high; leaves simple, opposite, about 4 inches long, shiny, dark green, turning shades of purple and red in autumn; flowers 1/4 inch wide, white, borne in terminal, flat clusters about 4 inches in diameter, late spring; fruit oval, 1/2 inch long, initially pinkish but turning bluish black with slight white waxy surface, on pinkish red stalks; bark scaly or blocky

PROPAGATION seed, warm stratify for five to nine months then cold stratify for three to four months; softwood cuttings; division of clumps

NOTES Nannyberry, with its excellent flower display, glossy and dark green summer foliage, and decent fall foliage and fruit colors, is a fine, small native tree for sunny or partially shaded sites.

NATURAL RANGE Quebec to southeastern Saskatchewan and southcentral Montana, south to New Jersey, Virginia, Illinois, Missouri, Nebraska, Wyoming, and Colorado

Viburnum prunifolium

BLACKHAW
CAPRIFOLIACEAE

ZONES 3 to 9

SOIL dry to moist

LIGHT sun to partial shade

ATTRIBUTES short but wide-spreading crown, about 15 feet high; leaves simple, opposite, about 3 inches long, shiny, dark green, turning deep red and purple (or occasionally bronze) in autumn; flowers 1/4 inch in diameter, white, in a 2- to 4-inch-wide flat cluster, in spring; fruit oval, to 1/2 inch long, initially pink but turning bluish black with white waxy surface at maturity; bark somewhat blocky

PROPAGATION seed, warm stratification followed by cold stratification; softwood cuttings

NOTES All three tree viburnum species here tolerate dry soil (and much shade), and all three are excellent small-tree alternatives to the more site-demanding flowering dogwood and eastern redbud.

NATURAL RANGE Connecticut to southern Wisconsin, southern Iowa, and Kansas, south to Georgia and Texas

Viburnum lentago

Viburnum rufidulum

RUSTY BLACKHAW
CAPRIFOLIACEAE

ZONES 5 to 9

SOIL dry to moist

LIGHT sun to shade

ATTRIBUTES short but wide-spreading crown, about 15 feet high; leaves simple, opposite, about 3 inches long, shiny, dark green, turning deep red and purple (or occasionally bronze) in autumn; flowers 1/3 inch in diameter, white, in 2- to 5-inch-wide flat cluster in spring; fruit elliptical, about 1/2 inch long, dark blue with white waxy surface; bark blocky

PROPAGATION seed, warm stratification followed by cold stratification; softwood cuttings

NOTES Rusty blackhaw is very similar in appearance to blackhaw, except its buds are densely covered by short, rust-colored hairs. It is the least cold hardy of the three tree viburnums listed here and is naturally found on the driest sites.

NATURAL RANGE southern Virginia to southern Ohio, Missouri, and Kansas, south to Florida and Texas

Viburnum prunifolium in autumn

Viburnum rufidulum

APPENDIX

PLANTS THAT TOLERATE WET SOIL

A species' tolerance to wet soil depends in part on type of soil; for example, wet mineral soils high in clay are much different in important physical and chemical properties than soils high in organic matter, and soils high in organic matter generally are better aerated, even when fairly wet, compared to wet soils high in clay. The lack of oxygen is the primary reason so many plant species cannot survive in saturated soils, although many important plant physiological processes are also significantly affected by these conditions. Soils high in organic matter are higher in nitrogen especially, although it is not readily available to the plant when the soil is saturated; additionally, these soils generally are acidic, although in some regions they can be heavily influenced by underlying calcareous bedrock or glacial deposits, as is the case in upstate New York.

Most species that seem to thrive in wet and even flooded soils actually grow much better on well-drained soils if they do not have to compete with other plants (of course, aquatic plant species are an exception and have not been included in this book). The best single source of information about a plant species' affinity to wet soils is the USDI Fish and Wildlife Service's National List of Plant Species that Occur in Wetlands. This list was developed for all wetland and aquatic plant species in each region and is best accessed via the USDA PLANTS Database Web site (http://plants.usda.gov). Once reaching this site, one should click on the "Wetland Indicator Status" choice on the main page. The regions most pertinent to the geographical scope of this book are regions 1, 2 (northernmost portion), and 3.

Many species that tolerate wet soil naturally occur on mineral soils along streams within floodplains that are flooded to various depths and durations, especially early during the growing season. Many of these same species—*Fraxinus pennsylvanica* (green ash) and *Platanus occidentalis* (American sycamore), for example—tolerate the extremes of streetside conditions, thus are often selected for such use. Some species—*F. nigra* (black ash) and *Picea mariana* (black spruce), for example—occur naturally on both wet mineral and organic soils. Species names followed by a ✔ are those that thrive on wet organic soils (i.e., those that typically occur naturally on peat and generally grow best under these conditions). The species included in this "Wet Soil" category are excellent candidates for wetland restoration projects, as well as planting in wet spots in one's garden. While numerous manuals and books are available on restoring wetlands, those by Keddy (2000) and Mitsch and Gosselink (2000) provide the strongest foundation on which to engage in these activities.

SUN

Ferns and fernlike plants
Diplazium pycnocarpon (narrow-leaved spleenwort)
Dryopteris celsa (log fern)
Dryopteris cristata (crested wood fern)
Equisetum fluviatile (water horsetail)
Equisetum hyemale (scouring rush)

278

Equisetum scirpoides (dwarf scouring rush)
Equisetum sylvaticum (woodland horsetail)
Lycopodium alopecuroides (foxtail clubmoss)
Matteuccia struthiopteris (ostrich fern)
Onoclea sensibilis (sensitive fern)
Osmunda cinnamomea (cinnamon fern)
Osmunda regalis (royal fern)
Selaginella apoda (meadow spikemoss)
Thelypteris palustris (marsh fern)
Thelypteris simulata (Massachusetts fern)
Woodwardia areolata (netted chain fern)
Woodwardia virginica (Virginia chain fern)

Grasses and grasslike plants

Acorus calamus (sweetflag)
Andropogon virginicus var. *abbreviatus* (bushy beardgrass)
Carex aurea (golden-fruited sedge)
Carex crinita (fringed sedge)
Carex grayi
Carex muskingumensis (palm sedge)
Carex nigra (black sedge)
Carex stricta (tussock sedge)
Deschampsia cespitosa (tufted hairgrass)
Hordeum jubatum (foxtail barley)
Juncus effusus (softrush)
Muhlenbergia capillaris (hairgrass)
Panicum virgatum (switch grass)
Scirpus cyperinus (bulrush)
Spartina pectinata (prairie cord-grass)
Sporobolus airoides (alkali sacaton)
Typha (cattail) spp.

Wildflowers

Asclepias incarnata (swamp milkweed)
Aster umbellatus (flat-topped aster)
Boltonia asteroides (false aster)
Boltonia decurrens
Caltha palustris (marsh marigold)
Camassia scilloides (wild hyacinth)
Chamaelirium luteum (devil's bit)
Chelone glabra (turtlehead)
Coreopsis rosea (pink coreopsis)
Delphinium tricorne (dwarf larkspur)
Erigeron pulchellus (Robin's plantain)
Eupatorium coelestinum (hardy ageratum)
Eupatorium fistulosum (hollow-stemmed Joe-pye weed)

Eupatorium maculatum (spotted Joe-pye weed)
Eupatorium perfoliatum (boneset)
Eupatorium purpureum (purple Joe-pye weed)
Gentianopsis crinita (fringed gentian)
Gentianopsis procera (lesser fringed gentian)
Geum rivale (water avens)
Hedyotis caerulea (bluets)
Helenium autumnale (sneezeweed)
Helianthus angustifolius (narrow-leaved sunflower)
Helianthus giganteus (swamp sunflower)
Helonias bullata (swamp pink)
Hibiscus moscheutos (rose mallow)
Iris fulva (copper iris)
Iris lacustris (dwarf lake iris)
Iris prismatica (slender blue flag)
Iris setosa (arctic blue flag)
Iris versicolor (northern blue flag)
Iris virginica (southern blue flag)
Liatris spicata (blazing star)
Lilium canadense (Canada lily)
Lilium michiganense (Michigan lily)
Lilium superbum (Turk's cap)
Lobelia cardinalis (cardinal flower)
Lobelia siphilitica (great blue lobelia)
Maianthemum canadense (Canada mayflower)
Melanthium virginicum (bunchflower)
Menyanthes trifoliata (bog buckbean)
Physostegia virginiana (false dragonhead)
Podophyllum peltatum (mayapple)
Senecio aureus (golden ragwort)
Smilacina stellata (starry false Solomon's seal)
Smilacina trifolia (three-leaved false Solomon's seal)
Symplocarpus foetidus (skunk cabbage)
Thalictrum pubescens (tall meadow rue)
Trientalis borealis (starflower)
Trollius laxus (spreading globeflower)
Veratrum viride (false hellebore)
Veronicastrum virginicum (culver's root)
Viola cucullata (marsh blue violet)
Viola sororia (dooryard violet)
Zizia aptera (heart-leaved alexanders)
Zizia aurea (golden alexanders)

Vines

Lonicera dioica (glaucous honeysuckle)
Wisteria frutescens (American wisteria)

Shrubs

Alnus incana subsp. *rugosa* (speckled alder)
Alnus maritima (seaside alder)
Alnus serrulata (tag alder)
Alnus viridis subsp. *crispa* (green alder)
Amelanchier bartramiana (mountain juneberry)
Amelanchier canadensis (shadbush)
Andromeda glaucophylla (bog-rosemary) ✔
Aronia arbutifolia (red chokeberry)
Aronia melanocarpa (black chokeberry)
Betula pumila (bog birch)
Cephalanthus occidentalis (buttonbush)
Chamaedaphne calyculata (leatherleaf) ✔
Chionanthus virginicus (fringetree)
Clethra alnifolia (summersweet clethra)
Cornus amomum (silky dogwood)
Cornus drummondii (rough-leaved dogwood)
Cornus sericea (red-osier dogwood)
Cornus stricta (southern swamp dogwood)
Dirca palustris (leatherwood)
Fothergilla gardenii (dwarf fothergilla) ✔
Gaylussacia baccata (black huckleberry)
Gaylussacia dumosa (dwarf huckleberry)
Gaylussacia frondosa (dangleberry)
Hamamelis vernalis (vernal witch-hazel)
Ilex decidua (possum haw)
Ilex glabra (inkberry)
Ilex laevigata (smooth winterberry)
Ilex verticillata (winterberry)
Itea virginica (Virginia sweet spire)
Kalmia angustifolia (sheep-laurel) ✔
Kalmia polifolia (bog-laurel) ✔
Ledum groenlandicum (Labrador tea) ✔
Lindera benzoin (spicebush)
Lyonia ligustrina (maleberry)
Lyonia lucida (fetterbush lyonia)
Myrica gale (sweetgale)
Myrica heterophylla (southern bayberry)
Myrica pensylvanica (northern bayberry)
Nemopanthus mucronatus (mountain-holly)
Physocarpus opulifolius (eastern ninebark)
Potentilla fruticosa (shrubby cinquefoil)
Rhododendron arborescens (sweet azalea) ✔
Rhododendron atlanticum (Atlantic azalea) ✔
Rhododendron canadense (rhodora) ✔
Rhododendron periclymenoides (pinxter azalea) ✔
Rhododendron viscosum (swamp azalea) ✔

Ribes americanum (eastern black currant)
Ribes glandulosum (skunk currant)
Ribes triste (swamp red currant)
Rosa palustris (swamp rose)
Salix (willow) spp. (nearly all)
Sambucus canadensis (black elderberry)
Spiraea alba (meadowsweet)
Spiraea tomentosa (hardhack)
Vaccinium corymbosum (highbush blueberry) ✔
Vaccinium macrocarpon (cranberry) ✔
Vaccinium oxycoccos (small cranberry) ✔
Viburnum cassinoides (witherod viburnum)
Viburnum edule (mooseberry)
Viburnum lentago (nannyberry)
Viburnum nudum (smooth witherod)
Viburnum trilobum (American cranberrybush)
Xanthorhiza simplicissima (yellowroot)
Zenobia pulverulenta (dusty zenobia) ✔

Trees

Acer negundo (boxelder)
Acer rubrum (red maple)
Acer saccharinum (silver maple)
Betula nigra (river birch)
Carpinus caroliniana (American hornbeam)
Carya aquatica (water hickory)
Carya illinoinensis (pecan)
Carya laciniosa (shellbark hickory)
Celtis laevigata (sugarberry)
Chamaecyparis thyoides (Atlantic white-cedar) ✔
Fraxinus caroliniana (water ash)
Fraxinus nigra (black ash)
Fraxinus pennsylvanica (green ash)
Fraxinus profunda (pumpkin ash)
Gleditsia aquatica (water locust)
Gleditsia triacanthos (honeylocust)
Larix laricina (eastern larch) ✔
Liquidambar styraciflua (sweetgum)
Magnolia virginiana (sweetbay magnolia) ✔
Nyssa sylvatica (blackgum)
Picea mariana (black spruce)
Pinus serotina (pond pine)
Platanus occidentalis (American sycamore)
Populus deltoides (eastern cottonwood)
Populus heterophylla (swamp cottonwood)
Quercus bicolor (swamp white oak)
Quercus laurifolia (laurel oak)

Quercus lyrata (overcup oak)
Quercus macrocarpa (bur oak)
Quercus michauxii (swamp chestnut oak)
Quercus nigra (water oak)
Quercus pagoda (cherrybark oak)
Quercus palustris (pin oak)
Quercus phellos (willow oak)
Salix (willow) spp.
Taxodium distichum (baldcypress)
Thuja occidentalis (northern white-cedar) ✔

SHADE

Ferns and fernlike plants

Diplazium pycnocarpon (narrow-leaved spleenwort)
Dryopteris celsa (log fern)
Dryopteris cristata (crested wood fern)
Matteuccia struthiopteris (ostrich fern)
Onoclea sensibilis (sensitive fern)
Osmunda cinnamomea (cinnamon fern)
Osmunda regalis (royal fern)
Thelypteris palustris (marsh fern)
Woodwardia areolata (netted chain fern)
Woodwardia virginica (Virginia chain fern)

Grasses and grasslike plants

Carex lupulina (hop sedge)
Carex muskingumensis (palm sedge)

Wildflowers

Aconitum noveboracense (northern monkshood)
Calla palustris (water arum)
Caltha palustris (marsh marigold)
Chamaelirium luteum (devil's bit)
Chelone glabra (turtlehead)
Diphylleia cymosa (umbrella leaf)
Geum rivale (water avens)

Iris prismatica (slender blue flag)
Iris versicolor (northern blue flag)
Lilium canadense (Canada lily)
Lobelia cardinalis (cardinal flower)
Maianthemum canadense (Canada mayflower)
Panax trifolius (dwarf ginseng)
Podophyllum peltatum (mayapple)
Polemonium vanbruntiae (Appalachian Jacob's ladder)
Senecio aureus (golden ragwort)
Smilacina stellata (starry false Solomon's seal)
Symplocarpus foetidus (skunk cabbage)
Thalictrum pubescens (tall meadow rue)
Trientalis borealis (starflower)
Veratrum viride (false hellebore)
Veronicastrum virginicum (culver's root)
Viola cucullata (marsh blue violet)
Viola sororia (dooryard violet)

Shrubs

Dirca palustris (leatherwood)
Hamamelis vernalis (vernal witch-hazel)
Ilex decidua (possum haw)
Ilex verticillata (winterberry)
Itea virginica (Virginia sweet spire)
Nemopanthus mucronatus (mountain-holly)
Vaccinium myrtilloides (velvetleaf blueberry)
Viburnum cassinoides (witherod viburnum)
Viburnum edule (mooseberry)
Viburnum nudum (smooth witherod)

Trees

Magnolia virginiana (sweetbay magnolia)
Nyssa sylvatica (blackgum)
Picea mariana (black spruce)
Styrax americanus (American snowbell)

PLANTS THAT TOLERATE DRY SOIL

These species often naturally occur on rocky outcrops or deep sands, both of which subject plants to occasional very dry conditions. On rocky outcrops, plants that survive do so by exploiting crevices that accumulate organic material and soil, or that provide a path to a less hostile underlying substrate. The parent geological material of these rocks can also influence which species can grow under these already difficult conditions, especially relative to whether the materials promote either an acidic (low pH) or alkaline (high pH) condition.

Deep sands are often quite deficient in nutrients, as well as moisture, and few plant species tolerate these infertile, dry sites. Sands also tend to be acidic, although those along dune systems can be circumneutral. Species best adapted to these driest, infertile sites are noted by a ◆ following the name; these species are especially good options for restoring badly degraded, infertile, dry lands that may not even have any soil.

The soil pH has a significant influence on plant nutrient availability and on essential symbiotic relationships for many plant species, whether the soil is dry or wet. Although many species grow best in circumneutral or slightly lower pH soils, some species, like the many very showy members of the heath family, require very acidic conditions. At high pHs, many species become chlorotic as they cannot access soil iron and other nutrients. However, some species naturally thrive under these higher pH conditions. A ✖ follows the names of those best adapted to dry sites with circumneutral to alkaline soils.

Many more species than those listed below can tolerate dry soils if not growing in full sun. Individual species entries in this book for should be consulted for this larger group.

SUN

Ferns and fernlike plants
Cheilanthes lanosa (hairy lip fern)
Cheilanthes tomentosa (woolly lip fern)
Dennstaedtia punctilobula (hay-scented fern)
Lycopodium tristachyum (ground-pine)
Pteridium aquilinum (bracken fern)
Selaginella rupestris (rock spikemoss)

Grasses and grasslike plants
Andropogon gerardii (big bluestem)
Andropogon gyrans (Elliott's broomsedge)
Andropogon ternarius (split-beard broomsedge)
Andropogon virginicus (broomsedge)
Aristida purpurea (purple three awn)
Bouteloua curtipendula (side oats gramma)
Bouteloua gracilis (blue gramma)
Buchloe dactyloides (buffalo grass)
Deschampsia flexuosa (crinkled hairgrass)
Elymus canadensis (Canada wild rye)
Elymus glaucus (blue wild rye)
Eragrostis spectabilis (purple lovegrass)
Eragrostis trichodes (sand lovegrass)
Muhlenbergia capillaris (hairgrass)
Panicum virgatum (switch grass)
Schizachyrium scoparium (little bluestem)
Sorghastrum nutans (Indian grass)
Spartina pectinata (prairie cord-grass)
Sporobolus heterolepis (prairie dropseed)

Wildflowers

Anemone patens (pasqueflower)
Asclepias purpurascens (purple milkweed)
Asclepias tuberosa (butterfly weed)
Aster azureus (prairie heart-leaved aster)
Aster ericoides (heath aster)
Aster laevis (smooth aster)
Baptisia australis (blue false indigo)
Campanula rotundifolia (harebell)
Chrysopsis falcata (sickle-leaved golden aster)
Chrysopsis mariana (shaggy golden aster)
Chrysopsis villosa (hairy golden aster)
Coreopsis lanceolata (tickseed)
Echinacea pallida (prairie coneflower)
Gentiana puberulenta (prairie gentian)
Geum triflorum (prairie smoke)
Hedyotis caerulea (bluets)
Heliopsis helianthoides (oxeye)
Iris verna (dwarf iris)
Liatris aspera (rough gayfeather)
Liatris punctata (dotted blazing star)
Liatris pycnostachya (prairie blazing star)
Lilium philadelphicum (wood lily)
Lupinus perennis (blue lupine)
Monarda fistulosa (bergamot)
Oenothera fruticosa (sundrops)
Oenothera macrocarpa (Missouri evening primrose)
Oenothera speciosa (white evening primrose)
Opuntia humifusa (eastern prickly pear)
Oxalis violacea (violet wood-sorrel)
Penstemon hirsutus (hairy beardtongue)
Phlox pilosa (prairie phlox)
Phlox subulata (moss-pink)
Potentilla tridentata (three-toothed cinquefoil)
Ratibida pinnata (prairie coneflower)
Rudbeckia hirta (black-eyed Susan)
Silene virginica (fire pink)
Silphium laciniatum (compass plant)
Silphium terebinthinaceum (prairie dock)
Solidago canadensis (Canada goldenrod)
Solidago nemoralis (gray goldenrod)
Solidago rigida (stiff goldenrod)
Solidago rugosa (rough-stemmed goldenrod)
Solidago sempervirens (seaside goldenrod)
Solidago speciosa (showy goldenrod)
Tradescantia ohiensis (smooth spiderwort)
Viola fimbriatula (ovate-leaved violet)

Viola palmata (wood violet)
Viola pedata (bird's-foot violet)
Viola sagittata (arrow-leaved violet)
Waldsteinia fragarioides (barren strawberry)

Vines

Campsis radicans (trumpetcreeper)
Celastrus scandens (American bittersweet)
Parthenocissus quinquefolia (Virginia creeper)

Shrubs

Amelanchier humilis (bush juneberry)
Amelanchier sanguinea (roundleaf serviceberry)
Amelanchier stolonifera (running serviceberry)
Amorpha fruticosa (indigobush) ◆
Arctostaphylos uva-ursi (bearberry) ◆
Aronia arbutifolia (red chokeberry)
Aronia melanocarpa (black chokeberry)
Ceanothus americanus (New Jersey tea) ◆
Ceanothus herbaceus (prairie-redroot) ◆
Celtis tenuifolia (dwarf hackberry)
Chionanthus virginicus (fringetree)
Comptonia peregrina (sweetfern) ◆
Cornus racemosa (gray dogwood)
Cornus rugosa (roundleaf dogwood) ✖
Corylus americana (American hazelnut)
Gaultheria procumbens (teaberry)
Gaylussacia baccata (black huckleberry) ◆
Hypericum densiflorum (dense hypericum)
Hypericum frondosum (golden St. John's wort)
Hypericum kalmianum (Kalm's St. John's wort)
Hypericum prolificum (shrubby St. John's wort)
Ilex glabra (inkberry)
Juniperus (juniper) spp. ◆
Kalmia latifolia (mountain-laurel)
Myrica pensylvanica (northern bayberry) ✖
Paxistima canbyi (mountain lover)
Physocarpus opulifolius (eastern ninebark)
Potentilla fruticosa (shrubby cinquefoil) ✖
Prunus maritima (beach plum)
Prunus pumila (sand cherry)
Quercus ilicifolia (scrub oak) ◆
Quercus prinoides (dwarf chestnut oak) ◆
Rhus aromatica (fragrant sumac) ✖
Rhus copallina (shining sumac) ◆
Rhus glabra (smooth sumac)
Rhus typhina (staghorn sumac)
Ribes odoratum (clove currant)

Robinia hispida (bristly locust)
Rosa (rose) spp. (except *R. palustris*, swamp rose)
Salix cordata (dune willow)
Shepherdia canadensis (buffalo berry) ✖
Spiraea alba (meadowsweet)
Symphoricarpos albus (snowberry)
Symphoricarpos orbiculatus (coralberry)
Vaccinium angustifolium (low sweet blueberry) ◆
Yucca filamentosa (Adam's needle) ◆
Zanthoxylum americanum (prickly-ash)

Trees
Acer nigrum (black maple) ✖
Amelanchier arborea (serviceberry)
Aralia spinosa (devil's-walkingstick)
Betula populifolia (gray birch) ◆
Carya glabra (pignut hickory)
Carya ovata (shagbark hickory)
Carya pallida (pale hickory)
Carya texana (black hickory)
Carya tomentosa (mockernut hickory)
Celtis occidentalis (hackberry) ✖
Cotinus obovatus (American smoketree) ✖
Crataegus (hawthorn) spp.
Diospyros virginiana (persimmon)
Fraxinus pennsylvanica (green ash)
Fraxinus quadrangulata (blue ash) ✖
Gleditsia triacanthos (honeylocust) ✖
Gymnocladus dioicus (Kentucky coffeetree)
Juniperus virginiana (eastern redcedar) ◆
Liquidambar styraciflua (sweetgum)
Nyssa sylvatica (blackgum)
Ostrya virginiana (eastern hophornbeam)
Oxydendrum arboreum (sourwood)
Pinus banksiana (jack pine) ◆
Pinus echinata (shortleaf pine)
Pinus pungens (Table Mountain pine)
Pinus resinosa (red pine)
Pinus rigida (pitch pine) ◆
Pinus virginiana (Virginia pine) ◆
Platanus occidentalis (American sycamore)
Populus deltoides (eastern cottonwood)
Populus grandidentata (bigtooth aspen)
Populus tremuloides (quaking aspen)
Prunus pensylvanica (pin cherry) ◆
Quercus bicolor (swamp white oak)
Quercus cinerea (bluejack oak)

Quercus coccinea (scarlet oak)
Quercus ellipsoidalis (northern pin oak)
Quercus falcata (southern red oak)
Quercus imbricaria (shingle oak)
Quercus laevis (turkey oak)
Quercus lyrata (overcup oak)
Quercus macrocarpa (bur oak)
Quercus muehlenbergii (chinkapin oak)
Quercus palustris (pin oak)
Quercus phellos (willow oak)
Quercus prinus (chestnut oak)
Quercus shumardii (Shumard oak)
Quercus velutina (black oak)
Quercus virginiana (live oak)
Robinia pseudoacacia (black locust) ◆
Sassafras albidum (sassafras)
Thuja occidentalis (northern white-cedar) ✖

PARTIAL SHADE TO SHADE

Ferns and fernlike plants
Dryopteris fragrans (fragrant wood fern)
Dryopteris intermedia (evergreen wood fern)
Dryopteris marginalis (marginal shield fern)
Pellaea atropurpurea (purple cliff brake)
Pellaea glabella (smooth cliff brake)
Polypodium polypodioides (resurrection fern)
Polystichum acrostichoides (Christmas fern)
Woodsia spp.

Grasses and grasslike plants
Carex eburnea (sedge)
Carex flaccosperma (sedge)
Carex laxiculmis (sedge)
Carex pensylvanica (sedge)
Carex plantaginea (plantain sedge)
Carex platyphylla (broad-leaf sedge)
Elymus hystrix (bottlebrush-grass)

Wildflowers
Anemone canadensis (Canada anemone)
Aquilegia canadensis (wild columbine)
Aster divaricatus (white wood aster)
Chimaphila maculata (spotted wintergreen)
Chimaphila umbellata (prince's pine)
Chrysogonum virginianum (gold-star)
Eupatorium rugosum (white snakeroot)
Galax aphylla (wandflower)

Geranium maculatum (wild geranium)
Hepatica americana (round-lobed hepatica)
Heuchera americana (alumroot)
Maianthemum canadense (Canada mayflower)
Podophyllum peltatum (mayapple)
Porteranthus trifoliatus (Indian physic)
Potentilla tridentata (three-toothed cinquefoil)
Rudbeckia hirta (black-eyed Susan)
Sedum ternatum (wild stonecrop)
Smilacina stellata (starry false Solomon's seal)
Solidago caesia (blue-stemmed goldenrod)
Solidago flexicaulis (zig-zag goldenrod)
Solidago ulmifolia (elm-leaved goldenrod)
Viola adunca (hookspur violet)
Waldsteinia fragarioides (barren strawberry)

Shrubs

Chionanthus virginicus (fringetree)
Cornus rugosa (roundleaf dogwood) ✖
Corylus (hazelnut) spp.
Diervilla lonicera (bush-honeysuckle)
Dirca palustris (leatherwood)

Gaultheria procumbens (teaberry)
Gaylussacia baccata (black huckleberry) ◆
Hamamelis virginiana (witch-hazel)
Hydrangea arborescens (smooth hydrangea)
Kalmia latifolia (mountain-laurel) ◆
Staphylea trifolia (bladdernut) ✖
Vaccinium arboreum (farkleberry)
Vaccinium pallidum (dryland blueberry)
Vaccinium stamineum (deerberry)
Zanthoxylum americanum (prickly-ash)

Trees

Acer nigrum (black maple) ✖
Amelanchier arborea (serviceberry)
Aralia spinosa (devil's-walkingstick)
Celtis occidentalis (hackberry)
Ilex opaca (American holly)
Ostrya virginiana (eastern hophornbeam)
Oxydendrum arboreum (sourwood)
Picea glauca (white spruce) ✖
Viburnum rufidulum (rusty blackhaw)

PLANTS THAT TOLERATE SHADE

Besides the species covered under wet and dry soil conditions, additional species tolerate partial to full shade on moist, well-drained soils. Of course, the previously listed species that tolerate extreme conditions grow even better when cultivated on moist, well-drained soils. Many other species could be included here, especially under the shrub and wildflower categories, but a species' ornamental attributes, especially flowering, fall color, and form, typically are greatly diminished by increasing amounts of shade. Many spring-flowering wildflower species will tolerate deep shade during the majority of the growing season but require the open canopy conditions that typically exist during their flowering and leaf development periods in early spring. Very few species in nature tolerate prolonged periods beneath evergreen canopies, which are not just dark beneath but much drier than below deciduous tree canopies. Species that tolerate extended periods of only light shade are excluded here.

Ferns and fernlike plants
Adiantum capillus-veneris (southern maidenhair fern)
Adiantum pedatum (maidenhair fern)
Asplenium bradleyi (Bradley's spleenwort)
Asplenium ×ebenoides (dragontail fern)
Asplenium montanum (mountain spleenwort)
Asplenium platyneuron (ebony spleenwort)
Asplenium rhizophyllum (walking fern)
Asplenium ruta-muraria (wall-rue)
Asplenium scolopendrium var. *americanum* (American hart's-tongue fern)

Asplenium trichomanes (maidenhair spleenwort)
Asplenium viride (green spleenwort)
Athyrium filix-femina (lady fern)
Botrychium dissectum (dissected grape fern)
Botrychium virginianum (rattlesnake fern)
Cryptogramma stelleri (slender rock brake)
Cystopteris bulbifera (bulblet bladder fern)
Cystopteris fragilis (fragile fern)
Cystopteris protrusa (lowland bladder fern)
Deparia acrostichoides (silvery spleenwort)
Dryopteris campyloptera (mountain wood fern)
Dryopteris carthusiana (spinulose wood fern)
Dryopteris expansa (northern wood fern)
Dryopteris filix-mas (male fern)
Dryopteris goldiana (Goldie's fern)
Gymnocarpium dryopteris (oak fern)
Gymnocarpium robertianum (limestone oak fern)
Lycopodium complanatum (northern ground-cedar)
Lycopodium digitatum (southern ground-cedar)
Lycopodium lucidulum (shining clubmoss)
Lycopodium obscurum (ground-pine)
Osmunda claytoniana (interrupted fern)
Phegopteris connectilis (narrow beech fern)
Phegopteris hexagonoptera (broad beech fern)
Polypodium virginianum (rock polypody)
Polystichum braunii (Braun's holly fern)
Polystichum lonchitis (northern holly fern)
Thelypteris noveboracensis (New York fern)

Grasses and grasslike plants
Chasmanthium latifolium (northern sea oats)
Luzula acuminata (hairy wood-rush)
Luzula echinata

Wildflowers

Actaea pachypoda (white baneberry)
Actaea rubra (red baneberry)
Anemone quinquefolia (wood anemone)
Anemonella thalictroides (rue anemone)
Arisaema triphyllum (Jack-in-the-pulpit)
Aruncus dioicus (goat's beard)
Asarum canadense (wild ginger)
Aster cordifolius (blue heart-leaved aster)
Aster macrophyllus (big-leaved aster)
Cardamine concatenata (cut-leaf toothwort)
Cardamine diphylla (broad-leaf toothwort)
Caulophyllum thalictroides (blue cohosh)
Cimicifuga americana (American bugbane)
Cimicifuga racemosa (black cohosh)
Clintonia borealis (blue bead lily)
Clintonia umbellulata (speckled wood lily)
Coreopsis auriculata (lobed tickseed)
Dicentra canadensis (squirrel corn)
Dicentra cucullaria (Dutchman's breeches)
Dicentra eximia (bleeding heart)
Dodecatheon meadia (shooting star)
Echinacea purpurea (purple coneflower)
Erythronium albidum (white trout lily)
Erythronium americanum (yellow trout lily)
Eupatorium rugosum (white snakeroot)
Hepatica acutiloba (sharp-lobed hepatica)
Hepatica americana (round-lobed hepatica)
Hexastylis arifolia (arrow-leaved ginger)
Hexastylis shuttleworthii (mottled wild ginger)
Hexastylis virginica (Virginia wild ginger)
Hydrastis canadensis (goldenseal)
Hydrophyllum canadense (maple-leaved waterleaf)
Hydrophyllum macrophyllum (hairy waterleaf)
Hydrophyllum virginianum (eastern waterleaf)
Iris cristata (crested iris)
Jeffersonia diphylla (twinleaf)
Mertensia virginica (Virginia bluebells)
Mitella diphylla (miterwort)
Monarda didyma (Oswego tea)
Oxalis acetosella (northern wood-sorrel)
Pachysandra procumbens (Allegheny spurge)
Panax quinquefolius (ginseng)
Phlox divaricata (wild blue phlox)
Phlox stolonifera (creeping phlox)
Rudbeckia laciniata (cutleaf coneflower)
Sanguinaria canadensis (bloodroot)

Sedum ternatum (wild stonecrop)
Smilacina racemosa (false Solomon's seal)
Stylophorum diphyllum (celandine poppy)
Thalictrum dioicum (early meadow rue)
Tiarella cordifolia (foamflower)
Tradescantia virginiana (Virginia spiderwort)
Trillium spp.
Uvularia (bellwort) spp.
Viola canadensis (Canada violet)
Viola conspersa (dog violet)
Viola pubescens (yellow violet)
Viola rostrata (long-spurred violet)

Vines

Aristolochia macrophylla (Dutchman's pipe)
Bignonia capreolata (cross-vine)
Decumaria barbara (climbing hydrangea)
Linnaea borealis (twinflower)
Lonicera sempervirens (trumpet honeysuckle)
Mitchella repens (partridgeberry)

Shrubs

Calycanthus floridus (sweetshrub)
Clethra acuminata (cinnamon clethra)
Cornus canadensis (bunchberry)
Euonymus americanus (American euonymus)
Euonymus atropurpureus (eastern wahoo)
Euonymus obovatus (running strawberry-bush)
Leucothoe axillaris (swamp dog-laurel)
Leucothoe fontanesiana (drooping leucothoe)
Lindera benzoin (spicebush)
Rhododendron spp. (including azaleas)
Rubus odoratus (flowering raspberry)
Sambucus racemosa (red elderberry)
Taxus canadensis (Canada yew)
Viburnum acerifolium (mapleleaf viburnum)
Viburnum alnifolium (hobblebush)

Trees

Abies balsamea (balsam fir)
Abies fraseri (Fraser fir)
Acer pensylvanicum (striped maple)
Acer saccharum (sugar maple)
Aesculus pavia (red buckeye)
Aesculus sylvatica (painted buckeye)
Amelanchier arborea (serviceberry)
Amelanchier laevis (smooth serviceberry)
Carpinus caroliniana (American hornbeam)

Cercis canadensis (eastern redbud)
Cornus alternifolia (alternate-leaf dogwood)
Cornus florida (flowering dogwood)
Fagus grandifolia (American beech)
Halesia carolina (Carolina silverbell)
Ilex montana (mountain winterberry)
Ilex opaca (American holly)
Magnolia fraseri (Fraser magnolia)

Magnolia macrophylla (bigleaf magnolia)
Magnolia tripetala (umbrella magnolia)
Magnolia virginiana (sweetbay magnolia)
Picea glauca (white spruce)
Stewartia ovata (mountain stewartia)
Styrax americanus (American snowbell)
Tsuga canadensis (eastern hemlock)
Tsuga caroliniana (Carolina hemlock)

PLANTS WITH FLOWERS THAT ATTRACT BUTTERFLIES AND HUMMINGBIRDS

The following species have flowers with high-quality nectar for butterflies and hummingbirds. Of course, other flower pollinators, like bees, will think you have invited them also. Red flowers that are tube-shaped are especially attractive to hummingbirds. Many species not listed below are also primary food sources for the larvae of many of the butterflies and moths native to this region. Further details on which species are significant food sources for larvae of these species are in Stokes et al. (1991) and Henderson (1987).

Wildflowers

Amsonia tabernaemontana (bluestar)
Aquilegia canadensis (wild columbine)
Aruncus dioicus (goat's beard)
Asclepias (milkweed) spp.
Aster spp.
Chelone glabra (turtlehead)
Cimicifuga racemosa (black cohosh)
Coreopsis (tickseed) spp.
Echinacea purpurea (purple coneflower)
Eupatorium (Joe-pye weed, boneset) spp.
Helenium autumnale (sneezeweed)
Helianthus (sunflower) spp.
Heliopsis helianthoides (oxeye)
Liatris (blazing star) spp.
Lilium (lily) spp.
Lobelia cardinalis (cardinal flower)
Lobelia siphilitica (great blue lobelia)
Lupinus perennis (blue lupine)
Monarda didyma (Oswego tea)
Monarda fistulosa (bergamot)

Phlox spp.
Physostegia virginiana (false dragonhead)
Rudbeckia (coneflower, black-eyed Susan) spp.
Sedum ternatum (wild stonecrop)
Solidago (goldenrod) spp.
Spigelia marilandica (Indian pink)

Vines

Bignonia capreolata (cross-vine)
Campsis radicans (trumpetcreeper)
Lonicera (honeysuckle) spp.

Shrubs

Callicarpa americana (American beautyberry)
Ceanothus americanus (New Jersey tea)
Cephalanthus occidentalis (buttonbush)
Chamaedaphne calyculata (leatherleaf)
Clethra spp.
Diervilla lonicera (bush-honeysuckle)
Fothergilla spp.
Itea virginica (Virginia sweet spire)
Lindera benzoin (spicebush)
Physocarpus opulifolius (eastern ninebark)
Rhododendron spp. (including azaleas)
Spiraea alba (meadowsweet)
Symphoricarpos orbiculatus (coralberry)
Vaccinium (blueberry, cranberry) spp.

Trees

Aesculus (buckeye) spp. (especially *A. pavia*, red buckeye)
Prunus pensylvanica (pin cherry)
Salix (willow) spp.

PLANTS WITH FRUITS
THAT ATTRACT BIRDS

Fruits of some species are devoured before they fully ripen: rarely do I pick many serviceberries or blueberries at my home before the invasion by catbirds, a bird species that I once really enjoyed seeing. Fruits of other species (hawthorns, crabapples) are not touched until late into the winter, months after the fruits have matured. Although birds are the primary consumers of some fruit, small mammals will eat the seeds within these fruit (dogwoods, for example). And the fruit of some plant species (those that produce cones, i.e., conifers) are only factories for the seeds that many bird (and some small mammal) species enjoy throughout the late fall into winter. Trees and shrubs especially also are essential to provide cover to bird species, even if they do not have any food to offer. Henderson (1987) discusses the many ways to enhance bird and other wildlife visits to one's property.

Vines

Celastrus scandens (American bittersweet)
Parthenocissus (Virginia creeper, grape-woodbine)
   spp.
Vitis (grape) spp.

Shrubs

Alnus (alder) spp.
Amelanchier (serviceberry, juneberry) spp.
Aronia (chokeberry) spp.
Betula pumila (bog birch)
Callicarpa americana (American beautyberry)
Chionanthus virginicus (fringetree)
Cornus (dogwood) spp.
Corylus (hazelnut) spp.
Gaylussacia (huckleberry) spp.
Ilex (holly) spp.
Juniperus (juniper) spp.

Lindera benzoin (spicebush)
Myrica pensylvanica (northern bayberry)
Nemopanthus mucronatus (mountain-holly)
Prunus (cherry, plum) spp.
Rhus (sumac) spp.
Ribes (gooseberry, currant) spp.
Rosa (rose) spp.
Rubus (raspberry, blackberry) spp.
Sambucus (elderberry) spp.
Symphoricarpos (snowberry, coralberry) spp.
Taxus canadensis (Canada yew)
Vaccinium (blueberry, cranberry) spp.
Viburnum spp.

Trees

Abies (fir) spp.
Amelanchier arborea (serviceberry)
Aralia spinosa (devil's-walkingstick)
Betula (birch) spp.
Carpinus caroliniana (American hornbeam)
Celtis occidentalis (hackberry)
Chamaecyparis thyoides (Atlantic white-cedar)
Cornus (dogwood) spp.
Crataegus (hawthorn) spp.
Fagus grandifolia (American beech)
Ilex (holly) spp.
Juniperus virginiana (eastern redcedar)
Picea (spruce) spp.
Pinus (pine) spp.
Prunus pensylvanica (pin cherry)
Sassafras albidum (sassafras)
Sorbus americana (American mountain-ash)
Thuja occidentalis (northern white-cedar)
Tsuga canadensis (eastern hemlock)
Viburnum (nannyberry, blackhaw, rusty blackhaw)
   spp.

PLANTS WITH FRUITS
THAT ATTRACT MAMMALS

I am not sure that all readers will want to rush out and plant these species: you may not appreciate the deer, opposums, raccoons, and even squirrels that might accept your invitation for dinner. But in some cases, "mammals" includes the reader (and maybe the reader's neighbor), and the species followed by a ✻ are worth tasting, without any special preparation. Consult Henderson (1987) for a thorough review on how to maximize wildlife visits by the use of plants.

Shrubs

Arctostaphylos uva-ursi (bearberry)
Cornus (dogwood) spp.
Corylus (hazelnut) spp. ✻
Gaylussacia (huckleberry) spp. ✻
Vaccinium (blueberry, cranberry) spp. ✻

Trees

Acer (maple) spp.
Aesculus (buckeye) spp.
Amelanchier arborea (serviceberry) ✻
Asimina triloba (pawpaw) ✻
Carya (hickory) spp. ✻
Cornus (dogwood) spp.
Diospyros virginiana (persimmon) ✻
Fagus grandifolia (American beech)
Juniperus virginiana (eastern redcedar)
Malus (crabapple) spp. ✻
Prunus (cherry, plum) spp. ✻ (some very astringent)
Quercus (oak) spp.

USDA PLANT HARDINESS ZONE MAP

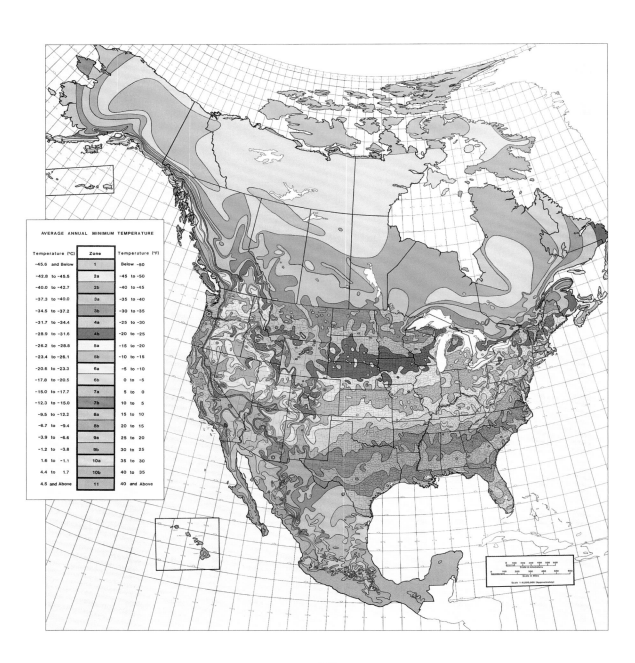

AVERAGE ANNUAL MINIMUM TEMPERATURE

Temperature (°C)	Zone	Temperature (°F)
-45.6 and Below	1	Below -50
-42.8 to -45.5	2a	-45 to -50
-40.0 to -42.7	2b	-40 to -45
-37.3 to -40.0	3a	-35 to -40
-34.5 to -37.2	3b	-30 to -35
-31.7 to -34.4	4a	-25 to -30
-28.9 to -31.6	4b	-20 to -25
-26.2 to -28.8	5a	-15 to -20
-23.4 to -26.1	5b	-10 to -15
-20.6 to -23.3	6a	-5 to -10
-17.8 to -20.5	6b	0 to -5
-15.0 to -17.7	7a	5 to 0
-12.3 to -15.0	7b	10 to 5
-9.5 to -12.2	8a	15 to 10
-6.7 to -9.4	8b	20 to 15
-3.9 to -6.6	9a	25 to 20
-1.2 to -3.8	9b	30 to 25
1.6 to -1.1	10a	35 to 30
4.4 to 1.7	10b	40 to 35
4.5 and Above	11	40 and Above

CONVERSION TABLE
FOR METRIC MEASUREMENTS

INCHES	CENTIMETERS	FEET	METERS
1/8	0.3	1/4	0.08
1/6	0.4	1/3	0.1
1/5	0.5	1/2	0.15
1/4	0.6	1	0.3
1/3	0.8	1 1/2	0.5
3/8	0.9	2	0.6
2/5	1.0	2 1/2	0.8
1/2	1.25	3	0.9
3/5	1.5	4	1.2
5/8	1.6	5	1.5
2/3	1.7	6	1.8
3/4	1.9	7	2.1
7/8	2.2	8	2.4
1	2.5	9	2.7
1 1/4	3.1	10	3.0
1 1/3	3.3	12	3.6
1 1/2	3.75	15	4.5
1 3/4	4.4	18	5.4
2	5.0	20	6.0
3	7.5	25	7.5
4	10	30	9.0
5	12.5	35	10.5
6	15	40	12
7	17.5	45	13.5
8	20	50	15
9	22.5	60	18
10	25	70	21
12	30	75	22.5
15	37.5	80	24
18	45	90	27
20	50	100	30
24	60	125	37.5
30	75	150	45
32	80	175	52.5
36	90	200	60

$$°C = 5/9 \times (°F - 32)$$
$$°F = (9/5 \times °C) + 32$$

BIBLIOGRAPHY

Armitage, A. M. 1989. *Herbaceous Perennial Plants. A Treatise on Their Identification, Culture, and Garden Attributes.* Varsity Press, Athens, Georgia.

———. 2000. *Armitage's Garden Perennials: A Color Encyclopedia.* Timber Press, Portland, Oregon.

Bailey, R. G. 1996. *Ecosystem Geography.* Springer-Verlag, New York.

———. 1998. *Ecoregions: The Ecosystem Geography of the Oceans and Continents.* Springer-Verlag, New York.

———. 2002. *Ecoregion-based Design for Sustainability.* Springer-Verlag, New York.

Barbour, M. G., and W. D. Billings, eds. 2000. *North American Terrestrial Vegetation,* 2nd ed. Cambridge University Press, Cambridge, United Kingdom.

Baskin, C. C., and J. M. Baskin. 1998. *Seeds: Ecology, Biogeography, and Evolution of Dormancy and Germination.* Academic Press, San Diego.

Bray, W. L. 1915. "The Development of the Vegetation of New York State." New York State College of Forestry Technical Publication No. 3, Syracuse.

Braun, E. L. 1950. *Deciduous Forests of Eastern North America.* Macmillan, New York.

Clausen, R. R., and N. H. Ekstrom. 1989. *Perennials for American Gardens.* Random House, New York.

Cullina, W. 2000. *The New England Wildflower Society Guide to Growing and Propagating Wildflowers of the United States and Canada.* Houghton Mifflin, Boston.

———. 2002. *Native Trees, Shrubs, & Vines. A Guide to Using, Growing, and Propagating North American Woody Plants.* Houghton Mifflin, Boston.

Curtis, J. T. 1959. *The Vegetation of Wisconsin. An Ordination of Plant Communities.* University of Wisconsin Press, Madison.

Darke, R. 1999. *The Color Encyclopedia of Ornamental Grasses.* Timber Press, Portland, Oregon.

Dirr, M. A. 1998. *Manual of Woody Landscape Plants,* 5th ed. Stipes Publishing, Champaign, Illinois.

Dirr, M. A., and C. W. Heuser, Jr. 1987. *The Reference Manual of Woody Plant Propagation: From Seed to Tissue Culture.* Varsity Press, Athens, Georgia.

Fike, J. 1999. *Terrestrial and Palustrine Plant Communities of Pennsylvania.* Pennsylvania Department of Conservation and Natural Resources, Harrisburg.

Flora of North America Editorial Committee. 1993. Introd. to *Flora of North America,* vol. 1. Oxford University Press, New York.

Fralish, J. S., and S. B. Franklin. 2002. *Taxonomy and Ecology of Woody Plants in North American Forests (Excluding Mexico and Subtropical Florida).* John Wiley & Sons, Inc., New York.

Gleason, H. A., and A. Cronquist. 1991. *Manual of Vascular Plants of Northeastern United States and Adjacent Canada,* 2nd ed. The New York Botanical Garden, Bronx, New York.

Greenlee, J. 1992. *The Encyclopedia of Ornamental Grasses.* Rodale Press, Emmaus, Pennsylvania.

Grounds, R. 1998. *The Plantfinder's Guide to Ornamental Grasses.* Timber Press, Portland, Oregon.

Harper-Lore, B., and M. Wilson. 2000. *Roadside Use of Native Plants.* Island Press, Washington, D.C.

Henderson, C. L. 1987. *Landscaping for Wildlife.* Minnesota Department of Natural Resources, St. Paul.

Hoshizaki, B. J., and R. C. Moran. 2001. *Fern Grower's Manual,* revised and expanded ed. Timber Press, Portland, Oregon.

Jones, S. B., Jr. and L. E. Foote. 1990. *Gardening with Native Wildflowers.* Timber Press, Portland, Oregon.

Keddy, P. A. 2000. *Wetland Ecology Principles and Conservation.* Cambridge University Press, Cambridge, United Kingdom.

Küchler, A. W. 1964. "Potential Natural Vegetation of the Conterminous United States." *Special Publication* 36, American Geographical Society, New York (with separate map at 1:3,168,000).

———. "Potential Natural Vegetation" (map at 1:7,500,000). Revised. National Atlas of the United States, U.S. Geological Survey, Reston, Virginia.

Ladd, D. M., and F. Oberle. 1995. *Tallgrass Prairie Wildflowers. A Field Guide.* The Globe Pequot Press, Guilford, Connecticut.

Leopold, D. J., and M. K. Wali. 1992. "The Rehabilitation of Forest Ecosystems in the Eastern United States and Canada". In M. K. Wali, ed., *Ecosystem Rehabilitation, Volume 2: Ecosystem Analysis and Synthesis.* SPB Academic Publishing bv, The Hague, Netherlands.

Leopold, D. J., W. C. McComb, and R. N. Muller. 1998. *Trees of the Central Hardwood Forests of North America: An Identification and Cultivation Guide.* Timber Press, Portland, Oregon.

Lloyd, C. 2000. *Christopher Lloyd's Garden Flowers.* Timber Press, Portland, Oregon.

Mickel, J. T. 1994. *Ferns for American Gardens.* Macmillan, New York. Reprinted 2003, with an updated source list, by Timber Press, Portland, Oregon.

Mitchell, R. S., and G. C. Tucker. 1997. "Revised Checklist of New York State Plants." New York State Museum Bulletin No. 490, University of State of New York, State Education Department, Albany.

Mitsch, W. J., and J. G. Gosselink. 2000. *Wetlands,* 3rd ed. John Wiley & Sons, Inc., New York.

Raynal, D. J., and D. J. Leopold. 1999. *Landowner's Guide to State-protected Plants of Forests in New York State.* SUNY-ESF, Syracuse.

Rickard, M. 2000. *The Plantfinder's Guide to Garden Ferns.* Timber Press, Portland, Oregon.

Shelford, V. E. 1978. *The Ecology of North America.* University of Illinois Press, Urbana.

Soper, J. H., and M. L. Heimburger. 1982. *Shrubs of Ontario.* Royal Ontario Museum, Toronto.

Still, S. M. 1994. *Manual of Herbaceous Ornamental Plants,* 4th ed. Stipes Publishing Company, Champaign, Illinois.

Stokes, D., L. Stokes, and E. Williams. 1991. *Stokes Butterfly Book: The Complete Guide to Butterfly Gardening, Identification, and Behavior.* Little, Brown & Company, Boston.

Thomas, G. S. 1990. *Perennial Garden Plants or The Modern Florilegium,* 3rd ed. Sagapress/Timber Press, Inc., Portland, Oregon.

Thompson, E. H., and E. R. Sorenson. 2000. *Wetland, Woodland, Wildland: A Guide to the Natural Communities of Vermont.* University Press of New England, Hanover, New Hampshire.

Vankat, J. L. 1979. *The Natural Vegetation of North America.* John Wiley & Sons, Inc., New York.

Woods, C. 1992. *Encyclopedia of Perennials: A Gardener's Guide.* Facts on File, Inc., New York.

INDEX